Making contemporary theatre

Manchester University Press

theatre
theory · practice
· performance ·

This series will offer a space for those people who practise theatre to have a dialogue with those who think and write about it.

The series has a flexible format that refocuses the analysis and documentation of performance. It provides, presents and represents material which is written by those who make or create performance history, and offers access to theatre documents, different methodologies and approaches to the art of making theatre.

The books in the series are aimed at students, scholars, practitioners and theatre-visiting readers. They encourage reassessments of periods, companies and figures in twentieth-century and twenty-first-century theatre history, and provoke and take up discussions of cultural strategies and legacies that recognise the heterogeneity of performance studies.

The series editors, with the advisory board, aim to publish innovative challenging and exploratory texts from practitioners, theorists and critics.

also available

The Paris Jigsaw: Internationalism and the city's stages
DAVID BRADBY AND MARIA M. DELGADO (EDS)

Theatre in crisis? Performance manifestos for a new century
MARIA M. DELGADO AND CARIDAD SVICH (EDS)

World stages, local audiences: Essays on performance, place, and politics
PETER DICKINSON

Jean Genet and the politics of theatre: Spaces of revolution
CARL LAVERY

'Love me or kill me': Sarah Kane and the theatre of extremes
GRAHAM SAUNDERS

Trans-global readings: Crossing theatrical boundaries
CARIDAD SVICH

Negotiating cultures: Eugenio Barba and the intercultural debate
IAN WATSON (ED.)

Making contemporary theatre

International rehearsal processes

Edited by
JEN HARVIE and ANDY LAVENDER

Manchester University Press
Manchester and New York

distributed in the United States exclusively by Palgrave Macmillan

Published by Manchester University Press
Oxford Road, Manchester M13 9NR, UK
and Room 400, 175 Fifth Avenue, New York, NY 10010, USA
www.manchesteruniversitypress.co.uk

Distributed in the United States exclusively by
Palgrave Macmillan, 175 Fifth Avenue, New York,
NY 10010, USA

Distributed in Canada exclusively by
UBC Press, University of British Columbia, 2029 West Mall,
Vancouver, BC, Canada V6T 1Z2

British Library Cataloguing-in-Publication Data
A catalogue record for this book is available from the British Library

Library of Congress Cataloging-in-Publication Data applied for

ISBN 978 0 7190 7491 2   hardback
ISBN 978 0 7190 7492 9   paperback

First published 2010

The publisher has no responsibility for the persistence or accuracy of URLs for any external or third-party internet websites referred to in this book, and does not guarantee that any content on such websites is, or will remain, accurate or appropriate.

Typeset by Servis Filmsetting Ltd, Stockport, Cheshire
Printed in Great Britain
by CPI Antony Rowe, Chippenham, Wiltshire

CONTENTS

List of figures   vii
List of boxes   xii
List of contributors   xiv
Preface   xviii
Acknowledgements   xix

Introduction – Contemporary theatre in the making   1
JEN HARVIE

1 The Builders Association – *Super Vision* (2005) – Digital dataflow and the
   synthesis of everything   17
   ANDY LAVENDER
2 Sidi Larbi Cherkaoui – *Myth* (2007) – Mapping the multiple   39
   LOU COPE
3 Complicite – *The Elephant Vanishes* (2003/4) – 'The elephant and keeper
   have vanished completely . . . They will never be coming back'   59
   CATHERINE ALEXANDER
4 Elevator Repair Service – *Cab Legs* (1997) to *Gatz* (2006) – Reversing the
   ruins: the power of theatrical miscomprehension   81
   SARA JANE BAILES
5 Forced Entertainment – *The Travels* (2002) – The anti-theatrical director 101
   ALEX MERMIKIDES

  6 Rodrigo García and La Carnicería Teatro – *Une façon d'aborder l'idée de
     méfiance* (*One Way to Approach the Idea of Mistrust*) (2006) –
     Approaching mistrust   121
     LOURDES OROZCO
  7 Gekidan Kaitaisha – *Bye Bye: The New Primitive* (2001) – Theatre of the
     body and cultural deconstruction   140
     ADAM BROINOWSKI
  8 Robert Lepage and Ex Machina – *Lipsynch* (2007) – Performance
     transformations and cycles   160
     ALEKSANDAR SAŠA DUNDJEROVIĆ
  9 Richard Maxwell and the New York City Players – *The End of Reality*
     (2006) – Exploring acting   180
     SARAH GORMAN
 10 Not Yet It's Difficult – *Blowback* (2004) – Unmaking *Blowback* – a visceral
     process for a political theatre   202
     PETER ECKERSALL
 11 Luk Perceval – *Platonov* (2006) – Rules for a theatre of contemporary
     contemplation   222
     ZOË SVENDSEN

Postscript   242
Select bibliography   244
Index   247

FIGURES

1.1 The Builders Association, *Super Vision*, rehearsal shot: Joe Silovski (TSA officer) and Rizwan Mirza (the businessman). Photo: Anna Henckel-Donnersmarck   23

1.2 Rehearsal shot: Moe Angelos as the grandmother and Tanya Selvaratnam as Jen. Photo: Andy Lavender   24

1.3 A scan of set designer Stewart Laing's notebook. Image: Stewart Laing   26

1.4 Computer rendition of a design idea from the Ohio workshop in 2004. Image: Stewart Laing   26

1.5 A scan of set designer Stewart Laing's sketchbook. Image: Stewart Laing   27

1.6 A still of an animation of the set made during the workshop at the Kitchen. Image provided by Stewart Laing   27

1.7 Rehearsal shot: Tanya Selvaratnam onstage. Photo: Andy Lavender   28

1.8 Rehearsal shot: David Pence tries out the arctic stage that, midway through the process, was envisaged for the end of the piece. Photo: Andy Lavender   30

2.1 Scene from *Myth*, © Koen Broos for Toneelhuis, Antwerp   40

2.2 Sidi Larbi Cherkaoui, © Koen Broos for Toneelhuis, Antwerp   42

2.3 Ulrika Kinn Svensson and Damien Jalet in rehearsal, © Koen Broos for Toneelhuis, Antwerp   45

2.4 James O'Hara and Christine Leboutte in *Myth*, © Koen Broos for Toneelhuis, Antwerp   48

2.5 Darryl Woods makes his mark in *Myth*, © Koen Broos for Toneelhuis, Antwerp   51

2.6 Patricia Bovi sings, accompanied by Ensemble Micrologus, in *Myth*, © Koen Broos for Toneelhuis, Antwerp   52

2.7   Marc Wagemans in front of Wim Van de Cappelle's set for *Myth*,
      © Koen Broos for Toneelhuis, Antwerp   53
2.8   *Myth*'s multiplicity as represented by its poster, created by Dooreman &
      Houbrechts, 2007   56
3.1   *The Elephant Vanishes* rehearsal shot: Mitsuru Fukikoshi and Atsuko
      Takaizumi exploring the husband and wife relationship in 'Sleep'.
      Photo: Sarah Ainslie   66
3.2   Rehearsal shot: a devising task. Left to right: Catherine Alexander,
      Keitoku Takata, Ryoko Tateishi, Victoria Gould. Photo: Sarah Ainslie   69
3.3   Rehearsal shot: a devising task for 'The Second Bakery Attack'. Photo:
      Sarah Ainslie   70
3.4   Design sketch by Michael Levine showing the horizontal wires and the
      flying man   72
3.5   Design sketch by Michael Levine showing the video projection screen
      making a rear wall, and a concentrated performance area with furniture   73
3.6   Rehearsal shot: filming wind-blown sand. Foreground left to right, Niall
      Black, Simon McBurney, Catherine Alexander. Photo: Sarah Ainslie   75
3.7   Rehearsal shot: Mitsuru Fukikoshi, with a projected image of wind-blown
      sand, in a devising task. Photo: Sarah Ainslie   75
3.8   Bilingual rehearsal notes. Photo: Sarah Ainslie   77
4.1   Elevator Repair Service's *Cab Legs* (1997): Tory Vazquez, James
      Hannaham, Scott Shepherd, Rinne Groff. Photo: Clemens Scharre, Salzburg,
      Austria   82
4.2   *Gatz* (2006): Scott Shepherd, Kate Scelsa. Photo: Chris Beirens, Brussels,
      Belgium   84
4.3   *Spine Check* (1992/3): Rinne Groff, Steve Bodow. Photo: John Collins, New
      York, 1993   85
4.4   *Total Fictional Lie* (1998): Robert Cucuzza, Susie Sokol. Photo: John
      Collins, Berlin, Germany   88
4.5   *Total Fictional Lie* (1998): Leslie Buxbaum, Rinne Groff (feet). Photo:
      John Collins, Berlin, Germany   93
4.6   *Highway to Tomorrow* (1999): Randolph Curtis Rand, Paul Boocock,
      Susie Sokol. Photo: Drew Fellman, New York, 2000   94
4.7   *Room Tone* (2002): Susie Sokol. Photo: Dona Ann McAdams, New
      York   95
4.8   *Gatz* (2006): Jim Fletcher, Scott Shepherd. Photo: Chris Beirens, Brussels,
      Belgium   98
5.1   Forced Entertainment's *The Travels* (2002). Photo by Hugo Glendinning   102
5.2   *The Travels*. Photo by Hugo Glendinning   103
5.3   The notebook. Photo by Alex Mermikides   107
5.4   'Dead Lane' map by Claire Marshall. Photo, Forced Entertainment   112
5.5   'Love Lane' map by Terry O'Connor. Photo, Forced Entertainment   113
5.6   *The Travels*. Photo by Hugo Glendinning   117
6.1   *Une façon* rehearsal day nine, 9 February 2006. Photo: Lourdes Orozco   125
6.2   Team discussion at the end of day eight. Photo: Lourdes Orozco   127

6.3   Mateus on day eight and her scene with the hens. Photo: Lourdes
        Orozco   129
6.4   García's storyboard on day five. Photo: Lourdes Orozco   131
6.5   Rehearsal day nine. Photo: Lourdes Orozco   132
6.6 & 6.7   Real and projected images of Ugeux in *Une façon*. Photo: Lourdes
        Orozco   135
6.8   Text and floating doughnut. Photo: Lourdes Orozco   137
7.1   *Bye Bye: The New Primitive*: Hino Hiruko in the scene 'Chimaera'. Photo:
        Miyauchi Katsu   147
7.2   Group choreography: *mure-kehai* ('pack' sensation). Photo: Miyauchi
        Katsu   149
7.3   The pack, wild and undomesticated. Photo: Miyauchi Katsu   150
7.4   From alpha to omega, the alphabet sequence. Adam Broinowski and
        Nakajima Miyuki. Photo: Miyauchi Katsu   151
7.5   Moving from 'Family' to the slapping scene. Adam Broinowski walks
        towards Nomoto Ryôko. Photo: Miyauchi Katsu   154
7.6   'Save our souls': the end of the slapping scene. Adam Broinowski and
        Nomoto Ryôko. Photo: Miyauchi Katsu   155
7.7   *Gunji* (holding and releasing): Hino Hiruko and Adam Broinowski.
        Photo: Miyauchi Katsu   156
8.1   *Lipsynch's* Newcastle cycle, February 2007: Ricky Miller as Jeffrey. Photo:
        Erick Labbé; courtesy of Ex Machina, Quebec City   162
8.2   Newcastle cycle: dubbing in a sound recording studio. Photo: Erick
        Labbé; courtesy of Ex Machina, Quebec City   166
8.3   The end of part one: Nuria Garcia as Lupe walks on top of the aeroplane.
        Photo: Erick Labbé; courtesy of Ex Machina   169
8.4   Newcastle cycle: Nuria García. Photo: Erick Labbé; courtesy of Ex
        Machina   172
8.5   Newcastle cycle: Nuria García as Lupe. Photo: Erick Labbé; courtesy of
        Ex Machina   174
8.6   Newcastle cycle: Nuria García. Photo: Erick Labbé; courtesy of Ex
        Machina   176
8.7   Montreal cycle, June 2007. Photo: Víctor Diaz; courtesy of Ex Machina 177
8.8   Montreal cycle. Photo: Víctor Diaz; courtesy of Ex Machina   177
9.1   The final scene of *The End of Reality*; choreographed fight sequence.
        Photo: Michael Schmelling   183
9.2   *The End of Reality* cast warm up. Photo: Sarah Gorman   184
9.3   Brian Mendes as security guard 'Brian'. Photo: Michael Schmelling 187
9.4   Mendes restrains Kempson. Photo: Michael Schmelling   187
9.5   Fletcher and Mendes' 'stillness' in performance. Photo: Michael
        Schmelling   191
9.6   Maxwell gives notes. Photo: Sarah Gorman   192
9.7   Kempson as guard with her back to audience. Photo: Michael
        Schmelling   195
9.8   Mendes' notes. Photo: Sarah Gorman   197

9.9   The cast discuss blocking alterations after the angle of the desk has been
        changed. Photo: Sarah Gorman   198

10.1   *Blowback* interrogation scene: Vivienne Walshe and Luciano Martucci.
        Photo: Lyn Pool   204

10.2   Shakespeare invented violence in *William Shakespeare: Hung, Drawn
        and Quartered*; Paul Bongiovanni (right) beats Greg Ulfan with the
        collected works of Shakespeare. Photo: Lyn Pool   206

10.3   Interviews in *Journey to Con-fusion #2* (Tokyo 2000), NYID in
        collaboration with Gekidan Kaitaisha, Louise Taube on the screen.
        Photo: Miyauchi Katsu   207

10.4   *The Australasian Post-cartoon Sports Edition*; Kha Viet Tran (right)
        teaches Katia Molino *Vovinam*. Photo: Lyn Pool   208

10.5   *Blowback*'s Scott and Charlene. *World of Our Own* soap opera actors
        played by Todd MacDonald and Roslyn Oades. Photo: Lyn Pool   211

10.6   *Blowback*, interrogation table. Military Intelligence Officer Casey James
        (Anita Hegh) interrogates Darko Reeve (Benjamin McNair). Photo: Lyn
        Pool   212

10.7   *Blowback*: American occupation forces' media division. Surveillance
        screen images contrast with live action. Tom Considine and Natalie
        Cursio. Photo: Lyn Pool   213

10.8   *Blowback* space, reverse angle. Photo: Lyn Pool   213

10.9   Televisual media in NYID performances. *Scenes from the Beginning of
        the End*. Photo: Lyn Pool   217

11.1   Luk Perceval' s direction of *Platonov*: Anna Petrovna (Karin Neuhäuser)
        waiting for Platonov (Act 1). Still from rehearsal footage. Image: Nikolai
        Eberth   225

11.2   Platonov dances himself to exhaustion (Act 2). Left to right: Osip
        (Thomas Thieme), Sascha (Christina Geisse), Jakow (Bernd Grawert),
        Platonov (Thomas Bading), Anna Petrovna (Karin Neuhäuser). Photo:
        Mira Voigt   228

11.3   Triletsky: 'What's wrong with Anna Petrovna today? She laughs, she
        sighs, kisses everybody . . . You know, I think she may be in love!' (Act 2).
        Left to right: Glagolyev (Erhard Marggraf), Petrin (Michael Renzenbrink),
        Vengerovich Jr (David Ruland), Platonov (Thomas Bading), Anna
        Petrovna (Karin Neuhäuser), Triletsky (Felix Römer). Photo: Mira Voigt   229

11.4   Platonov: 'What did I do? Nothing good. When did I ever do anything
        that I didn't feel ashamed of afterwards?' (Act 2). Left to right: Platonov
        (Thomas Bading), Sascha (Christina Geisse). Still from rehearsal footage.
        Image: Nikolai Eberth   233

11.5   Camera, action (Act 1). Left to right: Vengerovich Sr (Ulrich Voss),
        Vengerovich Jr (David Ruland), Benedict Haubrich (assistant director),
        Ivan Ivanovich (Horst Hiemer), Luk Perceval, Anna Petrovna (Karin
        Neuhäuser). Photo: Zoë Svendsen   235

11.6   Anna Petrovna: 'It's simple: a woman has come to you who loves you,
        the weather is gorgeous, what's the problem?!' (Act 2). Left to right:

Anna Petrovna (Karin Neuhäuser), Platonov (Thomas Bading). Still
from rehearsal footage. Image: Nikolai Eberth   236
11.7   Luk Perceval in conversation during rehearsal with Karin Neuhäuser
and Thomas Bading. Still from rehearsal footage. Image: Nikolai Eberth   239
11.8   Ivan Ivanovich: 'God has lost patience with us and has unleashed his
might.' Left to right: Marja (Lea Draeger), Platonov (Thomas Bading),
Anna Petrovna (Karin Neuhäuser). Photo: Matthias Horn   240
Postscript   A programme for making contemporary theatre   243

BOXES

1.1	On time (The Builders Association)	21
1.2	On laptops	25
1.3	On technical operation	33
1.4	Three memories	36
2.1	Les Ballets C de la B (Sidi Larbi Cherkaoui)	41
2.2	Tasks	45
3.1	The Seven Levels of Tension (Complicite)	68
3.2	On having technical support and equipment in rehearsals	74
4.1	'Quoting', 'lifting' and 'copying' (Elevator Repair Service)	86
4.2	Sources	90
5.1	Models of theatre-making (Forced Entertainment)	106
5.2	Tim's dream	107
5.3	The rules	114
5.4	Three terms	118
6.1	Director-performer dynamics: from fear to admiration (Rodrigo García and La Carnicería Teatro)	126
6.2	'Authenticity' versus 'theatre'	130
6.3	Animals on stage: can we eat them?	134
7.1	An approach to making (Gekidan Kaitaisha)	142
7.2	The practice of 'carrying'	145
7.3	Deconstructive scenography	152
8.1	The RSVP Cycles (Robert Lepage and Ex Machina)	163
8.2	Playing and accidental discovery	164
8.3	Open rehearsals	171
9.1	Rehearsal tasks (Richard Maxwell and the New York City Players)	190

9.2	Brian and Marcia's kiss	193
9.3	Finding a ceiling	196
10.1	Body listening (Not Yet It's Difficult)	203
10.2	Process and the politics of performance	208
10.3	The performance text	215
10.4	Performance and the rehearsal process	218
11.1	Perceval's prerequisites for rehearsal (Luk Perceval)	227
11.2	Perceval's rules of engagement	231
11.3	On giving notes	238

CONTRIBUTORS

CATHERINE ALEXANDER is Senior Lecturer in Acting on the BA (Hons) Acting for Collaborative and Devised Theatre at the Central School of Speech and Drama, University of London. Her work with Complicite includes: (Associate Director) *A Disappearing Number*, international tour and BITE festival, Barbican, 2007, and *The Elephant Vanishes*, Setagaya Public Theatre, Tokyo, BITE, and Lincoln Centre Festival, 2004/5; (Artistic Collaborator) *The Chairs*, Royal Court and Broadway, 1997; (Assistant Director) *The Caucasian Chalk Circle*, National Theatre and tour, 1997, and *Out of a house walked a man. . .*, National Theatre, 1994/5. As Artistic Director of Quiconque, 2000–2007: *Last Laughs, Window Play, Big Bad Duvet Terror, Hideaway* (produced on tour by Complicite) and *Biscuits of Love*. Other work includes: (Staff Director) *Coram Boy*, National Theatre 2006. In 2006 Catherine won the Jerwood Prize for a research project based on *Amedée* at The Young Vic.

SARA JANE BAILES is Senior Lecturer in Theatre and Performance at the University of Sussex, Brighton. Her research focuses on contemporary experimental perform-ance and performativity and utopia. She is co-editor of *Trafficking Boundaries* (*Women & Performance: A Journal of Feminist Theory*, 2002), author of *Performance Theatre and the Poetics of Failure* (Routledge 2010), and creative advisor with theatre ensemble The Special Guests. She writes for performance and has published on Forced Entertainment (*TheatreForum*) and Goat Island (*Performance Research* and *Frakcija)*. She is currently working on an oral history project, *Sounding Performance*, with Claire Macdonald and the British Library Sound Archive.

ADAM BROINOWSKI is a performer, director, translator and writer. He made the award-winning documentary *Hell Bento!* (Tetrapod. SBSiTV, 1995) and has made original solos (*non-dog, Vivisection Vision: Animal Reflections, Gherkin*) and group stage productions (*Know No Cure, Hotel Obsino, The Great Gameshow of Pernicious Influences, H20*). He has also worked with many theatre companies in Australia (Company B, desoxy, Dramalab, La Mama, Magpie, Not Yet It's Difficult, Playbox, Salamanca, Snuff Puppets, Stalker), Malaysia (Dramalab) and Japan (Gekidan Kaitaisha, Shinjuku Ryozanpaku, Rinkogun, Rakutendan, Mono), touring to festivals in South America, Europe, UK, USA, Asia, the Pacific and around Australia. He was a core member of Gekidan Kaitaisha and a research fellow at the University of Tokyo (2001-2005). He is a PhD candidate at the University of Melbourne/VCA critically analysing the space of war, memory and the body between theatre, philosophy and politics.

LOU COPE is a British dramaturg, lecturer, writer and director currently based in Belgium. Having directed collaborative performance projects in the UK for ten years, she now specialises in dramaturging, teaching and writing about, around or *as* collaborative practice. Lou will be Sidi Larbi Cherkaoni's dramaturg in *Babel* (2010), co-directed by Damien Jalet and designed by Antony Gormley. Recent or current articles cover training for collaborative practice, discussions of process with Alain Platel, and analysis of collaborative process for use in the visual acts. Lou also teaches in a number of HE institutions and is nearing completion of her PhD in facilitating collaborative practice.

ALEKSANDAR SAŠA DUNDJEROVIĆis Senior Lecturer in Theatre and Performance at the University of Manchester. His research focuses on contemporary theatre-making (interdisciplinary directing and devising), political theatre, and the crossovers between film and theatre. He is a theatre director who has worked in Canada, Serbia, Romania, Colombia and the UK, and author of *The Cinema of Robert Lepage* (Wallflower Press, 2003), *The Theatricality of Robert Lepage* (McGill-Queen's University Press, 2007) and *Robert Lepage* (Routledge Performance, Practitioners, 2009). He was visiting professor in the Theatre Postgraduate Program at the University of São Paulo in 2007.

PETER ECKERSALL teaches Theatre Studies in the School of Culture and Communication, University of Melbourne. He researches on Japanese theatre, contemporary performance and dramaturgy. Recent publications include *Theorizing the Angura Space: Avant-garde Performance and Politics in Japan 1960-2000* (Brill, 2006) and (co-editor with Edward Scheer) *The Ends of the 60s: Performance, Media and Contemporary Culture* (Performance Paradigm, 2006). He is dramaturg for Not Yet It's Difficult and an Australia Council Dramaturgy Fellow. Currently he is editing a book of plays by Kawamura Takeshi and researching performative interactions in art, theatre and politics in 1960s Japan.

SARAH GORMAN is Principal Lecturer in Drama, Theatre & Performance Studies at Roehampton University, London. Her research focuses on contemporary European and North American experimental theatre. She has published on Richard Maxwell and the New York City Players in *Contemporary Theatre Review*, on Forced Entertainment and Janet Cardiff in *Performance Research*, on 'new media' in *A Concise Companion to*

Contemporary British and Irish Drama (Holdsworth and Luckhurst [eds], Blackwell, 2007) and on Ljubljana's Mladi Levi festival in *Contemporary Theatres in Europe: A Critical Companion* (Kelleher and Ridout [eds], Routledge, 2006). She is currently writing *The Theatre of Richard Maxwell and the New York City Players* for Routledge.

JEN HARVIE is Reader in Theatre and Performance at Queen Mary, University of London. Her research focuses on contemporary performance and cultural identities. She is author of *Staging the UK* (Manchester University Press, 2005), co-author of *The Routledge Companion to Theatre and Performance* (2006, with Paul Allain) and co-editor of *Contemporary Theatre Review*'s special issue on Globalisation and Theatre (2006, with Dan Rebellato). She has published numerous essays, including on Robert Lepage and on DV8 Physical Theatre. She is co-editor with Rebellato of Palgrave Macmillan's series *Theatre&*, and author of *Theatre & the City* (Palgrave, 2009).

ANDY LAVENDER is Dean of Research and Professor of Contemporary Theatre at the Central School of Speech and Drama, University of London. He is artistic director of the theatre/performance company Lightwork (www.lightwork.co.uk). Writing includes *Hamlet in Pieces: Shakespeare Reworked by Peter Brook, Robert Lepage and Robert Wilson* (Nick Hern Books/Continuum, 2001) and essays on multimedia performance in Mary Luckhurst (ed.), *A Companion to Modern British and Irish Drama* (Blackwell, 2006) and Chapple and Kattenbelt (eds), *Intermediality in Theatre and Performance* (Rodopi, 2006). He is co-convenor of the Intermediality in Theatre and Performance working group of the International Federation of Theatre Research.

ALEX MERMIKIDES is a lecturer at Kingston University (London). Her research is on contemporary theatre-making, particularly script-writing and devising (the subject of her PhD from Goldsmiths College, University of London). She is co-editor of the forthcoming book *Devising in Process*, to be published by Palgrave in 2009. Her plays have been performed on stage (including at the Battersea Arts Centre, Lyric Hammersmith and Camden People's Theatre, all in London) and radio (BBC Radio 4). She is a member of Lightwork, the London-based multimedia theatre company directed by Andy Lavender.

LOURDES OROZCO is Lecturer in Theatre Studies at the Workshop Theatre (University of Leeds). Her research interests lie in cultural policy and contemporary theatre practice in Western Europe. She is the author of *Teatro y politica: Barcelona 1980-2000* (Madrid: ADE-Teatro, 2007) and co-editor (with Maria Delgado and David George) of *Contemporary Theatre Review*'s special issue on *Catalan Theatre 1975-2006: Politics, Identity and Performance* (2007). She has published articles on the work of contemporary theatre practitioners such as Rodrigo García and Albert Boadella and also on theatre buildings and policymaking in Spain and the UK.

ZOË SVENDSEN works internationally as a director, dramaturg and artistic collaborator, regularly translating plays from German (recently on attachment at the National Theatre Studio). Zoë is currently Research Fellow in Drama and Performance at the University of Cambridge. Zoë is Artistic Director of Metis Arts, and is co-directing and writing the TippingPoint commissional performance, *3rd Ring Out*.

PREFACE

As with many labours, this book resulted from a hunch and a desire.

The desire was inquisitive. We wanted to know what people did in their rehearsal rooms – how they made theatre that we found exciting, or pleasurable, or new and unusual. Theatre is a job of work that involves many people, whose activities can be mapped and explained. These activities change in relation to what culture permits, technologies allow, fashion invites, fancy provokes. Creative processes are not magic, even though sometimes they appear to produce magical effects. That's not to say that we wanted to pin them down, like butterflies on a board. Rather, we wanted to be butterflies ourselves, flitting across rehearsal rooms, touching lightly on one part and then another, the better to see the whole.

What connections were there between the intimate, precious and seemingly secret world of one rehearsal room with other rooms where interesting things were happening? Or would we find something special and unique? We wanted to explore from the inside, over the – what? – five hundred or more hours leading up to the short concentration of minutes that an audience eventually sees.

The hunch was that there are many ways of looking at theatre. But they all start with the act of looking.

Andy Lavender

ACKNOWLEDGEMENTS

As the following chapters make clear, this book could not exist were it not for the immense generosity of the theatre-makers who opened their rehearsals to us and to the book's other writers. Thank you most importantly to the companies and artists: The Builders Association, Sidi Larbi Cherkaoui, Complicite, Elevator Repair Service, Forced Entertainment, Rodrigo García and La Carnicería Teatro, Gekidan Kaitaisha, Robert Lepage and Ex Machina, Richard Maxwell and the New York City Players, Not Yet It's Difficult, and Luk Perceval. The book would also not be possible without the intelligent and patient work of its observer/writers. Thank you Catherine Alexander, Sara Jane Bailes, Adam Broinowski, Lou Cope, Saša Dundjerović, Peter Eckersall, Sarah Gorman, Alex Mermikides, Lourdes Orozco and Zoë Svendsen.

Development of the project has benefited from discussion with many, many others who deserve thanks. Some of these are Paul Allain, Bobby Baker, Peter Boenisch, Scott deLaHunta, Rebecca Groves, Adrian Heathfield, Erin Hurley, Karen Fricker, Joe Kelleher, Lucy Richardson, David Roesner, Lois Weaver and Lee White.

The book's development has been supported by the Arts and Humanities Research Council (which funded research leave for Bailes) and the British Academy (which funded research travel for Gorman).

We are especially grateful to our series editors, Maria Delgado and Peter Lichtenfels, who have supported this book throughout its development. Thanks also to anonymous readers for Manchester University Press who gave useful feedback on the project at an early stage, and to staff at Manchester University Press, who have been supportive throughout.

We are very grateful to our colleagues at Queen Mary and the Central School of Speech and Drama (both University of London), as well as Jen's former colleagues at Roehampton University, who have supported our research and work in this area more broadly. For practical support, thanks especially to Julia Boffey and Nick Ridout at Queen Mary and Simon Shepherd at the Central School of Speech and Drama.

Important thanks to those with whom we have explored some of the methods discussed in this book, including our students, and members of Andy's theatre company, Lightwork.

Thanks finally to our families, for your patience, support and love: Deb Kilbride; and Tricia Reid and Grace and Thomas Lavender.

Introduction: Contemporary theatre in the making

Jen Harvie

Watching theatre-making

This book aims to reveal what happens in rehearsal in the making of significant contemporary theatre. Rehearsal is understood here broadly as never just the repetition of learned delivery but the *creation* of performance. This book's eleven chapters, each focusing on one company of international stature, therefore describe the work of each creative team, including directors, performers, designers, writers, choreographers, instructors and technicians. And they explore several phases in the creation of new work, from conception and training, through development, preparation and delivery, to reception. Each chapter is written by an eyewitness who has had exceptional insider access to the company's work, in several cases as a participating maker in the process. Thus, the case studies convey the practical details of what happens in rehearsal but also the excitement, tensions and challenges of making innovative theatre for the international stage.

Making Contemporary Theatre aims to give insider access to contemporary rehearsal practices because many of us do not otherwise have that access: we experience theatre predominantly as a created product – a show – but have little opportunity to learn how it is created. Even when we are makers ourselves, it is rare we get to learn firsthand in detail about other makers' methods. This is partly because many practitioners carefully guard admission to their rehearsals, generally to help their companies feel safe to experiment rather than to protect any particular trade secrets.[1] More often, though, as many of the case studies here indicate, gaining access to the development and rehearsal process is simply impractical; it happens in more than one global location, in several languages and over several months or even years. The eleven chapters here travel with the companies across time, space and a host of different languages, distilling their processes of making and revealing their ambitions, concerns, inspirations, genealogies, methods, rules, preoccupations and curiosities. This insight helps us understand the work of each company, but also the work of theatre more broadly, as both audiences and practitioners ourselves, whether we are professional or would-be theatre-makers, students and/or teachers. Taken individually or collectively, the following chapters offer a range of knowledge, skills and insights which might be applied or combined in different ways to create new ways of seeing and making theatre.

This book also aims to redress the fact that there is relatively little published about contemporary *processes of making* theatre – as distinct from books about theatre productions. What has already been published on practices of making theatre focuses predominantly – though certainly not entirely – either on well-established individual companies or directors, or on strategies of directing the sort of text-based theatre that assumes psychological realism as its inevitable mode of performance.[2] *Making Contemporary Theatre* shares concerns and practices with this existing literature and is indebted to it, but our book seeks a new path, responding specifically to *new* trends in contemporary theatre-making. These trends reveal a persistent questioning of some of the fundamental beliefs that appear to underpin conventional practices of much twentieth- and twenty-first-century theatre-making, such as accepting the director as visionary leader or author/*auteur*, using text as starting point, valuing psychological realism, structuring narrative around conflict, and practising theatre itself as an established set of conventional practices. This is not to say that the theatre-making discussed here rejects the director, writer, texts, psychological realism, narrative or theatrical convention; indeed, it repeatedly returns to and exploits their allure. But it also considers how their seductiveness is potentially coercive as part of a wider examination of their limitations, interrogating their relevance in a twenty-first-century context and exploring how they might usefully be re-deployed through new theatrical forms which Hans-Thies Lehmann has influentially called postdramatic (a term to which I will return).[3]

Because of this ongoing theatrical trend to interrogate the roles of text and director, many of the chapters examine the methods of groups who devise theatre collectively, often led by or working with a director, but always with self-reflexive attention to the dynamics and ethics of power and authorship circulating amongst all participating makers. The popularity of devising in the work represented here reflects its move within theatre-making from a fairly marginal position in the 1970s to one of significant disciplinary and institutional orthodoxy by the first decade of the twenty-first century. We understand devising to be a method of performance development that starts from an idea or concept rather than a play text; is from the start significantly open-minded about what its end-product will be; and uses improvisation – by performers, but also other creators, including writers, designers, directors and choreographers – as a key part of its process. Its composition often happens concurrently in a variety of creative areas, including live performance, mediation, and the development of props/objects, machinery, texts and images. Processual refining takes place over time and in actual space, so that theatre-*making* is understood to be as plastic and time- and space-oriented as the medium of its output. This relatively recent shift towards devising's received orthodoxy as a theatre-making method reflects a handful of crucial and concurrent changes within theatre culture and beyond. These include scepticism about logocentrism, or the primacy of the word or text; in a related shift, a recognition that it is not only, or even principally, the playwright who creates a performance, but all those who contribute to theatre's multiple arts, including its performance, directing and design; and a parallel recognition that the meanings of performance are produced not just by its 'backstage' and onstage makers, but also by its audience.

Making Contemporary Theatre's focus on devising means it contributes to a growing library of recently published books on devising theatre.[4] However, where others generally aim to give overview analysis, often referring to many examples, *Making Contemporary Theatre* focuses on offering insight through select case-study examples written through the advantage afforded by rehearsal room witnessing. I discuss what we hope are the advantages of this insider approach in a little more detail below.

A final ambition for this book is that, through exploring contemporary theatre-making practices, it will offer insights into contemporary theatre but also into contemporary culture more broadly. These are points I return to in the final section of this introduction. But first, to give a stronger sense of the detail of the book, I outline our selection criteria and introduce the individual chapters.

Selecting the companies

The first criterion for selection was that companies and/or directors had to be exemplary of current cutting-edge theatre and performance, actively redefining established practices and inventing new ones in the conception, creation, rehearsal and presentation of theatre productions. They had to make theatre that did something new and exciting, received serious critical response and offered fresh rehearsal techniques. The book therefore concentrates on companies which are pioneering emergent creative practices. Sometimes this means the importance of the company itself is emergent, is only well-known in limited circles, or has only been established quite recently (usually after 1990). Sometimes it means the company itself is well-established but is nevertheless committed to ongoing exploration and innovation. While the book is on contemporary theatre, therefore, our particular inflection on the term 'contemporary' emphasises not immediate temporality so much as a focus on innovative, emergent practice. The time span covered by our examples extends back as far as 1997 because we see at that time emerging important practices of theatre-making that became increasingly ubiquitous over the ensuing decade and, at the time of writing, remain innovative in still-interesting ways.

Second, though we concentrate throughout on group practices of theatre-making, we have deliberately selected companies where strategies of leadership vary: for some, leadership is dispersed; for others, an individual director is clearly in charge. This is representative of the variety of contemporary practice, but it also suggests an emerging tendency in contemporary group-based theatre: after aiming for years (since the 1970s at least) to disperse power, ostensibly in pursuit of democracy, practice appears increasingly to value leadership. What this trend indicates is not always that devised theatre has abandoned the pursuit of democracy, though this may sometimes be the case. More importantly, it suggests that, after decades of attempts at democratic practice which were at best sometimes frustrating and at worst grossly compromised, many practitioners are now exploring strategies for *negotiating* democratic practices and relationships, in recognition that dispersed power is not necessarily democratic power and also that negotiated leadership can facilitate group agency.

Third, we have deliberately aimed to represent an eclectic range of practices, including chapters on physical performance, dance theatre, text-based theatre, multimedia theatre, work at the boundaries of theatre and performance art, and work combining these categories. This eclecticism is partly representative, capturing some of the diversity and multiplicity of contemporary – especially postdramatic – performance practice, which Lehmann has identified as deliberately non-hierarchical in its adoption and mixing of multiple forms of representation.[5] But our eclectic selection is also designed to reveal the specificity of particular kinds of theatre-making, and to suggest how creative approaches pioneered for one area of disciplinary practice might be – and are – applied across different forms in the emerging patterns and trends of postdramatic performance-making. Indeed, though the work discussed across this book varies in its forms, it is telling to note how much it shares in practices of making and how much this commonality arises from other shared formal characteristics, such as a shift away from linear narrative and towards exploiting all available means of representation in the service of a postdramatic theatre often concerned less with content than with form and with the practices of perception it invites.

Fourth, the selection is deliberately international, representing a range of European, North American and Asian companies and practitioners which attract international attention from audiences and critics and involve collaboration and presentation on the international theatre festival circuit. Our selection therefore largely ignores theatre which aims to make only local address or is community-based or national (unless it is also international). This international emphasis is necessary given our aim to explore emerging innovative theatre practice. The cutting-edge theatre of contemporary late capitalist culture is increasingly globalised. Its global conditions of production, distribution and reception inevitably influence what this emerging theatre often is: multilingual, emphatically visual, multimedia, and entailing an international, multicultural mix of collaborators. At least partly because the only shared international language it can confidently presume is the language of theatre, this theatre is also frequently self-referential about theatre's practices; in other words, it is metatheatrical, drawing attention not just to its own modes of representation but also to audiences' acts of perception.[6]

A last but not least criterion for selection was access. Writers had to have the kind of privileged access to each company's or practitioner's processes of making theatre which would provide the most illuminating and engaging detail and savour, allowing for understanding and analysis of the company's work but also, simply, a *sense* of it. With thanks to both the companies/practitioners and the writers, *Making Contemporary Theatre* has this privileged access. Admittedly, the degree of each writer's insider access is variable: some writers are academic observers; some, participant-makers. Likewise, the ways different writers have deployed their access varies: some focus more on details, others on the bigger picture. We have deliberately embraced this variety of relationships and approaches in order to explore the range of insights they offer, not least by allowing individual authors to explore how to articulate the work of his or her company most appropriately and dynamically. Across the board, however, we have sought insider, experience-based, close engagement with the work. Critics might argue that this approach compromises our authors' objectivity. This is a deliberate critical turn on our part: we are interested here in exploring subjective, engaged critical approaches rather than ones which privilege a supposed – but also problematic – critical objectivity.

We have aimed to maintain for our readers a direct line to our writers' access, as well as to the *processes* of theatre-making this access conveys, by providing photographs of rehearsals and materials generated in rehearsals – as well as productions – and by offering in each chapter asides in the form of embedded boxes of text. These boxes provide additional detail, extend or summarise examples, and record conversations, reproducing in miniature the kind of multiple, layered exchanges, digressions, red herrings and eureka moments that happen over weeks and months of rehearsal. The photographs, likewise, document multiple stories of rehearsal and development processes. They illustrate each work's evolving relationships to and between particular company histories, spaces, forms of training, people, bodies, languages, images, technologies and scenographies. They demonstrate practical strategies for generating performance and the ways that ideas materially evolve. They show drafts and experiments, some discarded, some reworked and some appearing, virtually unchanged, in the final performance. They document our writers' processes as well as those of the theatre-makers. Graphically, they show us a view which this book is committed to and which we usually cannot see – a view inside the rehearsal room and inside its processes.

Witnessing the companies

In chapter 1, Andy Lavender explores the work of The Builders Association, the New York-based, internationally touring, devised, multimedia theatre company directed by Marianne Weems, focusing on its 2005 production, *Super Vision*. Since forming in 1994, The Builders Association has practically and thematically explored relationships between lived, social experience and technology. *Super Vision*'s thematic engagement with these relationships weaves three narratives about three different and apparently unrelated sets of characters, who each experience a contemporary condition the company calls 'dataveillance', where our lived and ephemeral dailiness generates a parallel, enduring stream of electronic traces. The company's combined interests and methods produce a visually rich and textured theatricality as well as a resonant thematic investigation of the seductions and perils of our mediated, technological age; but they also entail a host of challenges for the processes of devising. Lavender examines how *Super Vision*'s development inverted conventional theatrical production processes, prioritising the creation of a media-saturated scenography over the creation of character. The process is racked by decisions related to scenography and the use of multimedia. Lavender identifies an artistic ethos committed both to collaboration with artists, designers and technicians from a range of backgrounds, and to a hierarchical structure which is largely flat but is marked by the executive facilitation of the director. Everywhere, relations between the live and the mediated are manifest and in creative tension.

Lou Cope lives and works in Belgium and was invited to observe the development of the work she discusses in chapter 2, Belgian-Moroccan choreographer Sidi Larbi Cherkaoui's dance piece, *Myth* (2007), co-produced by Antwerp's prestigious Toneelhuis theatre and London's Sadler's Wells, amongst others. The process of progressing towards – or accumulating – the show begins with a given theme of trauma, but perhaps more importantly with the accretion through training classes of a shared movement vocabulary, much of it from yoga. It clearly aims to preserve the specific movement style, personality and skills of each performer while nevertheless moving towards a fixed group performance. Issues raised in this chapter – about the dynamic relationships between leader and group, generating and fixing material, pragmatic decision-making and abstract thinking, and the value of surprise and accident – resonate throughout the collection. The chapter also implicitly draws attention to concerns shared throughout the collection and contemporary performance studies about how to *write* about or document the *act* of performance which might be seen as evanescent (especially in rehearsal), how to select what to write about, and how to represent the writing not simply as one's own but also as that of its contributing interviewees and subjects.

Catherine Alexander is an associate director with one of the UK's most influential contemporary theatre companies, the London-based, highly visual, Lecoq-trained, multimedia Complicite. Founded in 1983 and now led solely by director Simon McBurney, the company is known internationally for such productions as *The Three Lives of Lucie Cabrol* (1994–96) and *Mnemonic* (1999). In chapter 3, Alexander writes about its 2003–4 UK/Japan co-production, *The Elephant Vanishes*, which was based, ultimately, on three short fictions by the contemporary Japanese writer Haruki Murakami. Drawing on her rehearsal notebooks, memories of the time and interviews with participating artists, Alexander explores how the company faced the challenges of selecting sources, developing script, casting internationally, and working across English and Japanese languages and theatre cultures, with their different forms of training, approaches to collaboration, and hierarchies. Like several other writers throughout this collection, she also observes how the company responded to the accidental, found conditions of rehearsal.

Sara Jane Bailes has been observing the work processes and productions of New York-based Elevator Repair Service (ERS) since 1997, and she writes in chapter 4 about their work on a number of shows since then, from *Cab Legs* (1997) through *Total Fictional Lie* (1998), *Highway to Tomorrow* (2001) and *Room Tone* (2002) to *Gatz* (2006). In contrast to a perceived tendency in some contemporary experimental theatre to be sombre and self-consciously distanced, the work of ERS is distinctively gleeful, thrashing, absurdist and almost tactile in its engagement of the audience, and yet at the same time, as Bailes puts it, 'tamed by a fierce precision' (p. 82). It presents a curious dialectic, expressing both the 'introspective neuroses and self-assured attitude of New York City' (p.83), and accommodating pragmatics and aesthetics, flexibility and control, and preparation and accident. Work is devised by the group, often drawing on canonical American cultural texts. But it does not adapt those sources in conventional ways. A sequence of movement sampled from *The Shining*, for example, is re-cut and repeatedly recurs in unexpected ways. Detailed dances and soundtracks are core features of ERS's work and Bailes explores how these are composed – like all elements of their shows – through a combination of both carefully planned preparation and accident. For ERS, 'miscomprehension' is deliberate, a way of re-understanding the world.

Alex Mermikides observed one of the UK's most internationally famous experimental theatre companies, Sheffield-based Forced Entertainment. Founded in 1984 and directed by Tim Etchells, the company has continuously explored contemporary social experience, focusing on the kinds of stories we tell ourselves in order to try to make sense of the world, and how we tell these stories, particularly through theatre. Making work that is both big and bold and small and intimate, Forced Entertainment's shows include *200% and Bloody Thirsty* (1987), *First Night* (2001), *Bloody Mess* (2004) and *The World in Pictures* (2006). Focusing in chapter 5 on *The Travels* (2002), Mermikides examines the company's interest in exploring the dynamic, potentially intimate and easily abused relationship between performers and their audiences; the capacity of theatrical conventions to produce both deadness and exhilaration; the fruitfulness of applying rules to generate performance; the challenges of composing a final show from a surfeit of devised material; and the benefits of working as a sustained group. She focuses on authorial control of Forced Entertainment's group-devised work, exploring how the company's members combine elements of a director- or *auteur*-led system with a commitment to collective creation.

Lourdes Orozco also explores the dynamic tensions between director and company in the work of director Rodrigo García, who was born in Argentina and is now based in Spain. Orozco focuses in chapter 6 on the 2006 production of his company, La Carnicería Teatro, *Une façon d'aborder l'idée de méfiance* (*One Way to Approach the Idea of Mistrust*). García combines an established creative team (manager, designers and so on) with performers he has not worked with before, embedding his work in the stability of continuity while injecting fresh ideas as well as what he seems to see as a productive anxiety. The dualism – or paradoxical nature – of this approach informs his work in other ways too: alone, outside rehearsals, he produces text and storyboard images, while in rehearsals he works with the team on actions and images; projected text conveys one message while onstage action seems to convey another; and work is grounded in the real – including references to multinational companies and globally recognised disasters – but is also replete with apparently abstract or non-referential texts and images (a turtle making slow progress across the stage, a performer balancing live chickens). Orozco explores how *Une façon* produces multivalent meanings through practices of casting, development, working with different performers, editing, design-integration, production and touring. As in so many other chapters which deal with intellectually ambitious work, she notes that rehearsals are nevertheless pragmatic, concentrating on actions and how best to frame images, not principally discussing abstract ideas; and she suggests how the failure to attend to the pragmatic business of re-rehearsing scenes for touring can undermine them. She also implicitly questions the balance in García's work between representing the abuse of power in contemporary culture and the risk of reproducing that abuse in microcosm through a somewhat autocratic mode of directing.

Adam Broinowski has been a member of the Japanese 'body-theatre' company Gekidan Kaitaisha since 2001 and in chapter 7 he discusses the making of its show from the same year, *Bye Bye: The New Primitive*, in which he performed. The company's work comes out of the Japanese dance form of *ankoku butoh* which emerged after the Second World War. *Butoh* poses a social critique of the violence of the nuclear attack on Japan through a bleak visual aesthetic, acute kinetic control and, perhaps most importantly, the ambiguity of its bodies – rendered at once primitive through their muscular, non-verbal but clear articulation of feelings, and other-worldly, through the use of white body paint and slow, de-naturalised movement. Broinowski demonstrates how the detailed physical preparation of their bodies is foundational to the work of Gekidan Kaitaisha's performers, allowing, only subsequently, a choreography and performance to be generated. And he explores how the body signifies socially in Gekidan Kaitaisha's performances in general and *Bye Bye: The New Primitive* in particular, especially as a site of socially imposed violence.

Aleksandar Saša Dundjerović has written widely on the work of eminent Quebecois director Robert Lepage and his company, Ex Machina. Although Lepage also directs film, opera and other forms, he is best known for the work he also puts most focus on himself, his highly visual, multimedia, devised theatre work, including the solo performances in which he initially stars – such as *Elsinore* (1995), *The Far Side of the Moon* (2000) and *The Andersen Project* (2005) – and group shows – for example, *The Dragons' Trilogy* (1985), *The Seven Streams of the River Ota* (1994), and *Lipsynch* (2007). In chapter 8, Dundjerović observes the development and initial public performances of *Lipsynch*, co-produced by Ex Machina with Northern Stage, Newcastle, and the small UK touring company Théâtre Sans Frontières. What *Lipsynch* might represent in the development of Lepage's work, importantly, is both a more explicit acknowledgement than that made previously to initial audiences of the provisional nature of performances they are seeing, and an explicit invitation to them to participate in the creative process by feeding back responses on their experiences of the work-in-progress. *Lipsynch* demonstrates a shift in Lepage's strategies for negotiating what all artists discussed in this collection also have to manage: a balance between processes of creativity and audience expectations, between creation and production, and between the creative work of the company and the perception and meaning-making of audiences. Dundjerović here details the application of the cyclical RSVP method of group-devised performance-making in the development of *Lipsynch* as an exploration of voice; the creative benefits of this method for contributing performers and other artists; Lepage's relationship to the role of director as *auteur*; Ex Machina's sensitive and continuous integration of technology and story; and the relationship of Lepage and his company to the particular politics of Quebec, as well as to the politics of global migration and intercultural exchange.

Sarah Gorman has written extensively about the work of director Richard Maxwell and his company, New York City Players (NYCP), and for chapter 9 she observed development rehearsals for their 2006 show *The End of Reality*. Maxwell is rather an anomaly in the context of contemporary experimental theatre because he writes plays – not abstract or collaged performance 'texts', but plays, with conventional stage directions and dialogue rich with linguistic specificity and emotional conflict, including *House* (1998), *Drummer Wanted* (2001), *Joe* (2004), *Good Samaritans* (2005), and *Ode to the Man Who Kneels* (2007). What he does share with many of his peer experimenters is a keen interest in the pleasures of onstage reality-effects which are, however, achieved without using conventional strategies of psychological realism, strategies which many contemporary experimenters see as producing a non-real effect and as masking the work of ideologies through a normalising or humanist perspective. Gorman examines the significant challenge presented to many of his actors by Maxwell's simultaneous engagement of realist text and rejection of psycho-realist acting techniques, a rejection that strips many actors of a learned and valued method. She argues that Maxwell works to keep his actors in the theatrical present – rather than the fictional present, or fictional psychological past – and to help them produce a compelling emotional *reciprocity* amongst themselves on stage, rather than what she identifies as Method acting's emphasis on emotional *productivity*. She demonstrates how he does this in rehearsal and performance through concentrating on tasks over psychology, on action over acting, on reality-effects over realism.

Peter Eckersall has been dramaturg with Not Yet It's Difficult (NYID), based in Melbourne, Australia, since the company was established in 1995. NYID makes multimedia performance that is both politically and aesthetically self-reflexive about its position in a multimedia age. The 2004 production of *Blowback* that Eckersall examines in chapter 10 posited a future in which dissidents in an Australia occupied by US forces seek to destabilise those forces by hacking into state media. The power of the media's representational forms and cultural saturation is explored through multiple onstage cameras and projections which allow audiences to experience the dissonance between multiple live events and their mediated images, a dissonance illustrated vividly in the simultaneous and/or juxtaposed performance of a soap opera scene and violent military interrogations caught by surveillance cameras. Eckersall details the complex onstage action of this show, including how it wraps around the audience to incorporate them as witnesses and citizens in its represented future. He describes how the company combines set strategies for composing the show with an openness to devising processes, participants' contributions and change. The company's core trio of director, dramaturg and designer collaborate throughout the process, integrating their expertise into all aspects of the work. Its productions consistently address political issues through combining content and forms which are conventionally recognisable as political with practices which engage and compel viscerally, sensually.

For our final chapter, Zoë Svendsen attended rehearsals of Belgian director Luk Perceval's 2006 production of Chekhov's early play, *Platonov*, at Berlin's Schaubühne am Lehninerplatz where Perceval has been director-in-residence since 2005. This is the only chapter in the book which deals with the production of a classic play. This representation is important because the example is not atypical – innovative directors and companies are frequently called on to produce classics with their proven sale-ability (where new plays are comparatively risky) – but also because it demonstrates that innovation thrives in producing classics too, and that classics can powerfully address contemporary feeling. Perceval is interested in conveying a sense of the real but not through the arguably stale tropes of psychological realism. Like Maxwell, he pursues a heightened sense of the real through an approach to acting which focuses on the actor's present – rather than a character's psychological past – and through a performance aesthetic which is pared down, bare, forcing focus on actors and text. To rehearsal, Perceval applies a somewhat formalist approach, described in Svendsen's chapter as both an exoskeleton and a scaffold. But what he seeks in production is some sort of meaningful (if uncomfortable) familiarity, neither an alien formality nor the faked real of much psychological realism, with its actually unrealistic degree of eye contact, movement and focus on interiority.

Though this book by no means identifies a singular method or system for making contemporary theatre, it does identify shared trends, patterns and ideas. Can these be summarised? In our postscript (which is also a programme), we attempt the task.

Thinking through theatre

The work explored in this book highlights contemporary theatre-making's most urgent artistic and ideological concerns and conditions. Here, I address two of them: the work's relationship to global and local markets, communities and sensibilities; and the work's practice – in both developmental and production phases – as postdramatic theatre.

Global and local markets of production

Devised theatre's meanings are necessarily influenced by its conditions of production and presentation and, as already noted, the work is consistently presented in international festival contexts. This indicates not only its perceived high quality as product – which persuades festival programmers the work is marketable, distinct and artistically and economically viable. It also indicates certain shared characteristics which the work typically reproduces through development specifically for these production contexts. For one, the work is consistently promoted as not only excellent but innovative; it reproduces innovation and engages – often self-reflexively – in an economy which commoditises and possibly fetishises the new. Second, because the work is made to tour, its design aesthetics are frequently marked by an apparent fluidity and quasi-

minimalism which reflect materially what the work also means to represent thematically as its (international) fluency and adaptability. Third, the fact that it is made for
different audiences in different geographical locations, often different languages and
sometimes different cultures means that it must work across slightly more abstract
registers than might otherwise be the case. Thus, the stuff of cultural exchange is often
worked in the fabric of the content; the shows are often 'about' transculturalism or
boundary crossing. Where the 'local' is presented, it is as a function of something
other than itself; the concrete political determinants of whatever 'local' is put before us
are often used like case studies which illustrate more broadly recognisable categories
of experience or relationships between people, places and issues.

That said, there are noticeable cultural specificities to the work included in this
book, and these too importantly determine its meaning. For instance, the shows
from New York feature – and deal with – irony in a way that is foreign to, say, the
Japanese production which is grounded in *butoh*, a specifically East Asian form. The
body-focused improvisation-base of Cherkaoui, García and Complicite has a distinct
European inheritance, while Perceval's directing responds partly to the unique history
and mandate of his theatre, Berlin's Schaubühne am Lehninerplatz. Likewise, Forced
Entertainment's deliberate false amateurism – or apparent lack of skill – responds to
its situation in Sheffield, where a manufacturing industry based in skilled labour has
been shot to pieces in a period just a little longer than Forced Entertainment's lifetime.
Ex Machina's metropolitan multiculturalism arises from and responds to its production in Quebec, at a nodal point of continental language differences and explicit political and cultural debate about what it means to be at once North American, European,
transatlantic and global. NYID uses its position in the antipodes to explore an artistic
sensibility which might resist US military and media global hegemony. These distinctive colourings in part enable the work to have its specific character (it is grounded,
not rootless). But in a more globalised market, the influence and interpenetration
of ideas and practices as this work comes together at festivals establishes a number
of productive tensions and crossovers between, for example, Eastern and Western
thought and practice, dance and theatre forms, modes of improvisation and writing,
and focus upon story or action. Practices and preoccupations brought together from
different sites in globally sourced casts and international festivals produce both
tensions and new hybrid practices; for example, Eastern training practices of yoga
and body-awareness become foundational to more than half the work here, and co-
production on single shows frequently spans multiple continents. The performance
practices and outcomes explored in this book illustrate how the forces of contemporary culture are, dynamically, at once globalising and localising.

Postdramatic theatre

Partly as an outcome of being devised and globally produced, the work is postdramatic, bearing out Hans-Thies Lehmann's analysis of trends in avant-garde theatre
practice from the late 1960s on.[7] Lehmann's *Postdramatic Theatre* has encountered
some significant negative criticism.[8] But we find some of its key ideas profoundly
resonant in relation to the work we discuss here, particularly the phenomenological

turn it takes in theatre/performance criticism, paying attention to what's in the theatre space and in interaction with an audience, allowing us to be more precise in our calibrations of the medium-specific form and effects of theatre, and its affects for spectators. We also think it is potentially distinctive from ideas of postmodern theatre, particularly in crediting audiences with a form of political engagement instead of the potentially continuously open contingency-verging-on-apathy that some have seen as a symptom of postmodern theatre. Further, we think that its characteristic aesthetic effects result often directly from its processes of creation, something that Lehmann does not extensively explore.

First, what is postdramatic theatre? Broadly, it no longer focuses on the dramatic text; more than this, it is not principally defined by (but may also play with) both character as it is conventionally understood through psychological realism, and narrative in its conventional linear organisation around conflict. In place of dramatic theatre's drama-focused narrative emphasis, postdramatic theatre focuses on theatre, emphasising the visual (for our media age) and sacrificing a sense of coherent narrative synthesis 'in order to gain, in its place, the density of intensive moments',[9] particularly moments of *theatrical* intensity. Lehmann's book gathers a critical discourse and frame of reference that facilitates discussion of theatre precisely as theatre, cognisant of how movement, rhythm, architectonics, aural elements and so on all contribute to the fabric of the event. Postdramatic theatre, Lehmann contends, 'becomes more presence than representation, more shared than communicated experience, more process than product, more manifestation than signification, more energetic impulse than information'.[10] In all aspects of this description we can recognise the work discussed here in this book.

Part of the value of this theatre-focused perspective is that it pays proper attention to theatre's many meaning-making systems. Beyond this, for Lehmann, it offers social value for its spectators, who are invited to practise 'evenly hovering attention',[11] interpreting not in a linear fashion through obvious narrative or argument, but unpredictably, cumulatively, postponing the production of meaning and discovering gradually how different aspects of the performance relate and meanings evolve. Thus, we see in postdramatic theatre a consistent metatheatricality which produces for the audience a self-conscious *'politics of perception'*.[12] We are no longer addressed as in a dramatic theatre which claims to speak to (and construct) us as a unified mass, and which ignores our differences; but nor are we addressed as in a postmodern theatre which might have all its audience members producing individual, always provisional meanings in an abandonment of the politics of any shared group understanding or identification, let alone responsibility. Instead, we are constructed as 'a common contact of different singularities who do not melt their respective perspectives into a whole but at most share or communicate affinities in small groups'. Postdramatic theatre's potentially 'perturbing strategy of the withdrawal of synthesis', Lehmann argues, tenders 'the offer of a community of heterogeneous and particular imaginations'.[13] 'Theatre', he claims, 'becomes a "social situation" in which the spectator realizes that what s/he experiences depends not just on him/herself but also on others.'[14] Thus, like what is conventionally understood as postmodern theatre, postdramatic theatre *is* contingent and usefully recognises differences (of interpretation, culture, and so on). But it also eschews the political apathy postmodern theatre is so often accused of; instead, it engages the political responsibility of audience members to interpret, make sense and form at least some (political) affiliations.

Meaning in this postdramatic theatre is open but not infinitely so; in fact, it demands attention to a set of repeating thematic concerns, many of which are self-consciously political, though not in ways we might have expected from previous generations of so-called political theatre. Noticeably, the work reflects on relationships of contemporary culture to theatre's particular qualities. It considers theatre as a communicative art, exploring reality, spectacle, media, technology, creativity, craft, the body, stories and images. It attends to theatre as a communicative act, addressing violence, authority, the past, anxiety, trust, intention, accident, aesthetics, politics, cooperation, resistance, communication, intimacy, emotion, ethics and pleasure. And it considers theatre as an industry, embedded in globalisation, commodity culture and economic markets. In other words, postdramatic theatre – including the work discussed in this book – engages deliberately and self-reflexively with theatre's aesthetic practices and forms, the ways it offers itself for perception. As the examples in this book make clear, this engagement is always explicit in rehearsal and remains so in production. Indeed, one of the things this book demonstrates is how the characteristic aesthetic effects and thematic concerns visible in postdramatic theatre *production* are a result of its characteristic *processes of creation*.

Throughout, the practitioners explored here demonstrate a concern with power – but this is a concern not to reproduce what many of them might consider a failed political theatre focused on content, but rather to produce a theatre attentive to its own ambivalent relationship to the power of its forms and the ways those forms affect audience perception, the audience's construction of meaning and the constitution of an audience as an individual and/or a member of a group. This theatre pays consistent attention to fixing meaning or leaving it open; in other words, to authorship, its democratic dispersal and autocratic control. Repeatedly, we see an ambivalent embrace of the – persuasive and manipulative, exhilarating and frightening – power of the representational techniques of storytelling, spectacle and technology: most theatre discussed here is devised but it never rejects text; many of the companies highlight the media's exploitation of spectacle and technology, but they exploit it too; and although some companies focus perhaps more on the physical or the textual, most of them thoroughly integrate both, rejecting redundant understandings of the physical and the intellectual as separate. Consistently, the companies work not to erase their conditions of production by portraying these as an 'empty space' but to highlight how each show is literally made by the conditions of its production – the dimensions and found furniture of rehearsal spaces, the limits of rehearsal time, the challenges of international touring, the genuine social dynamics within the company, and the shared experience of makers and audience in the theatre. Repeatedly, we see a rejection of conventional theatrical practices of psychological realism for producing a 'real' theatre, but we also see an urgent seeking for other methods of producing something that feels genuinely important in different ways, that trades in authenticity and that deserves our attention now – perhaps 'more manifestation than signification, more energetic impulse than information'.[15] This is postdramatic theatre that is working out its ambivalent relationships to dramatic theatre, that is committed to purging or at least questioning what makes dramatic theatre redundant, but also to acknowledging and indeed expanding what makes theatre itself meaningful, effective and affective.

We observe in this collection a range of productions that are comfortable with eclectic sourcing and referencing, working with metaphor, metanarrative and metatheatre, but presenting broadly coherent worlds and narratives – perhaps a slightly more synthesised theatre than Lehmann would have. This is a theatrical theatre that is postdramatic and beyond postmodernism, that moves from the postmodern paradigm of performance towards a newer paradigm of presentation – that is still in-the-moment, but witting, organised, made for phenomenal engagement, spectatorial consumption and cognition; that can include representation, rather than hoping to supersede it, as in some postmodern theatre, or be effaced by it, as in much realism. As part of this shift, we observe a turn from narrativity to thematicity – the pieces we include still put some narration and narrative in play, but are usually strongly organised around a core of thematic concerns.

A significant, repeating feature of postdramatic theatre is that it encourages (or even necessitates) synaesthesia, the audience's gradual recognition and pulling together of correspondences across the work. We can see the origins of this produced effect in the processes witnessed throughout this book. Dispersed and multiple processes of creation become constitutive of the work in more ways than one – they are its process of making, and they remain in its product, requiring from its audiences a quality of 'evenly hovering attention'. Process has become more evidently defining and determining in postdramatic theatre – and it betokens a mode of production that alters the fixity of what is produced, so that the contingency of the end-product is a function of the easier (re)turn to process in the making. There is a shift in the nature of relationships between participants, though neither director nor author is 'dead'. Rather, our productions suggest that the nature of the creative *transaction* has evolved. We observe working processes that entail multiple inputs on a more level basis, usually with a director as facilitator – so creation is distributed, 'evenly hovering', but nevertheless facilitated. It entails openness but within programmatic parameters. In resonance with certain aspects of digital culture, it depends upon networks of connections between participants that can be variously made and remade; it is therefore differently generative than much theatre that has gone before – it inherently enables plural, simultaneous strands of development and the more evidently organic growth of the whole. Theatre-makers within such a culture work both collectively and semi-autonomously. This is nothing new, except that foregrounded here is the more immediately relational aspect of their work, always contingent, always capable of reiteration, always part of an ongoing transaction.

The devising modes witnessed here literally make postdramatic theatre. At the same time, these modes were necessary to postdramatic theatre and so it made them, to articulate a theatre sympathetic to the latter-day understanding of culture as lacking either grand narratives or answers, but committed nevertheless to some form of 'social situation' which acknowledges our connections and mutual responsibilities for making our knowledges and the realities of our experiences.

Notes

1 Giving access to theatre rehearsals has long been an industry taboo. Susan Letzler Cole's influential 1992 collection of essays based on observations of ten directors' processes, *Directors in Rehearsal*, is subtitled *A Hidden World* and cites objections to giving rehearsal access to outsiders by both George Bernard Shaw and Molière (Cole, *Directors in Rehearsal: A Hidden World* [London: Routledge, 1992], pp. 2–3). Based on the evidence of *Making Contemporary Theatre*, however, this taboo may be fading.

2 Important texts focusing on directing include: David Bradby and David Williams, *Directors' Theatre* (Basingstoke: Macmillan, 1988); Cole, *Directors in Rehearsal*; Judith Cook, *Directors' Theatre: Sixteen Leading Directors on the State of Theatre in Britain* (London: Hodder and Stoughton, 1989); Maria Delgado and Paul Heritage (eds), *In Contact with the Gods? Directors Talk Theatre* (Manchester: Manchester University Press, 1996); Gabriella Giannachi and Mary Luckhurst, *On Directing: Interviews with Directors* (London: Faber, 1999); Shomit Mitter, *Systems of Rehearsal: Stanislavsky, Brecht, Grotowski and Brook* (London: Routledge, 1992); Rebecca Schneider and Gabrielle Cody (eds), *Re:Direction: A Theoretical and Practical Guide* (London and New York: Routledge, 2002); David Tushingham, *Food for the Soul: A New Generation of British Theatremakers (Live: 1)* (London: Methuen, 1994); and, in part, Susan Letzler Cole, *Playwrights in Rehearsal: The Seduction of Company* (London: Routledge, 2001). See also Cambridge University Press's Directors in Perspective series (which includes texts on Robert Wilson, Tadashi Suzuki, and Ariane Mnouchkine and the Théâtre du Soleil), and Routledge's Performance Practitioners series (which includes short books on Jacques Lecoq and Mnouchkine). A detailed history of past rehearsal practices in England is Tiffany Stern's *Rehearsal from Shakespeare to Sheridan* (Oxford: Clarendon Press, 2000).

3 Hans-Thies Lehmann, *Postdramatic Theatre*, trans. Karen Jürs-Munby (Abingdon: Routledge, 2006).

4 This includes: Tina Bicât and Chris Baldwin, *Devised and Collaborative Theatre: A Practical Guide* (Ramsbury, England: Crowood Press, 2002); Emma Govan, Helen Nicholson and Katie Normington, *Making a Performance: Devising Histories and Contemporary Practices* (Abingdon: Routledge, 2007); Deirdre Heddon and Jane Milling, *Devising Performance: A Critical History* (Houndmills: Palgrave Macmillan, 2006); Leslie Hill and Helen Paris, *The Guerilla Guide to Performance Art: How to Make a Living as an Artist* (London: Continuum, 2nd edn, 2004); Alison Oddey, *Devising Theatre: A Practical and Theoretical Handbook* (London: Routledge, 1994); and Alex Mermikides and Jackie Smart (eds), *Devising in Process* (Houndmills: Palgrave Macmillan, forthcoming 2010). See also Nick Kaye (ed.), *Site-Specific Art: Performance, Place and Documentation* (London and New York: Routledge, 2000), Andy Lavender, *Hamlet in Pieces: Shakespeare Reworked by Peter Brook, Robert Wilson, Robert Lepage* (London: Nick Hern Books, 2001) and Caridad Svich (ed.), *Trans-global Readings: Crossing Theatrical Boundaries* (Manchester: Manchester University Press, 2003). Some useful examples are developed in Chris Johnston, *House of Games: Making Theatre from Everyday Life* (London: Nick Hern Books, 1998) and Theodore Shank (ed.), *Contemporary British Theatre* (Houndmills: Macmillan, 2nd edn, 1996). Useful books on and/or by individual artists, directors and companies include: Michèle Barrett and Bobby Baker (eds), *Bobby Baker: Redeeming Features of Daily Life* (Abingdon: Routledge, 2007); Stephen Bottoms and Matthew Goulish (eds), *Small Acts of Repair: Performance, Ecology and Goat Island* (London and New York: Routledge, 2007); Claudia Castellucci *et al.*, *The Theatre of Societas Raffaello Sanzio* (London and New York: Routledge, 2007); Robert Lepage and Remy Charest, *Robert Lepage: Connecting Flights*,

trans. Wanda Romer Taylor (Toronto: A. A. Knopf Canada, 1998); Paul Clements, *The Improvised Play: The Work of Mike Leigh* (London: Methuen, 1983); Tim Etchells, *Certain Fragments: Contemporary Performance and Forced Entertainment* (London and New York: Routledge, 1999); Andrew Quick, *The Wooster Group Work Book* (New York and London: Routledge, 2007); and David Savran, *Breaking the Rules: The Wooster Group* (New York: Theatre Communications Group, 1988).

5 Lehmann, *Postdramatic Theatre*, pp. 86–7 and 111–12.

6 That said, we have focused on broadly experimental productions (rather than commercial or demotic work), as these seemed most evidently to engage with innovation in both form and process and to be more readily influential in the field of new theatre-making. We do not gainsay the developments in content generation, delivery and brand management of larger-scale international theatre, including the marketable touring shows of Cirque du Soleil and cloned versions of mega-musicals from the stables of Andrew Lloyd Webber and Cameron Mackintosh. But discussion of these works is for a different book.

7 *Postdramatic Theatre*, Lehmann's book-length analysis, first published in German in 1999 and in English in 2006 (with several other translations in between), ranges principally across European, North American and Australian theatre and performance, including Tadeusz Kantor, William Forsythe, Heiner Goebbels, Robert Wilson, Sarah Kane and Heiner Müller. Given the longer arc of his survey, Lehmann inevitably embraces earlier postmodern work than we do, but our geographical scope is similar.

8 In her 2008 review in *TDR: The Drama Review*, for example, Elinor Fuchs suggests the book problematically proposes a generalising and colonising grand narrative, subsumes performance to theatre, and lays claim to the term 'postdramatic' in some spurious ways; she also takes issue with the book's translation, copy-editing and editing in English translation (Fuchs, review of Lehmann, *Postdramatic Theatre*, trans. Jürs-Munby, *TDR: The Drama Review* 52:2 [T198, 2008]: 178–83).

9 Lehmann, *Postdramatic Theatre*, p. 83.

10 *Ibid., p. 85.*

11 *Ibid.*, p. 87.

12 *Ibid.*, p. 185, italics original.

13 *Ibid.*, p. 83.

14 *Ibid.*, p. 107.

15 *Ibid.*, p. 85.

1

The Builders Association – *Super Vision* (2005) – Digital dataflow and the synthesis of everything

Andy Lavender

The new-spec practitioners

It was an easy decision to seek to observe The Builders Association for this book. My first encounter with the company's work was seeing *Jet Lag* at the Barbican Theatre, London, in 2000. I was struck by its precise bravado. Here was a crafted meld of performance, scenic design, sound and video, applied to a resonant concept and brought off with a cool commitment. This looked like a very modern sort of theatre – pleasurable in the intelligent play of its ideas, staging solutions and mixing of media. What was obvious, too, was that an experiment was afoot. The Builders Association seemed interested in meaning, narrative and emotional contour (not necessarily the priorities of all postmodern performance practitioners), whilst rampantly exploiting audio-visual technologies, the stuff of contemporary communications, in order better to tell its stories. The work resonated like a contemporary harmonic: collaborative creation, deconstructed narration, technological adaptation and aestheticised media-tion. How was it made? What were its principles? What could it teach us, by way of what it was and was not?

Founded in 1994, The Builders Association is a New York-based company that makes what might be described as 'theatre-plus'.[1] The shape of a signature starts to form across the early productions. The company's inaugural project, *Master Builder* (1994), based on Ibsen's play, was set in a partially constructed three-storey house, marooned on the stage like an atoll with, inside, the odd TV monitor mediating faces. *The White Album* (1995) wryly fused references to the Beatles' eponymous classic and Noël Coward's *Blithe Sprit*. *Imperial Motel (Faust)* (1996), the company's first inter-national co-production (with the Theater Neumarkt, Zurich), remediated an array of sources deriving from and including Goethe's play. The company subsequently refined this work in *Jump Cut (Faust)* (1997), which satisfied itself merely with Murnau's film *Faust* (1926) and John Jeserun's latter-day rendition.

Across these pieces is a deliberate deconstruction of classical and canonical material, continual location of productions in a very present cultural moment, and a focus on mediation as much as content. The multimedia fusion (sound, video, performance and architectonic design) helps bring the subject matter of the pieces to a state of resonant jeopardy, as it simultaneously magnifies, ironises and undercuts the material. It provides the shows with another signature feature: they dwell on ways in which contemporary communications technologies shape and define one's life within a culture.

The latter theme has risen to the fore in more recent productions. With *Jet Lag* (1998, with architects Diller + Scofidio), The Builders Association left the fictional havens provided by Ibsen, Goethe and (in a 1998 workshop) O'Neill to devise a series of reality-based shows. The company also embarked on what would be the first of several interdisciplinary collaborations with partners outside theatre. *Jet Lag* draws on actual (and most peculiar) incidents concerning travel of different kinds and sets something of a template for subsequent projects, cleverly interrelating actual and fictional circumstances, pre-recorded digital graphics and live video projection of the performers.

By the time the company produced *Alladeen* (2003) in collaboration with motiroti, the London-based Asian dance company led by Keith Khan, it was established internationally as a purveyor of classy multimedia spectaculars. *Alladeen* focused on the work of individuals in an international call centre in Bangalore, who are trained to speak and converse like Americans. In the same year the company's *Avanti: A Postindustrial Ghost Story*, a site-specific performance in the old Deluxe Sheet Metal Factory near the Studebaker factory in South Bend, unpacked a story of decline and change in America's industrial belt. *Continuous City* (2007–) explores contemporary urban environments across continents (fieldwork embraces Mumbai, Lagos and Mexico City) with the electronically facilitated involvement of spectators who are variously co-present and geographically remote.

Super Vision (2005) falls within the scope of these latter pieces. Characteristically, they grapple with large-scale social trends. They turn to relevant technological forms – video diary, radio logs, geo-mobile telecommunications, internet calling – figuring these thematically and theatrically as resources for multimedia performance. The warp of contemporary communications is worked into the weft of the shows themselves.

Artistic director Marianne Weems has directed all The Builders Association's productions to date. Weems was a dramaturg with the Wooster Group prior to establishing her own company, to which she brought a commitment to continual mediation of the bodies and voices that we see and hear on stage. This inheritance entails what Kim Whitener, a producer with both companies, describes as 'a little sensitivity – because the world out there has generally pronounced the Builders' work as a kind of second generation of the Wooster Group. And no-one wants to be considered a follower.'[2] Certainly Weems' post-Wooster theatre is intrinsically different from that of her erstwhile colleagues, in spite of the trace inheritance. There is a turn towards larger-scale pieces, more coherent narrative structures and a deliberate engagement with cultural and social themes. There are different modes of mediation – usually video projection on large rear cycloramas – and a more restless embrace of softwares in pursuit of what Weems describes as 'the presence of the technology and letting that be the protagonist'. As Wooster Group director Elizabeth LeCompte says, Weems' visual world 'is much more spectacular than mine. She takes structure from television and music video. It's a hybrid, a new genre entirely.'[3] That slightly overstates the case, although the *synthesised* mixedness of The Builders Association's work confers a distinct identity. In fashioning her hybrid, Weems herself is something of a compound: a mix of a European dramaturg-director, big on background research, theme and structure; and an old-style American show(wo)man, presenting modish high-tech spectaculars with pizzazz.

Contexts for *Super Vision*

Made in New York, *Super Vision* was decidedly unparochial.[4] The project was co-produced by the Wexner Center for the Arts in association with the Advanced Computer Center for the Arts and Design at The Ohio State University, the Walker Art Center (Minneapolis), Liverpool (under its European Capital of Culture 2008 banner), the Brooklyn Academy of Music Next Wave Festival, the New Zealand International Arts Festival, and the Mondavi Center for the Performing Arts, University of California, Davis. This is a show made to travel, and meant to make a splash around the US and at international festivals around the world. Its themes must be sufficiently accommodating to suit the show's touring footprint. Likewise its aesthetic configurations must appear new and exciting. The package – common on the international festival circuit – is of necessary performance innovation within a signature that guarantees brand identity.

In developing *Super Vision* The Builders Association undertook another major collaboration, following successful partnerships with Diller + Scofidio and motiroti. In this instance the main partner was dbox, an agency specialising in graphic design, animation and brand development, in particular in the luxury property sector.[5] The two companies had previously worked together when dbox provided animations for *Jet Lag* and *Alladeen*, after which James Gibbs, a dbox director, expressed his interest in being involved from the outset in any future collaboration. 'It's unusual for a design company like ours to be seeking challenges like *Super Vision*', says Gibbs. 'It's not something that's going to develop into a business for us. But it's a way of keeping the studio fresh.'[6]

Weems and Gibbs started discussing the project in 2003. 'James suggested the idea of surveillance as a field that we were both very interested in', Weems recounts. 'And surveillance and the theatre being a natural match . . . I started to research the data body and started looking at this more invisible form of surveillance.' Her research included John McGrath's book *Loving Big Brother: Surveillance Culture and Performance Space* in which, as she recounts, McGrath mentioned 'the idea that we are shadowed by an electronic doppelganger'.[7] Weems soon thought of this as 'dataveillance', a term that took root as (ostensibly) the thematic core of the show. It conjures the vapour trail that is left by credit card exchanges, mobile phone communications, visits to doctors, hotels, theatres – anything that allows a mark to be made on an electronic system that is then ripe for scrutiny and perhaps policing. The project had found its starting point.

Phases of development

With dataveillance as its theme, *Super Vision* was developed in a series of workshops. A ten-day phase, hosted by the Wexner Centre in Columbus, Ohio, in July 2004, principally focused on design ideas and content development. It was attended by Stewart Laing, a Scottish director-designer who had previously worked on Richard Jones's Broadway production of *Titanic* (1997); Chris Kondek, video designer on previous Builders projects (who subsequently withdrew from this one); Dan Dobson, the company's sound designer; two performers (Tanya Selvaratnam and Joe Silovski, who is also the company's technical manager); and two writers who subsequently left the project. This initial sketching was followed by a ten-day workshop that principally addressed the generation of text, held in New York in November 2004.

'There was this huge pool of dramaturgical information about data', says Weems, 'but it took us that long to find three stories that we really liked and believed in. So that resulted in a very small invited reading. It was weird – the first and only time I'll ever do that. We didn't even have microphones, we were just in a room, reading, it was terrible, but people liked it.'

The three storylines may have been identified, but the writing team left the project after this phase. Weems was after what she describes as 'a metaphorical level', at which point she hired Constance De Jong, a writer and performance artist best known as the librettist for Philip Glass's opera *Satyagraha: M.K. Gandhi in South Africa* (1981). 'This kind of group, what the end product is and what the process is, does not ask for a playwright,' says De Jong. Nevertheless, for its next concentrated phase of development, a two-week workshop in March 2005 at The Kitchen (a performance venue in westside Manhattan), the company worked with a script that De Jong and Weems had prepared. As Weems acknowledges, this marked 'a huge difference' from the company's usual improvisation-based process. The workshop entailed the full-size realisation of a 'draft' version of the set and a set-up for video projection. There were two additional performers, regular collaborators Kyle deCamp and Rizwan Mirza, along with video designer Peter Flaherty (who had worked on *Alladeen*).

This phase was not without its tensions. The company planned to present a showcase of its work at the end of the fortnight to an invited audience that would include potential funders. During work on a particularly vexing scene De Jong lamented 'the stupid pressure of the deadline of Saturday'. Weems, however, was at pains to insist that the showcase would be an opportunity to share some shapes and ideas rather

---

Box 1.1: On time

Super Vision's process of collective creation means that time-consuming changes must be made on the march. At one point during rehearsals at St Ann's video designer Peter Flaherty asks to change the timing of a video transition. 'Just a second,' he calls.

'Someone's gonna start a lexicon of Builders' terms,' says Marianne Weems dryly. '"One second" means at least two minutes.' She might be talking for anyone working with video in theatre.

'"How much longer?" means "Fuck you",' says sound designer Dan Dobson. They laugh. Time is always of the essence. In most ball games, the ball is in play for much less than game time. So in devising. We forget this at our peril.

---

than present finished stagings. The 'pressure of the deadline' means that decisions are made more swiftly. It suits a process that depends upon concretising the work in three dimensions. And it allows for feedback to be garnered that will inform future development.

A further two-week workshop followed at St Ann's Warehouse in Dumbo, Brooklyn, in September 2005, culminating in two performances to invited audiences. By this stage the cast had been consolidated by the addition of David Pence and Moe Angelos. This, in effect, was the final phase of development, entailing detailed reali-sation of the production prior to its get-in and first performances at the Walker Art Center in Minneapolis in October.

Circles of collaboration

It is usual in theatre-making for a team of individuals, each with their own specialism, to work together in the realisation of a production. The Builders Association, however, features a deeply embedded form of team-working that offers a good deal of creative leeway to many participants. The hierarchy is fairly flat, although Weems is clearly in charge. She works by way of facilitation, negotiation, questioning and occasional task-setting rather than *auteur*-like diktat. She goes through a forthcoming day's schedule at the Kitchen, for instance, then asks, 'What else? Questions, answers, thoughts, feel-ings?' The company is encouraged to share concerns or ideas. After a run of a scene that's been rehearsed, Weems asks, 'Thoughts, feelings? Want to try anything, look at anything different?' She runs the rehearsal room as a facilitator.

The group also works according to what production manager Neil Wilkinson describes as 'different circles of collaboration'. On *Super Vision*, accordingly, those circles are constituted by the director and the dbox team; the set, sound and video designers; the technical and production managers. This describes a set of inter-articulating groups, working loosely in small cells towards the realisation of an overarching vision. Wilkinson describes the work of his circle as that of moderation, given that 'the technology often fights each other' – lighting, video and scenic arrangements require careful dovetailing. This necessitates a committed process of ongoing communication and, often, personal compromise on the part of the designers.

In this instance, the performers are less intrinsic to the development of the work. As Silovsky observes, 'there's so much focus on the technology that the actual acting is hurt. There's not really much focus left over to figure out what the actors are doing.' 'Hurt' may indeed be the right term here, but I suspect that rather depends on your preferences. It is true that in the phases I observed the performers were required to deliver pre-scripted material without much – if any – work on back-story or underlying actions, the stuff of conventional characterisation. Instead their work in rehearsal was largely to do with calibrating movements, timings and tone. This seems inevitable in a process so determined by the task of integrating design elements in a synchronous whole. It makes for a certain evenness to the mode of acting, which forms a useful counterpoint to the different sorts of mediation in play ('flat' performance gets coloured differently by mediation) but arguably means that the shows do not make themselves available to a fuller range of emotional resonances. Perhaps, too, a diminution of the performers' creative input on this show is symptomatic of a company gestation where relationships are rebalanced in every project, with significant above-the-title collaborators – in this instance, dbox – affecting the internal dynamics of the creative process.

The stories

Super Vision begins with a prologue. A representative from Claritas (a market research company), played by Tanya Selvaratnam, addresses the audience, noting how it can be segmented following analysis of its credit card transactions in booking tonight's tickets along with other demographic markers. This opening catches the audience a little off-guard – it looks as though personal details have already been processed by the production team – and establishes the dataveillance theme in a savvy and ironic way.

The show then sets in motion three separate narratives. The first concerns the upper-middle-class Fletchers, Carol (Kyle deCamp), John Sr (David Pence) and their son John Jr (Owen Philip, who appears by way of video projection rather than in person). The family lives in an upscale, expensively furnished house whose virtual interiors, designed by dbox, are projected on an expansive rear cyclorama. John Sr is usually at his workstation, where he digitally adapts his son's identity to create false bank accounts and multiple trades. His remote adventuring spirals out of control until he flees the family home and ends yet more remotely in the arctic, where a horde of data, initially appearing as a bird-like flock in the distance, swarms around him.

The second narrative concerns a Ugandan-Asian businessman who travels in and out of the US. Each scene has the same set-up: an exchange between the businessman and a Transportation Security Administration (passport or border control) officer.

1.1 Rehearsal shot: Joe Silovski (TSA officer) and Rizwan Mirza (the businessman). Mirza's face is mediated by way of a camera offstage. Silovsky is sitting at the forestage desk, on the extreme right of the image, and performs to a camera a little way along the desk. The performers make apparent eye-contact when Mirza looks at the virtual Silovsky in the passport booth whilst Silovsky looks to his left, off-camera, at a pre-arranged mark. The image also shows a draft of the sorts of data and surveillance iconography developed in the video design.

Rizwan Mirza plays the businessman from onstage. Joe Silovsky plays a variety of officers from the desk that runs along the forestage, changing character in a playful riff of adaptations by way of hairstyle, facial hair and eyewear. He performs to a camera directly facing him, with his image located in a passport control booth that appears on a screen onstage (see figure 1.1).[8] The officers latch on to the merest hint of behaviour that might be construed as terrorist-like and seem to know everything about the businessman, from his cholesterol level to his sleeping requirements when booking hotels. This storyline resolves with the businessman slowly walking across the stage, remarking that 'now I profile in the US as one of your movers and shakers', meanwhile trailing personal data by way of a video projection that accumulates behind him like a dragnet.

The third narrative concerns Jen (Tanya Selvaratnam), a young Asian woman based in New York, and her grandmother in Sri Lanka (Moe Angelos). The pair converse by webchat. Jen is located at a workstation (with a camera) onstage, so that when she faces upstage to look at her computer monitor her own face is projected, as if on

1.2 Rehearsal shot: Moe Angelos as the grandmother and Tanya Selvaratnam as Jen. Angelos sits on the extreme left of the forestage desk. Selvaratnam is on stage at a workstation (facing a camera) where she can see Angelos's image. You can also see her other workstation – she moves between the two – behind the central sliding panel. The image of Angelos on the panels is broken up to denote her failing mental health. As with video calling formats, it includes a smaller image from one's own webcam (here, Selvaratnam's), so the image fuses both realist and metaphorical devices.

webcam, on to a screen onstage. Angelos sits at the desk on the forestage, also facing a camera, her image similarly projected. In a series of video-link conversations, we understand that Jen is helping her grandmother sort out the deeds to her house whilst digitally archiving family photos that trigger various reminiscences. Over the course of the piece the grandmother's mental coherence disintegrates through (we presume) the onset of Alzheimer's disease, figured here by a fracturing of the image of Angelos's face on the screen (see figure 1.2).

In the scenes between grandmother and granddaughter, and businessman and TSA officer, the performers connect by way of live mediation rather than direct eye contact, in a staging that performs both corporeal presence and virtuality, separation and conjunction. The relation is always to the mediating apparatus (the camera, the screen, the microphone) as much as to the fellow actor.

'I've done this kind of work a lot', says Angelos, 'but each time you do it you still have to deal with the foreignness of it. . . . I'm seated, and I have a tight shot on me. So it's very small what I'm doing, a lot of the time. . . . It's similar [to film acting] in that

Box 1.2: On laptops

The Builders Association rehearsal room bristles with laptops. Everybody, it seems, has one. The laptop of choice is a Mac, so an array of brushed aluminium PowerBooks quietly whirrs away. This could be a set for an advertisement.

The laptops are like a flourish across the room. During the workshop at St Ann's, Marianne Weems asks Rizwan Mirza to use his laptop at the forestage desk at which the operators sit along with the performers when the latter are not onstage. The video operators necessarily have their laptops, which are functional. Positioning one at the actors' seats is a bit of set dressing – designed to enhance the sense that everyone in this production is online, connected, hands-on with technology.

we have to hit a mark, we have to be someplace very precise for the camera to catch us, because otherwise you're not in the scene!' The performers' voices are amplified by small radio mics. 'That's lovely, actually,' says Angelos. 'You can be much more subtle. It's more sensitive and powerful, of course, to have your voice projected in a big way.'

The three storylines are interwoven but otherwise connected only by virtue of their contribution to the overarching thematic, concerning the exploitation of digital data and communication technologies. By the time I observe the workshops at the Kitchen and St Ann's Warehouse, then, the narratives are fairly consolidated and the work focuses more on their hypermedia staging.

'What we've been doing here is creating atmospheres,' says Kyle deCamp at the end of the workshop at the Kitchen. At this point, halfway through a development process, what challenges need to be cracked? 'The basic question,' responds deCamp. 'What is the relationship of these contemporary people to the ongoing, galloping situation of data?' An answer to this question – and perhaps a constraint in addressing it – lay in the ways the company wrestled with its design domain.

A set for spectating

One of the first ideas for the set for *Super Vision* was a large curved deck that would open to reveal pockets or gaps in which scenes would take place (see figures 1.3 and 1.4). This required a series of moving elements that posed difficulties for a touring show. Weems asked set designer Stewart Laing to conceive something radically different. His response entailed a narrow performance strip running the width of the stage. This was backed by a large cyclorama for rear projection, with a front wall of sliding panels that could reveal and conceal the performers and also act as projection surfaces (see figures 1.5 and 1.6). The actors, then, would perform between two planes of digital images (see figure 1.7). The downstage panels would be housed within an aperture, so that the audience had a sense of watching the action through a sort of large letterbox.

interior section
open onwards?

mother + son
in interior
space.

father projected
on exterior plane.

Maybe project still images over entire
surface area?

1.3 A scan of set designer Stewart Laing's notebook, showing an early design idea for a curved stage that takes projection, with inset units for performance.

1.4 Computer rendition of a design idea from the Ohio workshop in 2004. The final design retained the presence of performers along the edge of the playing area, although eventually they were located at the front.

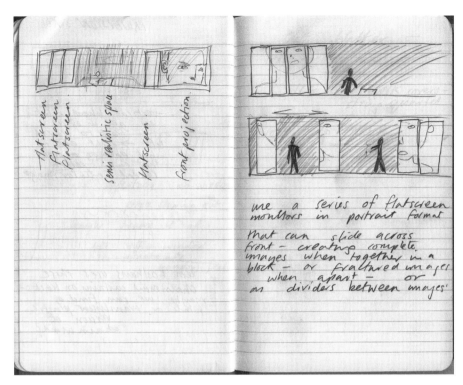

Flat screen
Part screen
Flat screen.

Semi robotic space

Flat screen.

Front projection.

me a series of flatscreen
monitors in portrait format
that can slide across
front – creating complete
images when together in a
block – or fractured images
when apart – or
as dividers between images'

1.5 A scan of set designer Stewart Laing's sketchbook, showing a sketch of sliding panels across the front of an aperture, from early in 2005.

1.6 A still of an animation of the set made during the workshop at the Kitchen, showing the principle of sliding panels that reveal spaces and actions, along with the forestage desk for operators and performers.

1.7 Rehearsal shot: Tanya Selvaratnam onstage. A rather poor-quality image – but it gives you a sense of how little room the performers onstage had in which to work, sandwiched between the rear screen and the sliding panels downstage.

This configuration was set up for the workshop at the Kitchen. It posed a number of challenges. How many projectors were required, front and back? How large and what proportions should the aperture be? How many sliding panels would be best, and what material should they be made from? How would they be operated? And, as Laing observed later, 'could we afford to project that amount of imagery, just in terms of square feet?'

At the start of the workshop there are three sliding panels, along with a scrim (a fine gauze) across the front of the aperture that allows you to see everything illuminated behind it but also acts as a large projection surface. Laing proposes that there be four sliding screens, rather than three (two made from Perspex, two from black gauze). 'Why did you decide that?' asks Jennifer Tipton. Laing observes that the smaller screens are better for touring. 'Only it's nice to have a centre,' Tipton suggests. Weems asks Wilkinson to mock up a panel that is seven feet wide. Wilkinson promises it for the next day.

Silovski and Wilkinson discuss means of fixing and operating the panels. 'There's only one instance where they don't move simultaneously,' says Silovski.

'That's gonna change,' says Wilkinson. 'And I'd rather design something that allowed for the possibility of change.' This is exactly the sort of production management – problem-solving, generous, accommodating – that this sort of process requires.

Sightlines are a problem: not everyone in the auditorium can see the rear screen through the aperture. Its proposed dimensions are currently 28 feet by 7 feet. Laing suggests altering this to 24x8, noting that at its most extreme a cinemascope screen entails a width to height ration of three to one. Weems is cautious about compromising the wide, non-televisual architecture of the frame. Later that afternoon, Wilkinson and Silovski resize the frame to 24x8. Developments in thinking are quickly made concrete in the space and tested in real terms as soon as possible. Later the next day, Weems notes her and Laing's view that the 24x8 aperture is not workable.

The set design and system for video projection require budgetary consolidation. Wilkinson reports at a company meeting that the projected expenditure on set is currently $35,000, whilst the available budget is $30,000. Whitener urges the production team to be creative in finding ways to keep within budget targets.

Flaherty reports on a series of options for projectors, including expensive models that can be refocused in mid-performance. Three projectors with a focal length of 18 feet would cost $29,000 – Flaherty's entire budget for video. Four consumer-level (lower-specification) projectors cost only $7,000. And a good deal of the budget needs to be assigned for software. One prospect is that the front projectors will be located on small stands on the floor in front of the audience. Whitener observes, 'We can't be in a situation where we find it doesn't work in the house, where we've got to lose seven or eight seats [to make it fit]. I've already had producers of *Alladeen* saying that it should be in the contract that we won't lose seats [so that the venue can maximise seat sales if the show sells out]. That's bad news.' As Flaherty points out, the location of the projectors will need to be 'part of the footprint of the set and part of the design'.

Laing observes that the budget would be alleviated if a recent idea to use electric glass for two of the panels were dropped, saving $6,000. The glass can be both opaque (so will become a projection surface) or transparent. Weems had been keen on using it. She concedes that it might go, looking like she is sucking on a lemon.

The following day the company explores fabrics for the front panels and scrim. There is much interest in an industrial material called textalene, a robust plastic sheeting with small oblong holes, which is used for garden furniture or as a wrapping around building sites. It acts like heavy-duty theatrical gauze. It takes a front-projected image as though it were a solid screen, but is sufficiently transparent so that if anyone behind it is illuminated they are clearly visible to the audience.

'That's really basic nineteenth-century theatre technology that we're using,' says Laing, referring to the gauzes of yore. 'Which is nice.' At this point the company considers using two screens in either textalene or LCD glass, and two that are solid. It also intends to remove the rear cyclorama to reveal (carried over from Laing's previous design concept) a steeply curved stage raking from floor to ceiling. This will be the arctic expanse to which John Sr escapes, providing a summative moment of scenic transformation (another echo, perhaps, from the nineteenth century) (see figure 1.8). The team needs to work out how to remove the projectors that are behind the rear screen, so that they are not in view at the 'reveal' – by raising ('flying') them, for instance.

'What about the houses that have no flying?' asks Weems.

'We'll just have to make something,' says Wilkinson, with sangfroid.

1.8 Rehearsal shot: David Pence tries out the arctic stage that, midway through the process, was envisaged for the end of the piece. This setting is informed by the early script and design workshops. The stage was eventually cut in favour of a video treatment of the Arctic. This image also shows the grid motif that provided a template for much of the video design.

Weems asks that the rear screen is rigged, 'so that we get used to the idea that the space isn't permanently open'. It's an important principle that you see things as the audience will see them, even in rough scratch phases of the process. It sounds simple, but what you see is what you get.

How were these various issues resolved by the time of the workshop at St Ann's? After the phase at the Kitchen, Laing built a model determining various configurations and sent it over from the UK. The dimensions of the aperture are now 30 feet by 10 feet – much better for sightlines, and nonetheless a distinctive 'wide-screen' configuration. There is no scrim across the front, and there are five sliding panels (each 6 feet wide), rather than four – so the panels have a centre. They are all made of textalene. They have a new electrical mechanism that allows for more precise gliding and stopping, and an operator who, in an enticing mix of old and new technologies, has electrical tape marking his TV monitor. This shows a shot of the stage. The tape on his screen indicates where he needs to position the panels for various scenes.

The arctic reveal, logistically complicated with its additional stage construction and flying projectors, has been cut. Instead the snowy waste is depicted by way of a video projection across the rear screen. There are three rear projectors covering the whole of the cyclorama, and two at the front with wide-angle lenses to cover the panels across the breadth of the aperture.

'The good thing about this design', muses Laing, 'is that it's pushed me in a different direction. But I also think it's pushed Marianne and the Builders in a different direction because they've never really had anything as sort of structured as this or indeed as big or technically, mechanically involved.' Laing observes that normally his work is not as defined by mediated images. 'What I've designed is a receptacle, and usually I'm doing more than that, I'm usually designing something that is giving the audience as much information as I want to give them. This time I'm designing the blank page and somebody else – well, a whole team of people – are filling in all the other information.' We turn to those people next.

Digital design and visual content

One challenge the company addressed was how visually to represent the phenomenon of data without simply *reproducing* data. Early on at the Kitchen, Laing notes to Flaherty that he likes the aesthetic of the grid, provided by a graph paper effect that Flaherty has created. The grid becomes (matrix-like) both a nexus of nodes and, when broken down to its simplest shape, a collection of separate squares that can then become cubes – an abstract representation of bits of interconnecting information. The grid helps cohere the entire video design, which in any case requires a meeting of different minds and processes.

Flaherty observes that he prefers not to work with 'found' footage but rather find 'an aesthetic from a design process'. Meanwhile, as he suggests, the dbox designers 'are exceptional at rendering a three-dimensional space on a two-dimensional surface. . . . The ideal scenario – and we'll see if this actually works out – is that they're building these virtual 3D spaces and I'm building two-dimensional video-based data spaces, and trying to determine how I can integrate live camera, real-time effects and make that work on stage.'

Weems and the visual design team gather at dbox's offices in Leroy Street, Manhattan, and watch some imagery that Gibbs and his colleagues have modelled. It shows interiors of the Fletchers' home, zooming into and panning around their chic and capacious dwelling. Gibbs is concerned that if the interiors are animated in this way in the eventual staging, the image loses its realist perspective in relation to the performers onstage. Weems, on the other hand, does not find such inconsistencies a concern. Theatre audiences, indeed, read spatial relationships with a form of poetic licence.

Gibbs moves items of virtual furniture into the lounge next to the kitchen, giving the virtual spaces greater proportionality. Weems asks for a rotation around the whole house – an estate agent's 360-degree view. 'Yeah, it's a beautiful image', she says, 'but I don't think that works in the theatre. The actors are in the wrong relation.' The process here entails a continual flow of ideas, changes of nuance that get tested quickly by way of small reconfigurations, slow nibblings at concepts and possibilities. It feels unpressured.

'What I'm after', says Weems, 'is some kind of motion. Whether it's something that comes out onto the front screen . . . It goes dead after it's been still for a while.' Gibbs shows two images of horizontal tree-like shapes that grow and develop branches. One looks very spiky and organic, the other like an accumulating cluster of wires. Weems asks to see this next to a body onstage. This motif will eventually become the basis for the branches of data that stream behind the businessman as he crosses borders, gathering transactions, reports and surveillance records in boxes and cubes as he goes.

At a pavement café nearby in Manhattan's revived Meatpacking District the team discusses the use of the rear cyclorama. 'Yesterday was the worst it has looked,' says Flaherty abruptly. 'There was no space. You don't get a sense of perspectival depth.'

I muse to myself that, if true, this reflects somewhat dismally on dbox's involvement, since providing graphical perspective is one of its signal endeavours. But Gibbs appears unfazed. He suggests projecting some elements on to the front scrim to create more depth. 'I'm not married to the panorama' (the wide stretch of the rear projection), he says. 'But it seems like we have to minimise options, because we have so many.' Weems intervenes to say that the panorama should be the template for all the design on the rear screen – a useful directorial mandate.

They discuss the real-time motion capture effects that they have been pursuing, where a camera is trained on a performer and the feed run through software that enables the projection of different outlines and shapes of the performer's body. Weems is a little sceptical, but still in search of a real-time relation between performer and screen. 'Allen Hahn [the lighting designer] said it best,' she observes. 'Yesterday it looked like an a-ha video. I don't want to keep saying the same thing about interactivity. I do not want the entire show to be people moving around in pre-recorded imagery.' What's afoot, then, is an attempt to use both pre-recorded video and live camerawork. Weems is right. There is a different texture and feel when both performance and video projection exploit synchronous real-time mediation – a palpable liveness and immediacy to the fusion of elements.

'I don't want to get locked into making everything human scale,' Weems continues. 'The overwhelming feeling in this piece is that technology is bigger than the human – that's what we have to hold on to.'

The following day in the rehearsal room they explore the principle of pulling images from the rear screen on to a front panel, along with a zoom into the Fletchers' virtual kitchen. As perspectives shift, a chair in the image cross-fades to appear on a panel downstage in larger proportion. An intern stands in as Carol Fletcher, and walks on the spot, her back to the audience as if going upstage into the kitchen. The effect is striking but slightly unreal, as Gibbs observes, since the intern's body size doesn't change in sync with the changing scale of the room. 'Yes, that's the point,' says Weems. A theatrical moment looms – one that suggests a naturalistic space, effects a transformation of it and in doing so reminds the spectator that this is a fabricated theatre configuration. Weems asks Gibbs to prepare three more such effects for Saturday's showcase.

By the St Ann's phase six months later, this effect has been finessed. For Carol's final scene, the backdrop shows a living room complete with grand piano in front of large windows. The image morphs to become a grid of white lines on black, then zooms into close-up as a smaller blue grid slides on from the sides. Meanwhile the downstage panels move into play along the front of the playing area. The sequence performs a series of small transitions in screen space and stage space that give the piece a dynamic feel and powerfully rhythmic flow. A slight strobing of the lines within the image makes this house – this life – seem unstable, volatile, more virtual than actual.

You can see how slow cooking eventually produces its dish. It is a process of

---

Box 1.3: On technical operation

Super Vision would be nothing without its operators. Not in the obvious sense that someone needs to press Go for sound, lighting, video and (here) sliding panels, but in a much more ingrained way through the process as a whole. Jeff Morey, who assists video designer Peter Flaherty and operates the show's video projections along with a colleague, undertakes continual problem-solving in the rehearsal room. He determines how some of the transitions play out in discussion with sound designer Dan Dobson. Unusually, Dobson operates his own sound design on tour, meaning that the relation between sound and performance is continually finessed, to the point where extremely subtle interactions and deft timings are possible. Design is only half the work. Grafting it into the fabric of production is the other half.

During the final phase of rehearsal at St Ann's Warehouse a minor difficulty arises in transitioning out of one of the businessman scenes. The company tries to find a line in the dialogue that will be a video cue point. The trouble is that the actors don't stick to the same script. It is agreed that video will take its cue on a count of three from an earlier line that is fixed. What's interesting here is that, rather than ask the actors to set what they do, their improvisation is taken as inherent to the performance, and the technical team works with and around it. Elsewhere in the show, cue points are rigorously marked. Nonetheless, this instance intimates the shift from a text-based production process to one that is more organic, interactive and, you might say, operational.

---

infusion, trying out ideas that lead to other ideas, one solution permeating another, all with the purpose of establishing – or discovering – core principles and closing in on the final outcome.

The audio in 'audio-visual'

The importance of Dan Dobson's sound to The Builders Association's multimedia identity can hardly be overstated. It is to some extent cinematic – ever-present, providing tone and rhythm, pace and punctuation. Yet it is more 'architectural' than many film scores, part of the structure of the piece rather than merely an accompaniment to it. When rehearsing one of the businessman scenes, for instance, Dobson provides an accompaniment: a pulsing riff, slightly ragged and jazzy, with a muffled underbeat and, at regular intervals, an electronic 'meow'. The composition is ambient, understated yet threatening, and crucial to the shaping of the scene.

'I always think of the sound as just an instrumental bed', says Dobson, 'and the text is really the lyrics of these songs. It's musical, the whole process. . . . the stuff I do is very cyclical and loopy because it can provide some sense of – I don't want to say "motion" – but feel. I always find that strong melodies just sort of take over and speak too much. We tend to like the ambient stuff.' He develops computer-generated electronic music for *Super Vision* – 'a blibbity blibbity thing' – that sits well with the technological feel of the production, along with separate motifs for the show's three narratives. 'We make so much stuff, and we throw so much of it away', he says, 'but you need to have that kind of repertoire to pull from.' Importantly, sound is developed alongside other production elements. In rehearsal Dobson sketches as he goes and tries things out, and Weems prefers to run scenes with sound wherever possible. Again the principle is one of continual iteration. It means that Dobson provides an acoustic infrastructure that from the outset is ingrained in the DNA of the piece.

Reckonings

The show is run on Thursday 22 September 2005 towards the end of the fortnight at St Ann's. This is an early run-through and will be a little bumpy. At this point of the process the piece's inherent difficulties – perhaps weaknesses – show up in starker relief, before the machinery of production has smoothed them out. When the performers speak, given their amplified voices and the ironies of the piece, they all sound like Laurie Anderson. The quest regarding the deeds of the grandmother's house is not properly resolved, and questions remain concerning Jen's motivation and indeed her relationship with her grandmother. The traveller scenes nicely depict the sinister reach of the authorities but are a little lurid. The storyline of the Fletchers gives unlike-able characters actions that have little development in texture. Indeed, none of the characters seem developed in much depth, a function of the scene structure, I think, rather than the performances. Each narrative is somewhat mono-dimensional as a consequence of providing a vehicle for multimedia design and theme.

Yet what design. At the Kitchen, Flaherty voiced a principal challenge: 'How do you fill out a 6-foot shallow space so that it feels like a full perspective?' Part of the achievement of this work is that it produces dimensionality in a virtuoso mix of planes and perspectives. The extremely thin performance strip, sandwiched by flat projection screens, is sumptuously fleshed out front and behind, with depth and dynamic provided by the video compositions and moving panels. 'Yeah,' agrees Laing. 'I think that it gives everything a real stillness, in the performance. Because the surround is so busy and moving and the images are moving on the screens and the screens are moving. It gives the performers an opportunity to just be really still.'

That's true, but the show's pleasures are also to do with movement of a different sort. It is like a machine, with an ineffable fluency to the conjunction of sound, utterance, action and imagery. Moment by moment it creates powerful vignettes that playfully develop resonant themes. Its spatial and visual compositions appear beautifully balanced, then shift to be replaced by different configurations. The modulations of tone are carefully calibrated, whilst a prevailing irony confers beguiling coolness.

The show has panache, and there is an exciting grandeur to the contemporaneity of its form and subject matter.

Reviewers typically responded positively to *Super Vision*'s technical sophistication. Mark Swed, writing in the *Los Angeles Times*, described it as a 'dazzling high-tech extravaganza' and attributed to Weems' work

> a certain delicacy in that intersection of glee and creepiness. The glee is in the technology, which she uses better than just about anyone. . . . The video wizardry . . . calls attention to itself, because its use is so slick and efficient and brightly innovative . . . But Weems is most remarkable in creating her own personal interface between technology and traditional theatre. The video serves live theatre, not the other way around. [9]

Michael Grossberg, in the *Columbus Dispatch*, found that 'More for its innovative techniques than its subject, *Super Vision* ranks as one of the most fascinating and rewarding multimedia theatre works in years.'[10] In a eulogistic review in the *Wall Street Journal*, Terry Teachout describes the show as 'a computer-enhanced visual poem about the pitfalls and promises of life in the information age . . . in which six actors move through a breathtakingly complex series of digitally generated three-dimensional projections'.[11]

Reviewers also responded to the show's overt engagement with themes of surveillance, data exploitation and the erosions of personal space, although here opinion was divided. For Joyce McMillan, writing in the *Scotsman*, the show tackles its themes 'with real emotion, and a powerful elegiac sense of that richly rooted, sensual and affectionate dimension of life that somehow fails to transfer to the digital sphere'.[12]

By contrast, Neil Genzlinger suggested in the *New York Times* that 'for something so technically sophisticated, the piece is all too simplistic and familiar in its central idea: Data accumulation=bad. . . . [T]he data revolution is well under way by now, and most people are making peace with it day by day, taking advantage of its good points and viewing its negative ones realistically.'[13]

One difficulty in delivering the theme of dataveillance is that the three narratives didn't quite centre in relation to it, perhaps because the company was in thrall to the techne of the phenomenon they sought to expose. The businessman is subject to a form of border-checking whose dystopian futurism gives this strand a fantastical slant. John Sr is concerned not so much with dataveillance as data-trafficking, and he is brought down by those old enemies, greed and debt, rather than electronic policing. And the exchanges between Jen and her grandmother really concern a family history (and a set of title deeds) rather than anything more insidious or ('veillance'-like) subject to external inspection. Thematically, then, for all its apparent concentration *Super Vision* is a little loose, arguably as a result of a process that settled relatively early on the narratives themselves, and prioritised the problem-solving of design challenges over the ongoing development of material through performance.

There is another lens through which to see this production, however, whose filter is provided by Hans-Thies Lehmann in his book *Postdramatic Theatre*. In many respects *Super Vision* accords with Lehmann's description of the postdramatic: it is

Box 1.4: Three memories

1. The parking lot

Shortly before I get to the Kitchen on my first day of observation I pass a small parking lot. There are two layers of cars – clearly one layer parks, then is hydraulically lifted. I have never seen this arrangement before. What if you want to collect your car that's in mid-air before the drivers of the cars underneath have returned? I guess the parking lot attendant has to do some shimmying of cars and lifts. This set-up seems apt to a city that stacks up on top of itself, and evokes a theatre process that requires continual shifting of component parts. And it is a reminder in this digital age of the continued presence of mechanical technologies.

2. The company photograph

Everybody gathers *en masse* in front of a picturesquely distressed brick façade outside the studio at St Ann's Warehouse in Brooklyn – actors, designers, technicians, interns. As the newest guy on the block – and an observer, not a participant – I take the photo. A company photo can be many things: celebratory, sentimental, inclusive, creating the appearance of harmony, recording the fact of togetherness, marking the peculiar conjunction of bodies and energies that is a theatre project at a particular moment. Twenty-six people are gathered. I am given other cameras with which to record this collective moment.

3. Looking at new things

People are continually showing new things to others – websites, fabrics, images of favoured discoveries. A scene is rehearsed that involves a blast of light on to a white surface. The reflected light illuminates the creative team and assorted interns scattered around the auditorium. They are watching intently. If there were a motif for this production process, it would be absorption in the face of new things.

multi-perspectival, depends at least as much upon its visual and visceral characteristics as its storylines and generates effect through its flow and sensory organisation. When Lehmann suggests that 'Postdramatic theatre is a theatre of states and of scenically dynamic formations', he could be describing *Super Vision*.[14]

In another respect, however, *Super Vision* points beyond Lehmann's conception of the postdramatic. 'The theatre of sense and synthesis has largely disappeared – and with it the possibility of synthesizing interpretation,' Lehmann argues. 'Synthesis is cancelled. It is explicitly combated. . . . Enclosed within postdramatic theatre is obviously the demand for an open and fragmenting perception in place of a unifying and closed perception.'[15]

Super Vision suggests an alternative perspective, a third way that combines *both* synthesis and fragmentation. This is a theatre for the age after postmodernism, post the postdramatic. Its paradigms are coordination, synchronicity, systematicity. Synthesis is very definitely not cancelled but a key feature. *Super Vision*'s creative process is intended to facilitate coherence (thematic, formal, narratival, operational).

That said, the piece and its process retain *difference* as a key determinant – its separate elements are discrete and internally coherent. There is, then, a larger paradigm at work: a deeply scored functional interdependency. Different storylines, media and thematic tropes – along with a range of collaborators – are brought together such that their togetherness and, simultaneously, their distinctness give meaning and affect. *Super Vision* is an outcome of twenty-first-century collaborative digital theatre production. It depends upon everything being separate and everything coming together, in a powerful rendition of live performance that is always and also mediated as something more quintessentially itself.

Notes

1 The Builders Association website is at www.thebuildersassociation.org/flash/flash. html?homepage (accessed 23 March 2008).

2 All quotations from members of The Builders Association are from interviews with the author and observations of workshop development between 28 March and 2 April 2005, and 21 and 23 September 2005, unless otherwise stated. I am most grateful to the company, and Marianne Weems in particular, for allowing me to observe and being unfailingly helpful and considerate.

3 Quoted in Jason Zinoman, 'All the World's a New Technology Incubator', *New York Times* (20 November 2005).

4 Go to www.superv.org/ (accessed 23 March 2008) for the company's information on the project. For a useful video trailer advertising *Super Vision* go to www.youtube.com/ watch?v=jlTpsTAKDGY (accessed 23 March 2008). For an article discussing *Super Vision*, and including extensive interviews with the creative team, see Nick Kaye, 'Screening Presence: The Builders Association and dbox, SUPER VISION (2005)', *Contemporary Theatre Review* (17:4, 2007), pp. 557–77. This material, along with more extensive documentation and video trailers from *Super Vision*, is featured as part of The Presence Project, an online enquiry into presence in performance. Go to http://presence.stanford.edu:3455/ Collaboratory/342 (accessed 23 March 2008).

5 dbox's website is at www.dbox.com (accessed 23 March 2008).

6 Quoted in Steve Dollar, 'Dancing about Architecture', *Print* (September/October 2006), p. 59.

7 See Kaye (2007), p. 561. See also John McGrath, *Loving Big Brother: Surveillance Culture and Performance Space* (London: Routledge, 2004).

8 Images are all from the development and rehearsal process. For some good production shots see www.superv.org/ and follow the link to images.

9 Mark Swed, 'The Unblinking Eye of Technology', *Los Angeles Times* (8 December 2006).

10 Michael Grossberg, 'Play Folds, Staples Identities in Digital Age', *Columbus Dispatch* (4 November 2005).

11 Terry Teachout, 'Making Ideas Beautiful', *Wall Street Journal* (10–11 December 2005). See also Mark Blankenship, 'Super Vision', *Variety* (1 December 2005), p. 4, and Hedy Weiss, '"Super" Stories Show Someone Has Your Number – Yikes!', *Chicago Sun-Times* (16 October 2006) for positive reviews of the production.

12 Joyce McMillan, 'Super Vision', *Scotsman* (27 May 2006).

13 Neil Genzlinger, 'A Triptych of Fables about the Too-Much-Information Era', *New York Times* (2 December 2005). See also Steven Winn, '"Super Vision" Scores an

All-Too-Familiar Point', *San Francisco Chronicle* (19 August 2006), and Adam Klasfeld, 'Super Vision', *TheaterMania* (30 November 2005), www.theatermania.com/content/news.cfm/story/7213 (accessed 10 March 2008), for less positive reviews of the production.

14   Hans-Thies Lehmann, *Postdramatic Theatre*, trans. Karen Jürs-Munby (Abingdon: Routledge, 2006), p. 68.

15   *Ibid.*, pp. 25, 83.

2

Sidi Larbi Cherkaoui – *Myth* (2007) – Mapping the multiple

Lou Cope

In both process and product they move in and out of each other, inviting, supporting, confronting, ignoring, loving, impressing, needing, manipulating and challenging each other. Each works to govern his or her own axis, keeping control of spine, gravity, arms, the relation of the neck to the body, the head to the neck and eyes to it all. And they work to keep in time with one another, to occupy the right amount of space, to think, say or do enough and not too much, to maintain the spatial and temporal relations of the group.

It makes me dizzy. (Lou Cope (rehearsal journal))

Introduction

Born in 1976, dancer and choreographer Sidi Larbi Cherkaoui has, despite his youth, already enjoyed a rich and varied career. Born in Antwerp, Belgium, to a Flemish mother and a Moroccan father, he trained at Anne Teresa De Keersmaeker's dance school PARTS in Brussels and, at the age of 19, was awarded the prize for the Best Belgian Dance Solo – an initiative set up by the director of Les Ballets C de la B, Alain Platel, with whom Cherkaoui went on to work throughout the next eleven years.

Having performed in Platel's *Iets op Bach* in 2000, he was invited by Les Ballets to choreograph his own show, *Rien de Rien*, which won the Special Prize at the BITEF festival in Belgrade (2000). Since then he has maintained a career both as a dancer and, I would argue, as two types of maker. First, as a choreographer, he has created work *for*, or – to use the traditional dance term – *on* some of Europe's most highly respected ballet companies in Monte Carlo, Geneva, Copenhagen and Stockholm. And secondly, as a collaborative performance director, he has worked *with* actors,

2.1 Scene from *Myth*.

dancers and musicians to devise 'performance dance'.[1] In this guise he created *Rien de Rien*, *Foi* (2003) and *Tempus Fugit* (2004) with Les Ballets C de la B; he made the award-winning *Zero Degrees* (2005) in collaboration with the three British artists, dancer Akram Khan, visual artist Antony Gormley and musician Nitin Sawhney; and he co-directed *Ook* (2002) with Nienke Reehorst (his assistant for the project I write about here), for Theater Stap, a professional Belgian 'theatre workshop where disabled actors and able-bodied theatre producers meet'.[2]

In 2006 Cherkaoui was invited by the artistic director of Antwerp's prestigious Toneelhuis theatre, Guy Cassiers, to become part of a creative team of six whose remit is not only to create and present their own work, but also to have input into selecting which other artists will be presented there. And it is to the context of Toneelhuis that I am invited to join Cherkaoui, to bear witness as he embarks upon his first major project in this role, the collective creation of a new show, co-produced by London's Sadler's Wells amongst others, that will premiere at Antwerp's De Singel Theatre in June 2007, and then tour internationally for two or more years. This show eventually came to be called *Myth*.

Before describing the process of *Myth*, it is useful to make brief reference to *Foi* – one of Cherkaoui's most successful previous collaborative projects – because for *Myth* he intended to develop some of the themes of *Foi*, work with some of the same performers and also build on some of the working practices he had developed creating *Foi* in 2003. *Foi* (French for 'faith') has five central characters and a chorus of dancing

---

Box 2.1: Les Ballets C de la B

In 2007 Alain Platel, Christine de Smedt and Koen Augustijnen are the Artistic Directors of this internationally respected dance theatre company, based in Ghent, Belgium. Sidi Larbi Cherkaoui was an Artistic Director until 2006. The directors create work independently but work under the collective company title. Their website describes Les Ballets as 'a unique melting pot of artistic movements that constantly interweave with and fertilise each other' (www.lesballetscedela.be). As well as producing the work of its Artistic Directors, the company gives other dancers and choreographers the platform to present their own work.

2007 productions include:
Vsprs – directed by Alain Platel
Import Export – directed by Koen Augustijnen
Aphasiadisiac – directed by Ted Stoffer
Patchagonia – directed by Lisi Esteras

---

guardians or angels who, against the backdrop of fourteenth-century Ars Nova music sung live by Belgian group Capilla Flamenca, guide the characters through their quests to find spiritual salvation in a kind of post-9/11 apocalyptic wasteland. Its blend of dance, live music and character won over audiences across the world, and it toured until 2007.

For *Myth*, then, the second part of what came to be foreseen as a trilogy, Cherkaoui reunited some of the key players of *Foi*, and introduced them to some new faces. 'I don't like to meet too many people at once', he tells me, 'but I do like to have a new friend once in a while.'[3] He even describes the company he has assembled for *Myth* as his 'dream team'. And what a team it is. At any one time in a Cherkaoui rehearsal room there can be eight dancers, five actors, sometimes five musicians, one assistant, one dramaturg, one carer, one production manager, one and often two observers, various guests, friends and different members of the production team. The principal collaborators come from Belgium, the USA, Australia, Sweden, Slovakia, France, Italy, Japan and the Netherlands. The languages used are French, Flemish and, predominantly, English.

Cherkaoui tells me that the starting point for the creation is 'trauma'. Guided by the work of his friend, the writer Joel Kerantoun, he is interested in exploring the ways people carry past trauma with them, in their minds or in their bodies. He wishes again to have the central characters surrounded by a chorus, but this time a chorus of shadows, and he wants to explore the idea of people taking control of how they respond to trauma and even – ultimately – to their own (real and psychological) shadows. Working with shadows leads him to thinking of light and dark, good and bad, and he intends to explore archetypes positioned around these dualities.

As is the case for many of Belgium's most prestigious creators, Cherkaoui sees his processes as 'ways of living'. A long and intense rehearsal process is considered not a luxury but a necessity. Rehearsals for *Myth* begin formally in September 2006, though

2.2 Sidi Larbi Cherkaoui.

there have been two previous smaller workshop weeks where some initial material was developed. The group as a whole kicks off with a week-long workshop in Antwerp, where all the performers get to meet one another. This is followed, across the next eight months, by twenty six-day weeks of rehearsal divided up into three different blocks – with up to two months' break in between each block. They rehearse in both Antwerp and Brussels.

This work schedule, including these breaks (and perhaps in part because of them), means that as I join the group in the early days there is the unnerving sense that these people are going to live through something quite intense together. I think I can see the slight fear of what Susan Melrose calls the 'not-yet-imaginable' etched on their faces.[4] Seasons will change, as no doubt will moods, hairstyles, injuries, relationships and ideas, and this is rather the point. Alain Platel describes his shows as being the 'condensation of what you live over the previous months',[5] and Cherkaoui, thanks to the support of Toneelhuis, seems to have chosen to continue in this tradition.

And thus it is that I join them on day two (frustratingly, though understandably, I have been asked *not* to join them on day one), and we all embark upon a journey of discovery. As well as being a fascinating glimpse into an international production process, this journey will allow me to unearth some of the key issues in devising contemporary performance: namely, the role of the director (and therefore also the performer) in collaborative devising; the initiation, generation and selection of material; transformation and multiplicity in both process and product; questions of signature in multiply authored work; and the notion of a product emerging to surprise its makers.

Efforts to write about this journey also highlight the difficulties of writing about process. What follows is an attempt to explore the different approaches, modes and perspectives afforded by my 'privileged-insider' position at the outside of the inside of this extraordinary melting pot.[6] (My small and changing patch – from where you can often hear the tap-tap-tapping of my laptop, which I am horribly conscious of and careful to stop at moments of silent intensity – is sometimes referred to as 'Lou's corner', a safe and warm haven where it is later joked that I will sell alcohol, drugs or kisses to anyone who needs them.)[7]

A day in the lives

The day begins with a warm-up, or 'class' as it is called, from 10.00 to 11.30. The company members then work in groups till about 13.00 before lunching for roughly an hour and going on to work until anything from 18.30 to 21.30. I intend to use this schedule to enable me to discuss the ways in which the sessions worked, and I use the progression of the day as a parallel to the progression of the process as a whole.

Class 10.00–11.30

In the early days, class is led either by one of the performers or by Cherkaoui. Often it is yoga or yoga-based (Cherkaoui spent months learning Hatha yoga from teacher/dancer Sri Louise – who is now performing in this piece). At the request of some of the dancers, some later sessions are more influenced by disco, hip-hop or contact improvisation. Occasionally someone's friend, perhaps someone who is in town on their own tour, will lead the class. Towards the end of the process, as production time draws nearer, professionals from outside the group are brought in on a regular basis.

The class was clearly important in a number of ways. Obviously it woke the performers and their bodies up, and prepared them for the intensity of the day that followed. It also enabled Cherkaoui to encourage a sharing of responsibility, interest, knowledge and skill that allowed the group to get to know one another better. Some of those that led a class spoke of nervousness before and relief after 'taking their turn'. It gave them opportunities to earn the respect of their peers, and it shared the burden of heaving their tired bodies into the next long day. Notable also from the very beginning was the openness of the group. Throughout the process, even towards the potentially stressful end, guests were welcomed to the space. There were friends, former collaborators and a couple of students (to whom Cherkaoui had given access to the process at weekends or whenever they had a free day). This was indicative of Cherkaoui's generosity and lack of possessiveness or protective fear, and his collaborators were simply expected not to mind.[8]

To the side of the main group of ten or more people, assistant Nienke Reehorst leads a different warm-up for the two actors with Down's syndrome, Marc Wagemans, with whom Cherkaoui has worked a number of times, and Ann Dockx. They work hard and their warm-ups too are often yoga-based. They work quietly but playfully, and are sometimes joined by other members of the company who are finding the main group's warm-up too challenging. At other times the two warm-ups merge completely.

28 September 2006: Cherkaoui is leading a really tough warm-up. It seems gravity is not for him. He is teaching the others Hatha yoga. They are all willing their bodies to do what their minds want them to do. Their skills evolve before my eyes.

Reehorst [Cherkaoui's assistant director] is simultaneously leading the warm-up with Dockx and Wagemans. She is getting them to do handstands against her as she leans on the wall. When they finish the warm up Dockx and Wagemans continue to move together to the music. It's completely focused and responsive – no task has been given, they respond purely to both each other and the music – mirroring, leading, following and touching. The other group are still lying on the ground and breathing. Reehorst and Cherkaoui are quietly watching, Cherkaoui gets up and starts to dance with Dockx. I cry for the first time during this process. I don't know why. Something to do with . . . the absolute commitment of these two people engaging so completely in the here and now. Gradually everyone in the room becomes aware of this unscheduled improvisation and they lie happily and watch it. Reehorst then suggests to dancer Satoshi Kudo that he joins in and he does. Kudo and Dockx move together for the next twenty minutes, while the others start their own work.[9]

Thus it was that the class often melted into the morning session. In this example an idea developed in the post-warm-up drifting formed a relationship between the two performers, Ann Dockx and Satoshi Kudo. The idea that originated here subsequently underwent months of gently changing permutations and found its way to the final product. This kind of journey was not uncommon in the development of performance material. In the latter stages of the process Cherkaoui rarely took part in the class, seeming not to have the time. Instead he had meetings (with technicians, publicists, designers), discussions with his assistant and, just occasionally, he snatched a moment of sleep, joining the others as they turned to face the rest of the day.

The morning session 11.30–13.30

26 September 2006: Having led the warm-up, dancer Alex Gilbert vacates the centre spot, but no one else fills it. Cherkaoui floats quietly around, kissing and joking with everybody.

They slip into activities. I don't see any 'start' moment, no 'assembly' where they sing a hymn and agree to do their best today, no directions or instructions given out by the Commander-in-Chief. I struggle to understand how work begins.

Box 2.2: Tasks

Examples of tasks given to generate material
- Please can you two work together and explore the arms.
- Can you do something in connection with your fear of animals?
- Make up a phrase with your legs.
- Work on a duet where *a* tortures *b*. Make it look painful without really being it.
- Group *a* manipulate, transport and lift *b* with only teeth and jaw strength.
- *A* invade *b* with your hair as if he might drown in it.
- Avoid something but involve the eyes by following the thing to be avoided.
- Create a phrase turning only to the left.
- Develop some ideas around Oprah Winfrey.
- I never see you angry. Write some angry text.

Examples of self-initiated starting points
- I always like to play with my hair, hands and toes.
- I wanted [my character] to be very different from the one in *Foi*. I wanted to be something more reduced, I didn't want to have high heels and I didn't want my hair out loose and I didn't want to be this hysterical red-haired woman with all the texts.

2.3 Ulrika Kinn Svensson and Damien Jalet in rehearsal.

In fact, the morning sessions always begin with Cherkaoui, and sometimes Reehorst, quietly initiating activities. Small groups are united by a given endeavour and at any moment there can be up to ten different groups (solos, pairs and larger groups) dancing, writing or improvising at the same time. There is rarely verbal discussion, even in the more theatrical, character-based scenes. Interaction is embodied, physical and exploratory. Little attention is paid to the 'why' or the 'what for'; instead, the 'what if' is given priority. As Sri Louise explains, 'Most of the movement has been constructed in a process where [Cherkaoui] pairs people, generally in twos, and he'll give you a task, but the task can be one word, or sometimes if he doesn't know what the task is he'll just put you with someone and say "find something".'[10]

Key to *Myth*'s process, and any analysis of the role of director therein, is how these morning sessions began. The central space – from where the director might issue requests or instructions, give feedback, encourage discussion or make decisions, by addressing the group as a whole and raising volume for all to hear – was rarely filled. Consciously or unconsciously, and most often I believe it was the latter, Cherkaoui chose not to place himself at the centre of the action, either physically or intellectually. Of course, these things all happened, decisions were made and so on, but they did not come from a central space. It was months before I saw him address the group as a whole for any extended period. Instead he flirted with his territory, and it was often difficult to locate him in the space. Thus it was he tried to maintain the balance between being the one in control, and being an open and receptive collaborator among collaborators.

> 28 September 2006: Cherkaoui divests responsibility. He lets, indeed forces, the performers to be individuals, teachers, sharers, devisers, directors, creators. He flits from one group to the other, picking up incredibly quickly where he left off. He is working somatically, simply creating, thinking with and through his body. He takes and then he gives. He takes an arm movement created by a dancer and extends it, or changes its tension, direction or relation with the head. He does this with his own body. And then, as he stands back to see how the dancer adopts his suggestion, he steps from the inside to the outside again, balancing the looking and the being, the seeing and the feeling. Perhaps he adds a few gentle words: 'Could you try keeping the head down?', 'What about following that through with the body?' There is no ivory tower that I can see, no vantage point of knowledge. He doesn't seem to be many, if any, steps ahead. Having sown a seed, or made a request, he then leaves the performer(s) to continue to explore without him. I look forward to harvest time.

I use the language of Michel de Certeau here, for the way it likens unknowing somatic practices – in our case, performance devising processes informed not by expertise or authority but by spontaneous and subjective interaction and decision-making – to the walking of a *wandersmanner*, a pedestrian (for de Certeau, male) who blindly strolls around a city with no real knowledge of what he is doing or where he is going.[11] There is no map (and no method) for him to follow; there was no training that could give him the expertise to make 'right' decisions, not least because here there is no such thing as 'right'; there is no aerial view that allows him to understand his context, his progress or his destination. When he turns left he doesn't know why he turns left. He works instinctively, taking advantage of opportunity and he 'makes do' by relying on his own intuition, taste and embodied knowledges. As Cherkaoui says: 'I don't have a fixed idea of how it has to end . . . .. I trust in the idea of moving, and as we move, we move forward. . . .. I don't prepare anymore. . . . I trust things will tell me what to do.'[12]

I can identify four ways in which Cherkaoui works with his performers. He responds to: his perception of who they are as people; what they tell him they want to do in this piece; his perception of what they are for, as performers; and opportunities and ideas that arise in rehearsal.

His perception of who they are as people

When I interviewed him in December 2006, Cherkaoui referred to Milan Herich, a Brussels-based dancer from Slovakia and part of the 'Les Slovaks' Dance Company. Herich had been working on a solo piece involving moving piles of books and restoring them to their shelves when they had been knocked down by the recklessness of other characters. As Cherkaoui observes:

> He really *is* the one who would pick up the books. Ulrika [Kinn Svensson] would step against them and make them fall and he would put them back up . . . There is a relentless building back up of what others break, and holding on to something, protecting it, without any sense of 'I'm sacrificing myself'.[13]

In the final production, Herich plays a character who seems to represent a contemporary time, a trusted filter through whom we see this strange and other world with its dark and mischievous shadows causing chaos, and he is indeed restoring books to their rightful places, creating order, respect and a sense of dignity. Similarly, Cherkaoui described Flemish dancer Iris Bouche as 'always taking care of people', and indeed in the performance her shadow character is torn between taking care of those she should shadow and throwing off her responsibilities in favour of more selfish, hedonistic behaviour.

Throughout his processes Cherkaoui makes quiet, and mainly private, analyses such as these and he tries to feed both the work and the workers accordingly. In his notebook he draws illustrations of what each person represents to him, and how they fit in with each other. He assigns each a number, a sign (earth, volcano, air), a description (book-keeper, knowledge, evil queen) and a drawing that comprises of a colour, a costume and a bodily position.

In other words, he tries to get to know each person, and then make appropriate suggestions and requests. It isn't easy to know how he does this. Cherkaoui is a very busy man with many dance, choreography, curating and visual arts projects running simultaneously. But somehow he finds time to develop relationships with those he works with, perhaps over a coffee after rehearsal, or in a car as they go to see a show, and he tries to ensure that he gets the opportunity to listen to how they are feeling and what they wish they were doing. A lack of time clearly limits how thorough this can be, and though he beseeched people to come to talk to him if they had problems, I spoke

2.4 James O'Hara and Christine Leboutte in *Myth*.

to more than one dancer who felt uncomfortable standing in a queue to trouble a busy man with their own, seemingly trifling, questions or doubts. That said, the notion that his intention was to listen and respond, as much as was possible, was clearly stated.

What they tell him they want to do in this piece

James O'Hara, for example, at Cherkaoui's request and with his input, developed a piece with a handheld fan that Cherkaoui really liked. O'Hara trained in both ballet and contemporary dance, and has a lightness and grace that Cherkaoui wanted to exploit. But O'Hara felt uncomfortable with some of Cherkaoui's suggestions. 'I wasn't fully in my skin,' he later explained, 'it felt "dancey" and superficial.' So despite Cherkaoui feeling that the material worked, that the piece needed its lightness, and that it was a shame O'Hara wanted to deny his obvious skill in this way, he respected O'Hara's desires and let it go. O'Hara was given the space to explore the 'different ways of being' he sought. What resulted was a solo piece that became a key moment in the final production, with James exploring an unusual physical vocabulary, involving him journeying from newborn to adult, as he kicked and heaved both his body and his being into consciousness. Both O'Hara and Cherkaoui later stated that they felt this sequence spoke more clearly of this 21-year-old dancer's search for individual expression and a place within this particular group than the fan dance could ever have done.[14]

His perception of what they are for, as performers

And then there is the idea of Cherkaoui exploiting what he sees as the performers' playing strengths. Ulrika Kinn Svensson is a friend of Cherkaoui's; they worked together on *Foi* and he describes her as not having a single mean streak. Yet her character in the piece personifies evil, she is the bad guy, the 'evil queen', and this is because Cherkaoui recognises in her performance skills a gaze that pierces the fourth wall with such charged candour and condescension that it sends shivers down every spine in the audience; the ability to play power and authority in ways that are simultaneously frightening and sexy; and the capacity to commit herself completely – physically and vocally – making herself extremely vulnerable onstage. He also wanted to exploit the richness of her flowing red hair. This negotiation between what Kinn Svensson wants and what Cherkaoui wants for her went on to form her character and indeed the backbone of the entire show, as it is *from* her and *in* her that we see explored many of the show's main themes; for example, faith versus reason, weakness as strength, and the comfort of knowledge versus the frightening insecurity of love and liberty.

With Ann Dockx, to take another example, it's her timing, vocal skills and the innocence of her appearance that Cherkaoui chooses to play with. He exploits and subverts Dockx's apparent holiness and innocence, exchanging them with comical, violent or sexual sequences that slap us in the face and challenge our perception of both Dockx and her character. At the same time any remaining prejudices we may have about the roles people with disabilities can play in contemporary performance are cheekily confronted.

Opportunities and ideas that arise in rehearsal

And of course Cherkaoui remains alert to the accidental moments that arise in a process and embody the whole point of devising performance. Staying with Dockx, there is a moment when she is on the floor and Cherkaoui asks Kinn Svensson, 'What could you do with her? Maybe you could kick her.' It delights both performers and it's in, it stays. For the next two years of touring Dockx will regularly be 'beaten' by Kinn Svensson, and it's one of the most amusing, challenging and well-received moments of the piece.

Material is initiated and generated in ways such as these throughout the sessions, with individuals working on several different ideas in any given single two-hour session. Frequently, especially in the early phases, they gather together to film material just before lunch. There are so many of them that those watching easily create an audience and, unavoidably, different moments get different responses. Some receive polite applause, others whoops and cheers. Thus it is that the selection process – the airing, editing and adopting of material – begins.

Interesting, and surprising to me as an observer, was how little discussion took place within the space. The group as a whole almost never gathered together to discuss anything, and on the rare occasions that they did, it was normally to discuss logistics and schedules, not ideas or themes. There were occasional semi-official meetings held outside the space, at someone's house maybe, and of course there were numerous smaller informal group discussions – between those who shared apartments or train journeys. But Cherkaoui was clear that there was no room, or time, for discussion or reflection in the space. Indeed he saw confrontation or disagreement as failure. The performer's state of not-knowing was deliberately maintained. Unsurprisingly, this approach suited some and not others, and comments I received in interview ranged from 'I feel in the dark about most things that go on . . . and this can raise competitive factors and mistrust', to support of the no-discussion tendency: 'If I'm in a process I don't question things too much, even if I don't trust everything . . . I don't allow myself to go there because if I go there I can't do what I want to do. If I started to [discuss and question things] I wouldn't trust in what I was doing and it would get so complicated.' Cherkaoui himself is resolute on the subject:

> The space for me is to work . . . to be concrete. . . . I don't want anyone talking during the work . . . it is a dance class not a theory class.
>   If the theatre score is being made then you should allow yourself to do anything . . . and then invest in that and not question it intellectually at all because it breaks the space for you to discover it and there are things that the brain cannot imagine. . . . I've tried![15]

But, of course, though there may not be much group discussion, opinions *are* being formed and decisions *are* being made. And as Cherkaoui makes his way instinctively through the material that is being created, he, consciously or otherwise, gives life to, or sounds the death knell of, individual ideas. Perhaps he doesn't see something, can't yet see a place for something, or simply doesn't 'like' it. I am led to examine what people are, again consciously or otherwise, working towards.

> 2 November 2006: What's interesting is how the dancers who have worked with Cherkaoui before are creating ideas. Are they working to what they think he wants, what they think he likes, or what *they* like, what *they* want, what feels right? And those that haven't worked with him before – what are they doing/feeling? How are they making decisions? Are they trying to second-guess what they think a 'Sidi Larbi Cherkaoui show' should be?

In my darker, less charitable moments, it was possible for me to see the whole process as a horrifically protracted audition. In the absence of discussion, or clearly stated intentions, I worried that the performers' fight for a slice of pie, which at best was likely to be about a sixteenth, led to a vulnerability and insecurity that was not always necessarily healthy. The dramaturg had somewhat controversially made it clear to all that he was there for Cherkaoui not for the performers, thus denying them another potential source of feedback or global vision that many felt would have been useful in such a large group, and promoting a perplexingly contradictory 'understanding hierarchy'. Though Cherkaoui's assistant Reehorst clearly did her best to be there for the performers, some of them told me that second-guessing what Cherkaoui might be looking for made the process occasionally stressful and even painful for them. Others, however, said it opened exciting 'third doors' that belonged neither to Cherkaoui nor them. Some spoke of fighting for their material to stay in, others of deciding not to bother. Either way, in time I learned that while there had indeed been a clear attempt to decentralise the process, Cherkaoui, or the performers' perception

2.5 Darryl Woods makes his mark in *Myth*.

of Cherkaoui, remained at the centre of everything. However, while I do not suggest that he was solely motivated by a desire to 'keep everyone happy', nor that he was entirely successful in doing so, Cherkaoui worked hard to find space for the strengths, personalities and signatures of everyone in the piece, saying, 'It is like salt in the soup – you can be a little bit of salt in the soup but if you are not there the soup is horrible. They can be omnipresent and at the same time be a sixteenth of the bigger whole.'[16]

Tellingly, when I interviewed actor Darryl Woods a few months into the tour, we had the following exchange:

'Does the show bear your signature?'
'Yes.'
'And do you think it bears the signature of all the performers?'
'Yes.'
'And does it bear Cherkaoui's signature?'
'Yes.'

It struck me that that this, at its very essence, is the sign of successful directed collaboration.

It is not all, however, about group devising. There are some choreographed pieces already extant that were made in the original workshop weeks. One of these is choreographed by Cherkaoui (though this did not make it into the final show); the others are amalgamations of material made by other individuals. These are now taught to, and in some cases developed by, the rest of the group, and form a significant part of the final production. Thus some individuals actually get to 'choreograph' material, as opposed

2.6 Patricia Bovi sings, accompanied by Ensemble Micrologus, in *Myth*.

to simply improvising it, though of course all material is ultimately presented as part of Sidi Larbi Cherkaoui's *Myth*.[17]

The afternoon session 14.30–evening

Sometimes there are singing sessions. Patricia Bovi, singer and co-founder of Ensemble Micrologus, who are the musicians for this project, specialises in ancient and traditional Italian music and she joins the rehearsals every few weeks to lead singing workshops. Some of the performers are quite reluctant singers, and some are extremely experienced (like the singer and vocal expert Christine Leboutte who was also in *Foi* and who acts as Bovi's lieutenant when she is not there). Bovi guides them through detailed exercises that develop breathing, the use of the mouth and tone. She also teaches the performers the songs.

> 23 January 2007: Patricia talks about the space needed within the voice. If she sings 'forte' she takes space – it is on the outside. If she sings 'piano' – she tries to maintain that space – but she brings it inside. It is easy to hear it in her singing but not easy to do. Some of the performers giggle nervously. If you are a dancer, presenting yourself on a world stage as a dancer is one thing, presenting yourself as a singer is quite another. The standard clearly has to be very high. Patricia speaks very conceptually, and yet very technically at the same time, about feeling, experience, spatial thinking, emphasis, texture, intention, colour.

2.7 Marc Wagemans in front of Wim Van de Cappelle's set for *Myth*.

As the months go by, the space gets busier and busier. More and more material is explored, and a variety of objects creep their way in – long black wigs, hooped skirts, old hardback books – each a tantalising clue to the aesthetic that is being developed. Wim Van De Cappelle's set, a grand nicotine-stained library, or Sartre-like waiting room, with huge doors that hint at both entrapment and escape, gradually material-ises. The original title of *Traum* disappears, and is replaced by *Myth*, as the emphasis becomes more on the archetypal characters who find themselves trapped in this limbo, and less on early ideas about trauma. The rehearsal room remains busy.

What Cherkaoui created, to borrow the language of Deleuze and Guattari, was a rhizome. He created a network of people, possibilities and desires, a multiplicity of units between which he encouraged multi-directional (primarily bodily) com-munication and transformation.[18] It was a collective assemblage, that aimed not to have hierarchical or dialectical channels, but that existed as multiple, simultaneous experimentations with what was real. Deleuze and Guattari describe mapping rhizo-matic action as a means of constructing the unconscious – partly what this writing is engaged with, and exactly what the journey from process to product was here. The constant interaction of individuals, all of whom have their own desires, tastes, knowledges and abilities, and the constant clashing of one idea against another, leads to third, fourth and fifth ideas. This, combined with Cherkaoui's general themes and interests, created a multiplicity of intention, purpose and outcome. Cherkaoui's job, as the collaborative director, was to keep the plates spinning and know when to give an idea immortality by selecting and using it.

The rhizomatic multiplicity is omnipresent. It is in:

- the languages used in both the process and the product
- the nationalities
- the disciplines (dance, theatre, music, writing, design)
- the background, training, desire and ability of the collaborators and their phenomenological experience of the process
- the multiple and rarely fixed themes
- the simultaneous development of material, character and purpose
- the inevitable performer blindness that occurs as a result of this simultaneity (no
one knows what anyone else is doing or which ideas are being selected until material is presented in a showing), leaving the performers each to find their own way
to their own understanding of what it is they have created, thus creating multiple
realities
- the way in which the structure and nature of the process is present in the product
- the gradual catalysis of the piece structured by Cherkaoui's palimpsest-like
composition that eventually forms his signature product that is multi-focused,
multi-layered and consequently consciously denies the notion of one fixed truth
in favour of multiple equally (in)valid truths that are crucially open to multiple
interpretation.

As the months go by, the creation process moves from being global, general
and generative, to being about selection and composition. Cherkaoui reveals which
moments he wants to keep, more doors are closed than are opened, and the rhizome
gets fixed in varnish. The 'showings' that pepper the entire process, where the great
and the good of Belgian theatre assemble to see what is happening, get more and more
frequent. The product begins to emerge. In February 2007, there is a showing of over
three hours of material, and it is later noted that nearly all of this material found its way
into the final two-hour production. This is done by Cherkaoui placing one idea beside
another, layering and merging material, so that what we see on stage is rarely just one
moment but rather a dense and busy cacophony of action. He comes to rehearsal with
a hand-written running order that has columns to allow for simultaneous moments,
which is photocopied and distributed. After a brief explanation, the performers enact
that running order, papers in hand. But as that happens, Cherkaoui will also respond
to the now and will direct on the hoof, making his own 'sense out of nonsense' as he
describes it, entering the performance space to make a new request, move a body or ini-
tiate a sequence at a time different to that he had planned. The performers work busily,
doing what's asked. They will watch the film later to see what it was they created.

> 21 May 2007: Cherkaoui has shifted his mode and is directing the detail now. Embodying,
> moving, speaking, demonstrating, instructing: 'I would like . . .', 'Can you . . .'. He jumps
> up and in to make suggestions, now working in a very clear directorial mode. His volume
> is turned up, he gives specific instructions – 'Do one not two', 'Darryl don't say that'. He
> conducts them, imposing pauses with hand gestures, or by calling out, '. . . and NOW!'

Thus, as the sun sets on the day and the process as a whole, a show is born. And
as the child growing in my belly in the last few months of this journey will no doubt
surprise me, the work surprises its makers, introducing itself, seemingly with its own

identity, and often with its own intentions. It is a third thing, that exceeds the knowl-edge of all those who made it. And just as Cherkaoui has made his own sense out of nonsense, both we the audience and they the performers are left to make our own sense of what is being presented and experienced.

Many of the performers spoke about their own journeys towards understand-ing, and their attempts to find logic, to attribute meaning and to form links between themselves, the material and each other. One describes this as 'finding my own little soap stories', and, though once the show opens the material is more or less fixed, many admit that this search for meaning will continue throughout the tour. This troubles some and thrills others. Consequently, throughout the process and in the early stages of the tour, when I ask either Cherkaoui or the performers what the show is about, for them, today, I am met by a hugely wide range of answers, one of which remained for many, 'I don't know. Yet.'

22 June 2007 20.00–showtime

After two weeks of working with the full set and lights in De Singel, the curtain goes up on the opening night.[19] The intimidating 'presence of numerous international programme planners'[20] merely serves to highlight the preposterousness and impos-sibility of trying to represent, or do justice to, eight months of complex, collaborative and transformative process in two hours, and under one title – *Myth*. This dawns on some of the performers with some sadness as they prepare to face the post-premiere onslaught of 'what people thought'.

And what did people think? Peter T'Jonck of Belgium's newspaper *De Morgen* was bold with his interpretation: 'This is the message of the piece: you cannot ignore your shadows . . . what is weighing you down or what you don't want to recognise in yourself.'[21]Jean-Marie Wynants, from the Belgian newspaper *Le Soir*, acknowledged the multiplicity but didn't venture her own interpretation, though she did comment on her personal response to the visual cacophony: 'Drawing inspiration from (among other things) the tarot, religious imagery and martial arts films, Sidi Larbi Cherkaoui unleashes a veritable flood of images, thus generously providing us with all the raw material needed to construct as many narratives as there are spectators in the auditorium.'[22]

But what does Cherkaoui, not as author but as the *metteur en scène*, the editor, the 'gluer together of moments', say about its content?

> I never want to pinpoint one thing. I'd like it to be about human nature and interaction . . . and all the different philosophies of how to live your life. You can choose . . . and that choice will define your humanity. But then, I'd like to go even further and say that in the end it doesn't really matter. Cosmically, there is a bigger picture.

And perhaps it is this bigger picture, where our actions are recognised as small and inconsequential, that he is trying to paint with the bodies and minds of

2.8 *Myth*'s multiplicity as represented by its poster, created by Dooreman & Houbrechts, 2007

his collaborators. He speaks of enjoying the temporary nature of dance – calling it drawing in time – and how, through it, we can experience the present, loaded nevertheless with the past, and simply let it go into the ether, to live on in the minds of those who presented, saw, or even read in some book, about the moment in time that was the process and product of *Myth*.

Notes

1   Simon Murray and John Keefe, *Physical Theatres: A Critical Introduction* (London and New York: Routledge, 2007), p. 76.
2   www.theaterstap.com (accessed 3 August 2007).
3   Sidi Larbi Cherkaoui in interview with Lou Cope, October 2006.
4   Susan Melrose, 'Constitutive Ambiguities', in Joe Kelleher and Nicholas Ridout (eds), *Contemporary Theatres in Europe* (Abingdon: Routledge, 2006), p. 126.
5   Adrian Kear, 'Seduction & Translation: Conversations with Alain Platel', *Performance Research*, 7:2 (2002), 35 – 49, p. 45.
6   Susan Melrose, 'Introduction', in Rosemary Butcher and Susan Melrose (eds), *Rosemary Butcher: Choreography, Collisions and Collaborations* (Middlesex: Middlesex University Press, 2005), p. 20.
7   My thanks go to Wim Van De Cappelle for opening the door, to Sidi Larbi Cherkaoui, Nienke Reehorst and Mien Muys for welcoming me in, and to Sri Louise, James O'Hara, Darryl Woods, Ulrika Kinn Svensson and all the other collaborators for making my stay so enjoyable.
8   In fact, in November 2006, singer and actor Christine Leboutte told me that there had been so many guests lately she was beginning to feel a bit like a lab rat. She asked if she might see some of what I was writing. This raised interesting and important issues about the complexities of being a non-participant observer and the effect of the observer on the observed, but, despite my desire to be open to the performers, I elected not to show Christine my rehearsal observation notes for fear of increasing awareness of my presence and thereby threatening my non-participant status. Instead I gave her a document about my research as a whole which I believe helped a little, though she rightly said it was a bit dry and academic. I offered to meet and talk, but her interest, or perhaps her discomfort, waned and it was not to be.
9   Here and below quotations are from my rehearsal journal.
10 Sri Louise in interview with Lou Cope, December 2006.
11 Michel de Certeau, *The Practice of Everyday Life*, trans. Steven Rendall (Berkeley, CA: University of California Press, 1984), p. 93.
12 Cherkaoui in interview with Lou Cope, October 2006.
13 Cherkaoui in interview with Lou Cope, December 2006.
14 *Ibid.*; James O'Hara in written interview with Lou Cope, August 2007.
15 Cherkaoui in interview with Lou Cope, December 2006.
16 *Ibid.*
17 The 'contract for erasure', as Melrose describes it, does not go unnoticed, though most see the opportunity to create work in this way, as well as the two-year spell of paid work, as a fair exchange (Melrose, 'Constitutive Ambiguities', p. 124). As dancer Damien Fournier puts it, 'I am clearly playing in [Cherkaoui's] house', and he is happy with that. Nevertheless the decision not to include full biographies in the programme, thus minimising the role of the individuals in the authorship of the piece (though the show is billed as 'performed and created by' the performers), caused concern for many.

18   Gilles Deleuze and Félix Guattari, *A Thousand Plateaus* (*Capitalism and Schizophrenia*, vol. 2), trans. Brian Massumi (Minneapolis: University of Minnesota Press, 1987).

19   Production credits include the following: director/choreographer – Sidi Larbi Cherkaoui; created and performed by Alexandra Gilbert, Damien Jalet, Darryl Woods, Ulrika Kinn Svensson, Iris Bouche, Peter Jasko, Sri Louise, James O'Hara, Ann Dockx, Satoshi Kudo, Marc Wagemans, Milan Herich, Christine Leboutte, Damien Fournier; assistant director – Nienke Reehorst; music – Patrician Bovi and Ensemble Micrologus; set design – Wim Van De Cappelle, Sidi Larbi Cherkaoui; costume design – Isabelle Lhoas; lighting design – Luc Schaltin; dramaturg – Guy Cools.

20   Jean-Maria Wynants, '"Myth", a Sidi Larbi Cherkaoui Creation, in Antwerp', *Le Soir*, Belgium (22 June 2007).

21   Peter T'Jonck, 'Profound Frivolity', *De Morgen*, Belgium (22 June 2007).

22   Wynants, '"Myth", a Sidi Larbi Cherkaoui Creation, in Antwerp'.

3

Complicite – *The Elephant Vanishes* (2003/4) – 'The elephant and keeper have vanished completely . . . They will never be coming back'[1]

Catherine Alexander

When you are making theatre ideas are never the problem. There are hundreds of ideas. It's finding how to transmit them. It's all about how the idea is expressed. It's not a logical thing . . . most importantly it involves the imagination of the audience: once you plug into that theatre lives.[2] (Simon McBurney)

Complicite: a constant state of evolution

Complicite was founded in 1983 by Simon McBurney, Annabel Arden and Marcello Magni. Since then the company has been a constantly evolving ensemble of performers and collaborators, many of whom studied at L'École Jacques Lecoq, the theatre school in Paris led by the celebrated French teacher Lecoq. Complicite's work has mainly comprised devised theatre pieces, adaptations and revivals of classic texts. The company has also worked in other media, with radio productions including one of John Berger's *To the Wedding* (1997), a collaboration with the Pet Shop Boys in Trafalgar Square in central London (2004), and *The Vertical Line* (1999), a multi-disciplinary installation performed in a disused tube station. If the company is constantly percolating new collaborators, so too the work is in a constant state of evolution: from the actor-led, comic and highly physical early pieces to the vast recent collaborations directed by Simon McBurney which embrace intellectually challenging material and cutting-edge technologies.[3]

I first worked with Complicite in 1994 on *Out of a house walked a man* at the National Theatre. This was the start of a three-year period assisting Simon McBurney on performance and education projects including the company's productions of Brecht's *The Caucasian Chalk Circle* at the National Theatre and Ionesco's *The Chairs* at the Royal Court (both 1997). I trained as an actor at L'École Jacques Lecoq between 1997 and 1999 and founded my own theatre company, Quiconque, in 2000. Since 2003 I have been an Associate Director with Complicite for *The Elephant Vanishes* (2003-4) and *A Disappearing Number* (2007). In 2003 Complicite presented my devised production of *Hideaway* on a UK tour. This long connection with the company has shaped my working methodology and helped me to define my own voice as a theatre-maker.

I have spent much of my working life, then, in the intense environment of Complicite rehearsals and workshops but I still find it nearly impossible to reconstruct the development of each show. The nature of any creative process is that you constantly make and discard: the act of forgetting is as important as that of remembering. As soon as a day, week or month of rehearsal is over, the memory of the process vanishes and you only take forward the vital elements for the performance. Simon McBurney has written about his work over the years but frequently in retrospect where the process can be remembered in a seamless way. For this chapter on *The Elephant Vanishes* I have returned to my copious notes and rehearsal diaries in an attempt to reflect the creative chaos of the day-to-day work and describe the shape of the creative process from within.

The Elephant Vanishes: starting points

Some shows come very quickly and only require a single block of rehearsal. Others are more delicate and complex. *The Elephant Vanishes* took about ten years from the beginning of its journey to the first performance. The creation also involved a sizeable number of people: two sets of producers (Complicite in London and the Setagaya Public Theatre in Tokyo), a large creative and production team, the actors and many other collaborators from development workshops. This was an intercultural collaboration: West and East attempted to meet and find a common creative language. The show was initially created for performances in Tokyo and Osaka and a run for the BITE (Barbican International Theatre Event) festival in London.

Complicite first travelled to Tokyo in 1995 with its production of *The Three Lives of Lucie Cabrol* (an adaptation of John Berger's novel) at the Tokyo Globe Theatre. When the company brought *The Street of Crocodiles* (adapted from short stories by the Polish writer Bruno Schulz) to the Setagaya Public Theatre in 1998, Simon was invited to lead a workshop with Japanese actors and the prospect of a co-production was discussed for the first time. Cheiko Hosaka, producer for the Setagaya Public Theatre, expands upon the project's starting points:

> [Simon McBurney's] preliminary workshops looked at restoring our memories in the
> highly consumerist society of the Twentieth Century by exploring the world of Tanizaki

texts which were written in [the] 1930s. The more Simon and [the] Japanese actors explored the world of Tanizaki, the more we realized the difference between the contemporary world and that of Tanizaki. . . . In order to understand Tanizaki's world, we have to travel back thousands of years to explore the origins of the Japanese culture. The world we live in now has a sense of rootlessness and detachment from the past. Modern Japan is a floating world.[4]

In 2002 we started to explore short fiction by another Japanese writer, Haruki Murakami, in order to find a more immediate connection to the modern world. The eventual production was based on three of Murakami's stories: 'Sleep', 'The Elephant Vanishes' and 'The Second Bakery Attack'. It drew together impressions of modern Tokyo and thoughts about the consumption of electricity and the physics of light. My memories of *The Elephant Vanishes* in performance feature television monitors, images and actors moving relentlessly back and forth across the stage, caught up in a light storm. I remember mysterious shadows on a shoji screen and banal everyday events momentarily becoming extraordinary. I see a man literally floating on top of his memories as he narrates his own story; a woman ruptured into three elements, unable to sleep and enveloped in sequences from *Anna Karenina*. I hear a pumping and ear-splitting mix of Kendo drummers and music by Craig Armstrong, while I watch a husband and wife drive through the streets of Tokyo at night armed and ready to undertake a hold-up. Through all these images walks an elephant. It was in this dream-like layering that the show emerged: less a piece with a strong narrative drive than one with a series of rich visual and sensual evocations.

The early workshops: how to make words heard (2001)

The Japanese for shadow is *kage*, but according to our translators the term has a very different sense from how we use it in English. In the West a shadow is a defined shape, whereas in Japan it is connected to the word *shade* or *soft/filtered light*. It can also mean 'moonlight' or 'moon shadow'. This small example of a difficult word to translate was also typical of the subtle cultural differences that underpinned the project. In the 2001 Tokyo workshop, just days before the 9/11 World Trade Center attacks, we were working in a peaceful rehearsal room exploring differences between East and West. Our fortnight in Japan led us to consider some of the challenges we were to face over the following few years.

The first five years of this collaboration centred on Jun-ichiro Tanizaki's short story *A Portrait of Shunkin* and essay *In Praise of Shadows*. Tanizaki was writing in the 1930s during a period of extreme Japanese nationalism. His writing expresses nostalgia for the Japan of the nineteenth century and rails against the inward seep of Western culture in the early decades of the twentieth. He muses upon architecture, actions, objects, time, light and shadow, giving a fascinating insight into traditional

Japanese culture. Although it seems to be deliberately provocative, particularly in its polarised vision of East and West, this writing helped us to open up the question, 'What does it mean to be Japanese?'

In one exercise we took sections of Tanizaki's text and edited them into concise phrases. One group's edited section described a *tokonoma*, an alcove situated in the centre of a traditional Japanese house:

> *Tokonoma* . . . though we know perfectly well it is mere shadow we are overcome with the feeling that in this small corner of the atmosphere there reigns complete and utter silence . . . even we as children would feel an inexpressible chill as we peered into the depths of a *tokonoma* to which the sunlight had never penetrated. It is the magic of shadows. Were shadows to be banished from its corners, the alcove would in that instant revert to mere void.

We discussed the fragility of translation and how the words sound different to English and Japanese ears. We began to realise that when you don't understand the spoken text you listen to and direct work in quite a different way. One of the Japanese actors explained to us that there is no formal voice training in Japan. The average Japanese actor doesn't use gradation in volume – when an actor speaks there is nothing between a whisper and a shout.

Simon used this workshop to explore spoken language: how to read Tanizaki aloud and make the words easy to hear. We explored short passages in terms of rhythm and found five different ways to speak the text. For example:

1. Like newsreaders.
2. Punctuated by space, volume, intensity, rhythm.
3. Horror movie – first scared – then scary.
4. As two grumbling grandfathers and two young girls.
5. With the dynamic of ceramic – brittle and sharp.

After hearing the five versions the listeners decided which allowed them to hear the words best. As a group we experimented with how to use space, rhythm and style to play with language. Importantly this wasn't about a direct emotional connection with the language but concrete, observable dynamics. After we discovered various ways to approach speaking the words Simon layered in images, actions and music. One example, which used the *tokonoma* text, was as follows:

TEXT	The text is read by actors from four corners of the space.
ACTION	Masaki (one of the actors) comes home, removes shoes and sits and works at his computer (the only light source).
IMAGE	An image of a *tokonoma* is slowly formed using bamboos by a chorus of actors.
MUSIC	Clive Bell improvises on his *shakuhachi* [a Japanese bamboo wind instrument] as the *tokonoma* image starts to unfold.

Through these very simple juxtapositions we started to find the tension between the past and the present. In the early stages of the workshop Simon choreographed these collisions of the various elements, but as the participants become more fluent with devising they conducted more of this work independently in groups.

Throughout these early workshops in Japan there was a muted anxiety on the part of the actors that the inconsequential fragments we were compiling might end up on stage. Very few of them knew Complicite's work – nor its dependence upon long exploration and extensive provisional 'sketching' by way of trial performance – so Simon reassured them that this was simply research and definitely not for an audience's eyes. All we wanted to discover were the circumstances where we heard Tanizaki's words most clearly. This process feels like an archaeological excavation and is nearly always slow and painstaking.

A modern time: Murakami not Tanizaki (2002)

In 2002 a group of Japanese actors and producers from the Setagaya Public Theatre came to London for a two-week workshop. Complicite also invited Japanese actors who lived in the UK and France along with English performers, Chris Shutt (sound designer) and Clive Bell (musician). Simon chose to spend this two-week process exploring short stories from Murakami's collection entitled *The Elephant Vanishes*. We needed a break from Tanizaki and wanted to explore more immediate and contemporary material.

Hosaka confessed to being 'on the pins and needles' during the preliminary workshops with Murakami's texts, but the work seemed much more accessible and the results funny and fresh. The workshop made us appreciate how firmly fixed most of us are in the modern world and how well we communicate in this context. We also discovered that Murakami hints constantly at the shadow of a past world: in the stories there is an almost invisible imprint of the past upon the present. The characters in Murakami find a window into this other world whose evocation becomes almost mystical. The kitchen salesman in 'The Elephant Vanishes' is the only person who realises the elephant has disappeared. The newly married couple in 'The Second Bakery Attack' feel an insatiable hunger that they believe is a curse brought on by past actions. So where Tanizaki recognises the specific time that everything required in an idealised Japan of the past, Murakami expresses the unstoppable velocity of modern life by exploring characters who have paused for a moment. When the lost world of the past catches hold it does so with an obsessive and visceral quality – the need to hold on to it becomes very powerful for the characters.

Murakami's stories touched something in all of us but Simon worried that they weren't sufficiently 'Japanese' and were somehow *too* accessible. Simon needed to know why they were important to us, and this became an obsession in the late stages of the process. We read more Murakami and became interested in the short stories 'After the Quake' and 'Underground'. Faxes shot back and forth between the producers in Japan, London and Murakami who finally agreed that Complicite could adapt any of the stories from the collection published in the UK under the title *The Elephant*

Vanishes. This broad decision for the material for the show was arrived at in mid-2002. There were still misgivings, and a central concern was to find an overarching narrative that grounded the stories in a particular reality. We discussed using the Sarin gas attacks on the Tokyo metro that occurred in 1995 and passages about the physics of light and parallel universes from David Deutsch's book *The Fabric of Reality*. We had turned away from the Tanizaki texts but this early exploration – and in particular the appearance of shoji screens, shadows and glimpses of the past – infused our work on Murakami.

Casting (2002-3)

Finding the right actors for *The Elephant Vanishes* took an enormous amount of time and investment. The Japanese producers had to begin to understand and support Complicite's unusually demanding and lengthy process. In addition the best Japanese actors are booked up for years ahead, so making late casting decisions is very challenging. Finding actors who had the drive and desire to create rather than simply present, and the ability to work in a relatively chaotic devising process, took many years. This gave the show a slow and careful evolution. Trust had to be earned and built with each actor so that they were able to be instinctive and even anarchic. They had to learn to be autonomous and to speak their minds as directly as possible, which remained the hardest thing. I remember Simon asking direct questions and the whole company nodding and looking at the ground, then three days later explaining why they actually disagreed.

Following the London workshops Simon decided that three of the Japanese actors (Yuko Miyamoto, Keitoku Takata and Atsuko Takaizumi) were right for the main project. Yasuyo Mochizuki, a Lecoq-trained actor-dancer, had also impressed in the London workshops but we encountered the sharp edge of the Japanese theatre hierarchy. Yasuyo was situated outside the Japanese theatre system and was considered hard to place in a company of established Japanese actors. Yuko, Yasuyo and Atsuko had done some incredible work together in our workshops but the Japanese actors were unhappy about Yasuyo being cast in the project.

In autumn 2002 Simon went on a short trip to Japan to meet more actors. We considered the stories we were most interested in and thought we might need two young men (who could potentially play the dentist from 'Sleep' and the young man in 'The Second Bakery Attack') and an older woman. Casting for devised work is a shot in the dark: your choices both limit and inspire the work you are about to make and it is fatal to think too literally. At this point we only knew that we were missing a central and dynamic performer who could carry the show. The Japanese actors had a great capacity to follow and create as a company but we desperately needed a provoker of ideas and work – a maverick.

I went to Tokyo in December 2002 to hold an audition workshop to cast the rest of the show. I was filled with nerves and a little lonely staying in my salary-man hotel in Yoga. It was a crisp, cold December and I couldn't work the heating (apart from the heated toilet seat). I was jet-lagged and wide-awake at 4.00am, sitting on the loo to keep warm.

We worked in a large rehearsal room and I was struck again by the cleanliness and respect that Japanese theatre-makers have for the working space. You remove your shoes at the entrance and change into soft slippers, so the floor is spotlessly clean. It becomes a matter of shame now when I look at the soles of my bare feet, blackened by British rehearsal-room floors. There is something very calming about a clean room.

The actors turned up in dribs and drabs and then Mitsuru Fukikoshi (Fuki) arrived with his suited and booted manager. The manager stayed and watched the whole workshop, along with a line of Setagaya producers. I realised, after a series of games and exercises, that Fuki was auditioning me. Every actor in the room had a huge reverence for him and it made the workshop feel unbalanced. It was a fairly intimidating circumstance and I felt painfully aware of the need to represent Simon's work fairly. I went back to my hotel room that night, sat on the hot toilet seat and felt close to tears. The encounter had been utterly exhausting. The following day I managed to lead some more evolved exercises and was able to delve more deeply into Fuki's work. His improvisation and devising skills were phenomenal. He was head and shoulders above anyone we'd encountered so far and I managed to work with him to craft some of his improvisations. At the end he came up and said he had enjoyed the workshop and would like to do the project. I was delighted, as Fuki was clearly the challenging and brilliant performer who would provoke and interrogate the work. I was anxious to land back in London and get him contracted as soon as possible.

I was fairly sure that we had found three interesting performers. The first was Fuki. The second was Ryoko Tateishi, an older woman with an amazing versatility with spoken text. She carried a delicate tragedy with her and I knew from watching her play simple theatre games that she was natural, playful and truthful. The third was Masato Sakai, a young university-educated actor with great energy and enthusiasm. It was clear he was extremely bright and would be a marvellous tension-breaker: he would frequently fall over because he was laughing so much. The process of casting was nearly over. How the six actors would work together remained to be seen.

London: the exploration and creation of a company (March–April 2003)

The success of the London workshop led to the rehearsal period being arranged in two sections: five weeks working in London and five in Tokyo. This allowed the first five weeks to be playful and the devising process to progress in a non-linear way. As Sonoko Yamamoto, the stage manager, observed:

> Working in London allowed Simon to have some normality and minimised the amount of new things that he had to cope with. The actors enjoyed being in London too, it was

3.1 *The Elephant Vanishes* rehearsal shot: Mitsuru Fukikoshi and Atsuko Takaizumi
exploring the husband and wife relationship in 'Sleep'.

a different experience and it liberated them. . . . They enjoyed London, living together,
eating, rehearsing and drinking together. Most of the actors hadn't ever shared flats before
so it was a new and interesting experience.

As we started rehearsals for *The Elephant Vanishes* in March 2003 the question
about why this show needed to be made now became increasingly urgent. What made
it relevant? Who were the key narrative voices and why were they telling their stories?

Masato recently said that he'd never been asked these questions before and, though blindingly simple, they radically changed his approach as an actor.

In the early days of rehearsal we explored many voices. The company was constantly asked, 'Which voice allows us to hear the words best? Which accompanying images or scenes enable the stories to be transmitted?' The initial improvisations were almost painfully simple. We returned to the absolute bare essentials of theatre: a voice telling a story in direct address. We explored the private voices of people telling their story in a bar, or to a video diary; the interrogative voices of a journalist or prosecution lawyer; nostalgic voices or those of old men talking about their past. Then we coupled the voices and story fragments with the simplest of stage pictures. We were gradually learning about the stories and their important events, states and sequences.

Alongside this work was the ongoing physical preparation of the acting ensemble and the journey in building a shared theatre language. Every morning we worked together physically. Simon led yoga and Feldenkrais-style exercises to allow us to become more physically coordinated and free. We played games to build competitiveness and aggression, we moved together in pairs and groups and became more and more responsive to each other. These games and exercises awoke a sense of inner physical impulse, put us in the present tense and made us alert and ready. Sometimes a mat would be rolled out along the floor and the actors would roll, walk, run or fall on it in various sequences for half an hour at a time. Sometimes we would work in groups to remake photos or create soundscapes. Gradually we learned about each other and the theatrical territory that we were navigating.

At some point in workshops and rehearsals Simon always returns to a classic Lecoq exercise: The Seven Levels of Tension. When taught well, this is a beautiful activity, so graspable and widely applicable to character, text, voice, body and space. It is as useful for designers and writers as it is for actors because everything has a tension that implies a rhythm, a space, a colour and shape.

One of our first exercises using the tensions model considered the use of tension in the black-and-white photographs that lined the rehearsal-room walls. We translated the photos into movement texts, which led to an awareness of the space, rhythm, tempo, shape and contact of each image. The results were very specific and brought the actors smoothly away from a literal approach to movement and image-making.

The results of this exercise led to a discussion about literal or representational work and, in contrast, work which is dynamic and expressive. This distinction is central to understanding the training at Lecoq's school and to getting inside the reason why Complicite shows have a unique flavour. The company constantly searches for an inner dynamic (of images, text and physical or emotional states) and a way of making that explicit. This is an extra dimension that exists alongside all the more recognisable work on character, text, acting and staging. Though other directors may create an externally pleasing picture and choreograph the actors to move in particular ways, if an inner dynamic isn't *embodied*, the work remains superficial. Simon insists on this exploration for weeks and weeks of the process, often to the bemusement of producers. It is work that cannot be skimped and Simon approaches it with

Box 3.1: The Seven Levels of Tension

This exercise is an exploration of muscular tension. It asks a performer to take a particular muscular tension into the whole body, including the respiration, eyes and voice. The initial challenge is to allow one tension to inhabit the body in its entirety. Start by exploring the two ends of the scale: high and low tension. At the two extremes of the scale no movement is possible.

1. If you take all of the tension out of your body what happens? Clearly you can't remain standing – so you collapse. No movement is possible except the essentials of staying alive – a gentle breath, the blood moving around inside. Hardly any sound is possible and the eyes are unable to focus or stay open. Explore this lack of tension in pairs with one person staying in the lowest state of tension and the other manipulating them to ensure that they are not holding tension anywhere. This is zero.
2. What happens when you put maximum muscular tension into your body? Stay in the same pairs and take turns to tense every muscle and sinew in your body. Which positions allow the highest level of tension? Don't hold the high tension state for more than a few seconds – it's extremely tiring. Explore the breath. Can you breathe or just hold your breath? Can you see, hear or make sounds? As you observe your partner and try to move parts of their body, discover where there isn't maximum tension. In maximum tension no movement should be possible. This is level 7. While you are exploring, observe the postures that people begin to arrive at.
3. Now that you have the points of reference of 0 and 7, explore the rest of the scale. From 1 to 6 movement is possible, so explore the tension by moving around the space. Each tension has a specific relationship with gravity, a direction (for instance, moves in circles, or straight lines), occupies a particular space and has an inherent rhythm and tempo. Some tensions can't arrive at a fixed point and others have moments of stillness. Take your time as a group to explore, and try to come up with your own scale and the specifics of each number.
4. The list of names that are sometimes given to each level are:
   0. Catatonic   3. Economic   6. Passionate
   1. Fatigue   4. Alert   7. Petrified
   2. Relaxed   5. Suspense

Be cautious with these names. It is very easy to start characterising and externalising each tension and not really inhabiting them and taking them in to everypart of the body. For example, Tension 1 can be explored purely physically but by calling it 'Fatigue' an actor may arrive at a tension through a specific known state. This is potentially limiting. Of course, when an actor has accurately discovered the state of tension it may well suggest fatigue or drunkenness, but it is more useful to arrive at that purely by exploring muscular tension.

3.2 Rehearsal shot: a devising task, exploring Japan past and present and Schroedinger's Cat. Left to right, Catherine Alexander, Keitoku Takata, Ryoko Tateishi, Victoria Gould.

great generosity and patience, ensuring that everybody shares the principles of move-ment and a working language. Clive Bell describes an improvisation which explored the dynamic of the terrifying dream in the story *Sleep*:

> The heroine is terrified by an old man with a pitcher, standing at the end of her bed and pouring water onto her feet. I accompanied the action on a wooden flute, still just playable in spite of being filled with sand. Towards the end, a tilt of my head sent the sand trickling from the end of the flute. Messy, but worth it.

Before the rehearsal period and during these early weeks we also worked at the task of extrapolating the spoken text from the Murakami stories we were consider-ing. After the Seven Levels of Tension exercise Simon asked the actors to explore this dialogue purely in terms of tension: appropriate or inappropriate. It created a very strong and often funny vocal delivery – muscular, unpredictable and rhythmically varied.

As the explorations continued in London there was a growing sense of unease about the shape of the company. Things were not gelling and Simon expressed the need to cast a performer who really understood movement. We considered several Japanese dancers but conversations kept leading us back to Yasuyo – the Lecoq-trained actor-dancer from the first set of Murakami workshops. Finally she arrived in about week four of the process and subtly and sensitively worked her way into the core of the company. Six became seven, the perfect prime number, instantly making the company the right shape.

3.3 Rehearsal shot: a devising task exploring flying and projections for 'The Second Bakery Attack'.

Creating a spatial language

Space in theatre is tangible and material, and that goes for the space proposed by the rehearsal room. I noted in my rehearsal diary:

Amazing how a rehearsal room inspires you and influences the work. A tall room inspires vertical work, a dark room allows an exploration of light. In the Soho Laundry during the first Murakami workshop in 2002 we all became obsessed with using a three-seat sofa. People disappeared down the back of it and rolled over it . . . it was used in nearly every scene.

In our rehearsal room at the Playground in London we obsessively played a ball game each day based on a noughts-and-crosses grid taped on to the floor. Sometimes Simon would be lost in thought and we would play together for nearly an hour at a time. Each square was approximately 150 cm along each side and the grid was taped in the middle of the rehearsal room. If something that definite is placed on the rehearsal-room floor, then it is impossible to ignore. You find yourself walking along the lines or placing objects or bodies in relation to them in pleasing ways. The grid became our map. One exercise that grew out of the grid led directly to one of the repeated visual themes of the final show. Simon became interested in exploring seeing someone alone in their personal space:

EXERCISE
1. The actor would enter the space or start in the space (the 150x150 cm square).
2. They would dress or undress in an entirely realistic way, as if unobserved. The actors were asked to search for the extraordinary, surprising and broken rhythms that we adopt naturally when we are alone.
3. The exercise was taken one step further by placing the actors in adjacent boxes and asking them to do any activity they wanted in their square.

We watched their private lives unfold in front of us. One had a bath, another spoke on the telephone while brushing his teeth, one got dressed, one did some ironing and another did the washing-up. The results evoked a Tokyo apartment block: lots of people living in close proximity but still being totally isolated.

Simon's proposal for the next stage of the exercise was for three actors to occupy the same square but to be oblivious to each other. This pushed the idea of people living on top of each other. It foregrounded notions of interference and parallel lives, and expressed the sense of chance and magic that permeates Murakami's writing. We had discovered our first theatrical equivalent – the normal actions of people living their lives being made extraordinary by the manifesting of inexplicable links between them. This exercise grew into what we called 'the crossing sequence', which opened the show and linked each of the short stories. Fragments of people's lives and the actions within them crossed and travelled through each other – appeared and disappeared, linked momentarily and in an arbitrary manner. Although Murakami's stories are all set in modern Tokyo they don't connect in an obvious way. This exercise allowed the central characters and their narratives to appear appropriately, in an implicitly connected way, and gave the audience the sense of dropping in, as if at random, on people's lives.

The same grid on the floor also led to the central dynamic, shape and movement of the piece. Elements of the set and the actors' physical journeys emphasised a series of lateral movements across the stage and the opposite movement from upstage to

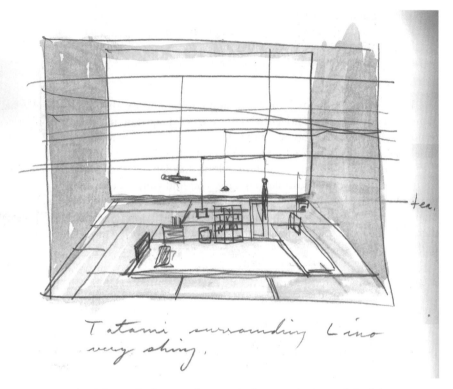

Tatami surrounding Lino very shiny.

3.4 Design sketch by Michael Levine showing the horizontal wires and the flying man.

downstage. Everything adhered to these straight lines. This pattern was strengthened and formalised in Michael Levine's design, which featured visible wires above head-height that traversed the stage from left to right, along with a series of sliding screens that moved along the same horizontal axis. (See figures 3.4 and 3.5.)

Chaos and discovery

Simon McBurney is uniquely gifted in the art of collaboration – not in a fluffy, egalitarian way but in a muscular, incisive and carnivorous way. He rips and trashes through the mounds of material and crafts a show. He wrestles with subject, form, space, sound and actor to make something new. Most importantly, he allows himself and everyone around him to struggle.

This wrestling with subject and form became increasingly evident as the weeks of rehearsal unfolded. The games and open-ended improvisations gradually became more pointed and specific. The work also became more demanding, emotionally and physically. Simon requires his company to be boring, repetitive, quiet, ponderous and

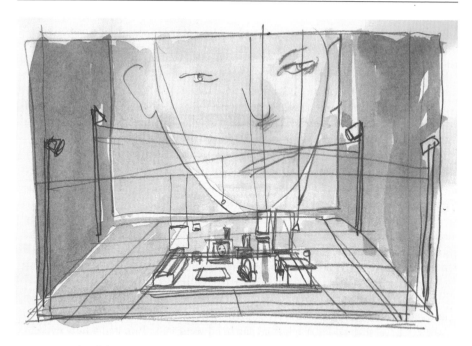

3.5 Design sketch by Michael Levine showing the video projection screen making a rear wall, and a concentrated performance area with furniture.

ineffective. And constantly to fail. Failing is better than being reductive and correct. As a director and a teacher I increasingly recognise the value of actors or students who allow themselves to fail, who willingly place themselves in a difficult and uncomfortable place.

The dominant feeling at this mid-stage of the process was that nobody, especially not Simon, knew what was going on. The most successful collaborators existed happily in the mêlée, created on a day-to-day basis and didn't play an endgame. The more practical or panicky offered pragmatic solutions and attempted to make sense of the chaos that surrounded them. Simon pushed us further into the chaos of unexpected discovery. As theatre-makers it is inevitable that we constantly repeat and revise work using learned patterns. Working with Simon is revelatory because as soon as we get comfortable we're forced to move on. Some people thrive in this circumstance and others hate it. As a collaborator with Complicite you learn to accept that, if you're lucky, five per cent of what you create has life and the rest is rejected. As Clive Bell observes:

Every preconception about what the show might include seems to be hurled out of the window, so as to create a scary blank page. Then the text is trampled, like grapes in a vat, till it releases its essence. A small group, say four performers, will spend half a day creating a ten-minute improvisation, in which two lines of text are translated into a series of unforgettable images. At the end of a long day, when everyone is exhausted and hungry,

Box 3.2: On having technical support and equipment in rehearsals

At any one time there was a range of people collaborating in the rehearsal room. Video, sound and lighting and other technical elements were included from the beginning of the process and became integral to the storytelling.

For *The Elephant Vanishes* we had a manual flying track installed in the rehearsal rooms in London which meant that we were able to fly people (suspend and move them in mid-air on a wire) even in initial improvisations (see figures 3.2 and 3.3). The flying operators became incredibly sensitive to Masato (the actor who performed the flying sequences in the show) and together they learnt to execute very complicated sequences. Every day after rehearsal there was a flying call for half-an-hour when certain moves could be perfected.

One movement involved Masato standing on the top of a fridge and leaning over until his body was horizontal, then bending to take out a beer. Later in the process a sequence was videoed to project onto the front of the closed fridge door, which developed this action further. The video showed a hand reaching underwater and dislodging a can of beer from a pile of pebbles, then bringing it out of the water. At the same time the actor plunged his hand behind the fridge and brought out a real can of beer, synchronising with the can of beer in the video image. Chris Shutt added a splash as the hand went in and we had a fully evolved piece of action that had been developed organically. This sequence illustrates a domino effect of ideas, inspirations and additions provided and realised by a range of collaborators.

When I worked at the National Theatre in 2005 on a show that incorporated flying I naively asked if we would have a flying track in the room. The response was laughter from the technical team. In the end the actors got to practise a couple of times on a static line in the dock to find their balance and then had an hour or two during the technical rehearsal. In this circumstance all you can achieve is going up and down. It's rather limited and seemed to me a bit dull and pointless – what was the flying really *saying*? A technical element needs as much detailed examination as any other element of the show. It is common practice to work in a really detailed manner to improvise back-stories or learn a historically accurate period dance – yet pay no attention to the dramaturgy of technical elements.

When you have the equipment in the room you can ask, '*Why* is this man flying? What is his relation to the people on the ground? How do you incorporate video into the flying work?' These become puzzles to be solved by the company. They can only be posed and then answered through exploration – through endless devising tasks, most of which seem to turn up barren earth. Then a gem appears and the meaning of the process becomes clear.

the scene is performed to the company. Then we move onto something different. What seems like months later the show itself may start to emerge. Rehearsals can feel like a long sea voyage, during which the show, that new continent, refuses to appear on the horizon. The rehearsals can be draining, confusing and exasperating . . . on average once a day there

3.6 Rehearsal shot: filming wind-blown sand. Foreground left to right, Niall Black, Simon McBurney, Catherine Alexander.

3.7 Rehearsal shot: Mitsuru Fukikoshi, with a projected image of wind-blown sand, in a devising task.

would be an epiphanic moment; a group movement or a stage interaction that was so right, so perfect, you wanted to throw your hat in the air and cheer.

Composition: making elephants appear

The following excerpts from my notebooks give a sense of the work in progress about five weeks into rehearsals.

Simon and I ate supper last night and riffed on how wonderful it would be to reveal a real living, breathing elephant on to the stage: shitting, warm and alive. It would be the most amazing *coup de théâtre* imaginable. So that isn't practical for a touring show . . . and anyway elephants are expensive and dangerous. So we have to find another way.

On the 3 April 2003 we all worked on making elephants. We formed small devising groups and were given a couple of hours to create various manifestations of the elephant.

Simon, Victoria, Yasuyo and Tim dressed in grey suits and played salary men and women in a bar. The people in the bar held the chairs and transformed them into elephant legs walking. They observed the precise movement of a walking elephant and transposed the weight, dynamic and rhythm into the chairs as they manipulated them. Chris Shutt added to the image by using deep vibrating sounds to each footstep. The group played with the idea by gradually reducing the scale of the image to beer bottles in their hands walked across the floor, then four saki cups walked across a table top. In the final image a single hand became the elephant. It created the visual story of an ever-diminishing elephant.

Atsuko, Ryoko and Masato worked with video designers Ruppert Bohle and Anne O'Connor and made a television documentary about the disappearance of the elephant. They filmed interviews with eye witnesses who saw the elephant before it vanished: a school girl, a school dinner lady and an old lady. On video a news reporter showed us the three-metre wall and the barbed wire which enclosed the elephant. The use of video to mediate text and image gave the story an authenticity which will be useful.

Yuko, Fuki and Keitoku made the most amazing discoveries today. They explored the elephant keeper and how his presence with broom and bucket can create the elephant. It's a simple idea but surprisingly tender and effective. They juxtaposed this image with the salesman sitting at his kitchen table with his scrapbook. The group explored ways of constructing and dissolving images of the elephant upstage of him – this was very strong and created the idea of the elephant existing in the salesman's memory.

This group also made an amazing discovery while exploring the situation of the sales-man at the zoo filming the elephant. He took his video and zoomed closer and closer to the elephant's eye and eventually into its eye and inside the head. This image morphed into the elephant's point-of-view shot where the elephant watched the keeper and the salesman watching him. It's fantastically exciting to think we can get inside the elephant's head. We realised that image of the elephant's eye on the monitor is very, very important. The image gives us the scale and aliveness of the creature.

This work bore fruit in the final production. As Ben Brantley noted in the *New York Times*:

A single, lonesome eye is all that is seen of the title character in *The Elephant Vanishes* . . . Immense and somber in fading shades of gray, a filmed image of the eye glides across the

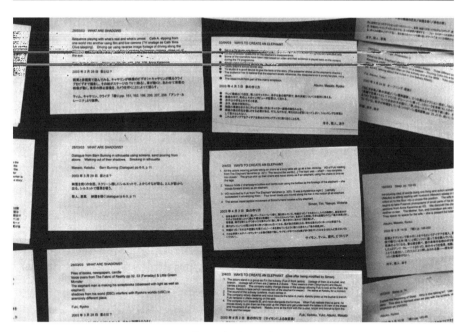

3.8 Bilingual rehearsal notes.

stage . . . somehow terribly sad in its incompleteness. The missing elephant re-materializes in a bewildering variety of forms . . . everything from a childlike outline to a remarkable pantomime creature briefly summoned into being by members of the ensemble with the help of a few office chairs.[5]

The final five weeks

When we arrived in Tokyo in April 2003 I was introduced to the literary translator Akiko Kondo. We sat next to each other on computers day and night for about six weeks, translating from English to Japanese and Japanese to English, discussing the tone and rhythm of each sentence. The actors were constantly running over to Akiko and me and handing us scraps of paper with phrases they had reworked. We would discuss each change very carefully: the rhythmic implications, the closeness to the Murakami original, the tone. It was extraordinary becoming fluent in parrot fashion with the rhythms and words of the Japanese script, knowing the intention and meaning of each line despite not speaking the language. In the end I forgot I was listening to a foreign language and even the translators became confused, translating English not into Japanese but into clearer English and then everyone realising their mistake after quite a few seconds had elapsed. There was a sense that the two languages were merging.

In the final few weeks of the creative process we gradually juxtaposed elements and scripted them. The show as a whole began to evolve and emerge. This is the most obscure part of the work and very difficult to describe: everybody is overwhelmed and catching up with the hundreds of ideas and images that are happening on the floor. In week eight we ran a long sequence for the first time and a sketch version of the whole piece emerged. This happened in the rehearsal room and although we were watching it from very close there was a sense of what would ultimately happen in terms of lighting, sound and video. There was an enormous engagement as everybody in the room – sound operators, stage managers and actors – improvised their way through new territory. Nobody had any perspective or sense of an overall shape or meaning, but the run was exhilarating because there was clearly something there.

This first assemblage was followed by the gradual process of putting the show on to the stage. In the Setagaya Public Theatre we had the luxury of a two-week technical rehearsal, but even this was barely long enough to render the highly complex video work. Sonoko Yamamoto describes the first preview as the most exciting moment of the process: 'We never did a dress rehearsal. And no one was sure we could get through the show from beginning to end. The first night was the first time we did the thing we'd never done, in front of an audience.'

After the first performance there is always huge relief that you have got through the show from beginning to end. There is a tangible exhaustion which is stronger than any sense of exhilaration. Having just climbed an enormous mountain you feel that you're just starting the real work. You also start to have sufficient distance from the piece to make essential shifts and changes.

The reception

The initial response to the first performances in Tokyo in 2003 was fascinating. Japanese audiences are notably quiet compared to those in Europe and America, which is disconcerting at first. Even so, the humour and lightness of the piece didn't communicate properly. Before we re-mounted the show at the Barbican, we added an opening monologue which worked in direct address. This created a tangible connection with the audience, brought them into the world of the play and contextualised the piece. This immediately changed the response to the piece and gave the audience permission to laugh. As Matt Wolf wrote:

> The Elephant Vanishes begins with deadpan stand-up comedy . . . so spontaneous is the opening riff that not everybody realised it is part of the show . . . only to deepen into a melancholy yet witty meditation on loneliness and loss.[6]

When we took the show back to Tokyo a year later I performed the opening speech in excruciatingly bad Japanese, which had a similar effect. The re-mount a year on also gave us the opportunity to rework in fine detail many of the sequences, and to add a new layer to the piece about electricity and light. The show seemed to grow in stature as the actors became more assured about what they were part of. Acting requires confidence and ownership and it took a long time for the actors to gain ownership of this highly complex piece. When they did, it flew.

The reviews and audience response inevitably focused on the visual and technical impact of the piece. Sarah Hemming wrote in the *Financial Times*:

> [I]t is a mesmerising, surprisingly beautiful piece that lays bare the price of urban aliena-
> tion. . . . [the staging] astutely conveys both the confusion of these individuals and the
> slick, frenzied world in which they live . . . screens of different sizes plough back and forth
> across the stage, buzzing with images of endless traffic, high rise buildings and tireless
> lights . . . this mechanised world divides the characters from themselves.[7]

Nonetheless, there was a recognition that the production's visual imagery did not detract from the power and coherence of the whole. As Michael Billington suggested in the *Guardian*, 'The result is an astonishing piece of theatre in which communal storytelling blends with hi-tech wizardry.'[8] The actors were celebrated for their skilled and truthful performances. The show clearly captured the disintegration and perpetual motion of modern urban life without losing any sense of narrative drive. Critics were quick to mention its wild comedy, communal storytelling, finely observed human detail. Most satisfyingly, there was no mention of this being a surtitled performance. Perhaps in this instance the visual mode helped to integrate this all-too-often irritating device and make it just another way of sharing a story.

The after-effects

When you step out of the constraints of your own country, your previous experience and status count for nothing. This is tremendously liberating as you are judged on the work and nothing else. *The Elephant Vanishes* gave all its collaborators an opportunity to meet on a middle ground and simultaneously pushed everyone beyond their boundaries (it felt boundless). It also felt unbelievably hard. I haven't written about the tears, the slipped disc, the relentless, long days and nights of work and the exhaustion. But then, all worthwhile theatre shows are a bit like that.

On a practical level *The Elephant Vanishes* gave me the chance to explore the huge potential of using video on stage: how to make this form three-dimensional and integrated with the narrative and staging dynamics. I also learned about script development, dramaturgy and the laborious process of working through translation, particularly developing new levels of precision and rigour with text. Most importantly this show has also given me a relationship with Japan that I have found stimulating and provocative. I'm now on my sixth visit and Tokyo feels almost like my second home. We are developing a new show based on the original Tanizaki texts, so in the end we have come almost full circle to our starting point. Nothing is wasted.

Notes

1 From Complicite, *The Elephant Vanishes* (2003).
2 Simon McBurney, quoted from the author's journal.
3 See Complicite's website, www.complicite.org, for more details of the company's work. Images relating to *The Elephant Vanishes* in this chapter are from the development and rehearsal phase. For production shots go to www.complicite.org/photos/?start=a&end=k&pagenum=3 (accessed 4 April 2008).
4 All quotations from members of the company are from interviews with the author or from work undertaken and observations made during the rehearsal process, noted by the author.
5 Ben Brantley, *New York Times* (23 July 2004).
6 Matt Wolf, *Variety* (9 July 2003).
7 Sarah Hemming, *Financial Times* (1 July 2003).
8 Michael Billington, *Guardian* (30 June 2003).

4

Elevator Repair Service – *Cab Legs* (1997) to *Gatz* (2006) – Reversing the ruins: the power of theatrical miscomprehension[1]

Sara Jane Bailes

In my view, the accident is positive. Why? Because it reveals something important that we would not otherwise be able to perceive. In this respect, it is a profane miracle. (Paul Virilio, *The Accident of Art*)

Introduction: 'Elevator who?'

In October 1997, not long after moving to New York City, I saw a performance called *Cab Legs*, the most recent production by downtown experimental theatre ensemble, Elevator Repair Service (ERS). Around eighty minutes long without interval, *Cab Legs* invents a compellingly neurotic world in which a strong internal logic possesses a group of nerdy characters who spill in and out of the performance space. They speak over one another, walk out into the audience, break into dances and organise detailed yet chaotic scenes which more or less resemble a play. The show's sensibility was distinct from European theatre, most notably in the immediate brutishness of the knockabout physical comedy, the undressed simplicity of the space, and the way the work was assembled, that is, its compositional strategies. Though often hilarious, the performance possessed a strange, quiet integrity grounded by the skill of its 'quoted' actorliness and character observation. *Cab Legs* draws inspiration from Tennessee Williams' play *Summer and Smoke* (1948), in particular the play's characters and text, though both are radically reinvented. What distinguished this performance was the dances. At times they were vigorously athletic, exploding out of nowhere as bold intrusions upon the course of events, performed in unison to an eclectic

4.1 *Cab Legs* (1997), Tory Vazquez, James Hannaham, Scott Shepherd, Rinne Groff in a signature ERS dance.

range of music which included Colombian dance music, Baltic folk tunes and lounge jazz. These choral pieces were contrasted by smaller gestural sequences and together brought an alternative language to the work.

ERS dances are enthusiastic arrangements that infuse movement with a blunt awkwardness; in fact, awkwardness as a concept is characteristic of the composition and delivery of the company's work. The dances function as disarticulatory interludes and are constructed out of well-practised movements made to retain their clumsiness: strange hand and exaggerated facial gestures resemble a body language fixed out of broken or discarded moves, filled with the effort of reverse momentum and a refined angularity – all elbows, contorted mouths and jerky limbs. These compose remnants of copied gestures relocated to body parts that are hostile to their demands. At times, an elaborate soundtrack insistently nudged the performance forwards: coughs, burps and whistles bumped up against the visual spectacle and imbued it with a sense of the ridiculous. *Cab Legs* felt both improvised and set at the same time, anarchic but tamed by a fierce precision.

If I were to try to broadly characterise the company's practice I might describe it as expressive of a particularly North American sensibility that reflects the interdisciplinary avant-garde histories it playfully invokes but then extends and dissolves those histories within a range of contemporary developments in music, art, literature and urban culture. It carries the influence of artists such as John Cage, Merce Cunningham, Yvonne Rainer and, before these mid-twentieth-century artists, Gertrude Stein's experimentation with the concrete topographies language can produce. But equally the company's theatre expresses a vernacular collaged out of the last piece of music listened to, the walk of a character in a favourite film, or a line of speech overheard on a subway ride. It favours multiplicity and plays with surface and depth (both rhythmically and philosophically), combining the language of mastered formal theatre technique with everyday colloquialism. Each piece is an assemblage of disparate worlds, genres and eras depicted through the hard edges of an adopted cartoon style, saturated by popular culture with keen attention paid to the surreal encounters generated by crowded urban living. ERS delivers a postmodern slapstick that reinvents that form from the perspective of the twenty-first century, shot through with the boisterous energy, abandonment, introspective neuroses and self-assured attitude of New York City. It is theatre that reminds an audience of what it is to revel and unravel – and then some; theatre that resonates with the city in which the company lives and works.

Formation and influences

Established during the early 1990s, ERS is a New York-based ensemble of practitioners from a range of artistic backgrounds who all share an interest in experimental theatre. At the time of writing the company has made twelve original shows and is currently working on its thirteenth.[2] For more than a decade and a half, the group has earned itself an increasingly influential role in Manhattan's low-budget downtown experimental theatre community, a vibrant scene that challenges more traditional and ideologically conservative models of theatre production on and off Broadway.[3] Their shows are described as 'fiercely intelligent', 'defiantly theatrical', 'hilarious', 'experimental without being pretentious, witty without being precious' and 'fantastically inventive', while the mood of their work is almost always identified as oddball, goofy and off-kilter.[4] The company describes what it does as theatre that straddles several traditions: vaudeville, visual spectacle, devised theatre and traditional drama and this cross-fertilisation is key to their aesthetic and structural approach.[5] As an ensemble, membership shifts according to the particular demands of each show and members' availability, though a more permanent core steers the direction of the work. Usually the company makes one show per year, though the process can take much longer and various shows can develop simultaneously. They devise and rehearse over extended periods in intermittent rehearsal blocks of up to five or six weeks, with work-in-progress showings providing an important feedback stage in developing and refining material.

In ERS's working process, time is constitutive to the development of ideas, which is to say that periods between rehearsals enable discoveries to sediment and gain (or lose) relevance in often tangential ways. Some shows evolve over a number of years, with materials taken up and played with for brief periods then suspended until conditions enable ideas to develop with specific group members. Such is the case with *Gatz* (2006), the company's touring show (at the time of writing), which began in a rehearsal room in 1999 when F. Scott Fitzgerald's famous American novel, *The Great*

4.2 *Gatz* (2006), Scott Shepherd who doubles as *The Great Gatsby*'s narrator, Nick Carraway, and an office worker reading the novel and Kate Scelsa as both Lucille and an office worker.

Gatsby, was brought in by company member, Steve Bodow, as a text of interest. Four years later, as director John Collins rehearsed with two performers in a small office above the Wooster Group's performance space (The Performing Garage on Wooster Street), ideas for how to situate the novel within a dramatic space were elaborated and key formal decisions made: first, to read the novel verbatim in order to preserve what Collins calls its 'bookness' instead of trying to adapt it for the stage; second, to set it in a cluttered office similar to the found office/makeshift space in which they found themselves rehearsing.

Blocks of performable material were created that began to animate the text while performers continued to read directly from the book. In 2004, these ideas developed more fully, the office setting inspiring Collins to determine further concepts for the show, principally the convention of dual narratives – that of an office, and that of the novel – co-existing and converging, most significantly in the mind of the spectator. The prolonged, six-hour encounter between these incongruous narrative worlds provides the compelling dramatic tension for the piece. Work-in-progress showings took place in spring 2004 and January 2005, and *Gatz* continues to tour internationally.[6] But while *Gatz* developed over a period of seven years, other shows take as little as six months to make, so the time span devoted to a making process can vary considerably. American literature – in particular Faulkner, Williams and Kerouac, whose writing captures the US during specific geographical and historical moments and in states of transition and cultural development – has, in recent years, provided inspiration and an objective for the development of ERS's approach to theatre-making.

The flexible membership the ensemble adopts allows for new talent and input

4.3 *Spine Check* (1992/3), Rinne Groff and Steve Bodow.

to strongly influence the direction of the company, and ERS has grown considerably since a handful of university graduates began devising theatre performances in a New York loft apartment during the winter of 1991.[7] The make-up of the company evolved slowly in the first three to four years, and began when several members graduated from Yale University's Drama and English departments and moved to New York intent on making original theatre together. Members come from a variety of backgrounds (not all are theatre-trained), and most hold full-time jobs that financially enable them to pursue theatre-making without artistic compromise. John Collins, artistic director and director of all ERS's shows to date, was pivotal in establishing the group and the artistic vision for the work they make.

Collins's influences, which include the absurd humour of the Dadaists, slapstick and Artaud's writings, were in service of an already strong belief that theatre's potential lies in its ability to communicate experientially. This suggested that it could therefore be driven and shaped by many things besides written text – such as music, objects, sound or movement – though not necessarily to the exclusion of dialogue. Such an approach has greatly influenced ERS's commitment to working from sources that are non-dramatic as a primary method for generating material while maintaining a strong interest in narrative structure. An eclectic range of materials, groups and events further influenced their early approach to making theatre. Key among these was a production of the Wooster Group's *Frank Dell's Temptation of St Anthony* (1987), which Collins saw several times. On seeing the Wooster Group's work, he became aware of something that completely altered the way he perceived both the making and reception of theatre. In his own words,

Box 4.1: 'Quoting', 'lifting' and 'copying'

The concepts of originality and authenticity in composition have been tested and played with by ERS and other theatre groups, influenced by a history of experimentation with form that decontextualises or 'repurposes' materials in art practice. This attempt to dislocate and recycle materials occurs regularly across different media throughout the twentieth century, in painting, music, dance and film. These three discrete but interchangeable terms – 'quoting', 'lifting' and 'copying' – imply a similar principle: material is isolated and lifted from an original context and resituated (sometimes entirely reworked) in the new work and context in surprising ways. An example which helps demonstrate the principle, drawn from popular music, is the way hip-hop samples from other dissimilar sound/music sources to create original compositions that nevertheless retain the quality of these borrowed samples. In sampling there is no attempt to *conceal* the influence or borrowed source. In theatre-making, such quotation can work across a range of elements: text, movement and gesture, sound, character designation, song, and so on.

> I realised that I could watch and listen to that show the way I looked at abstract art. It didn't have to make sense according to familiar rules of narrative or spoken or written language. This was a great thing to come to understand because the show was making sense to me in a way I hadn't experienced before. It was a piece of theater making sense *musically*.[8]

In terms of other local influences, ERS also acknowledges director/writer Richard Foreman's work with the Ontological-Hysteric Theatre at legendary performance venue, St Mark's Church, in the East Village, and several members of ERS interned with both companies in the early 1990s. Stylistically, ERS share certain formal characteristics that define these older and highly influential performance groups, most notably Foreman's disjunctive layered aural and visual landscapes; meticulous complex soundscapes; copied and highly affected delivery styles; lavish quotation from cinematic and/or other stage performances; and abstract 'lifted' movement sequences that signature the Wooster Group's heavily mediated style (see box 4.1). The contribution all three groups make to theatre experimentation is united by a desire to confront the challenge of how to construct a dynamic, decentred performative experience that nevertheless avoids a free-for-all mélange of ideas and frameworks that might only confuse the spectator. As Hans-Thies Lehmann notes in his characterisation of postdramatic theatre, a definition in many ways well-suited to ERS's work, no synthesis is offered, but rather 'a poetic sphere of *connotations* comes into being'.[9]

Ensemble work: ethos and economics

The financial challenge of establishing an experimental theatre ensemble in Manhattan in the early 1990s has clearly had an impact upon the aesthetics of ERS's theatre and the foundations of their praxis, as real estate prices have soared and arts funding continues to be drastically cut.[10] One senses the physical location of New York City within the fabric and rhythms of their shows. ERS performances are infused with the unpredictable diversity and cramped feeling of tight physical conditions, and the fast-paced multiplicity, fragmentation, and relentless energy of New York as an iconic 'city of cities'. Such a romantic view is offset by the everyday reality of the impoverished material conditions in which they have had to learn to make work – rehearsing for years in members' apartments without funding, props or set; juggling other jobs; lacking training in technical areas; and possessing little or no equipment. Yet over the years, these circumstances have been turned to the group's advantage. In part as a consequence of this, ERS's theatre remains performer-led rather than relying on lavish sets or design. 'Found' objects rather than sophisticated sets focus the space and rehearsal activities, and the compromises each rehearsal environment demands contribute to major artistic decisions, as in the example of setting *Gatz* in an overcrowded office because originally the piece evolved in just such a space. The group takes inspiration from an aesthetics marked by imperfection, the provisional nature of temporary and sometimes inappropriate circumstances, and the invention that recycling space, materials and dialogue can reveal. As a result of their inclusive, resourceful approach, the stand-in costumes and props adopted in early rehearsals are often maintained through to production or, at the very least, influence final design decisions. Costumes usually look borrowed or informal (even if they are not), and the visual style they manufacture is often intentionally slightly 'off', hovering between tacky, trendy and absurd. Like both the Wooster Group and Forced Entertainment, ERS indulge in the business of theatre, its licence for pretence and the permission this gives the artist to dress up and disguise without attempting to conceal the ruses and trickery of the game. Exaggerated theatrical costumes such as untidy wigs, false eyebrows or the odd pair of broken over-large geeky eyeglasses, sit alongside the mundane vestments of thrift stores. The nerdy quality performers adopt reflects an absurd sense of humour as well as a distinct awareness of Middle America's disposable, tasteless 'mall culture' which their pieces sometimes draw upon.

Despite a democratic ethos adopted in the production of work, ERS is led by Collins, though often fellow founder member Steve Bodow joins Collins to co-direct, most notably between 1997 and 2002. To some extent, therefore, even the directing has retained a collaborative approach. In the room, Collins and Bodow intuitively complement one another. While Bodow often concerns himself more with choices concerning textual material, Collins usually begins by bringing formal concerns to the table. An example of the fluidity and alliance between the two occurred in rehearsals I attended for the company's tenth show, *Room Tone* (2002). At the beginning of the process, Bodow brought in a William James text he had been reading about spiritual visions ('*The Varieties of Religious Experience*' – *A Study in Human Nature*, 1902). Partially influenced by the perceptual psychology and works of light artist James Turrell, Collins knew prior to rehearsals that he wanted to make a show that experimented with actual darkness. He wanted the stage so darkly lit that everything would be performed and seen through dim light, and focused much of his attention towards the lighting design and the effects of the interaction between performer and lighting state in scenic composition in order to experiment with an overall unsettling mood for the piece. Once this

4.4 *Total Fictional Lie* (1998), Robert Cucuzza, Susie Sokol.

process was under way, however, Collins shifted attention to work more closely with the performers to discover how James's dense, antiquated rhetoric might be handled. How, for example, might performers deliver passages of text written in an archaic formal language without trying to dramatise or 'act' through it, allowing its intrinsic literary quality to remain? Bodow joined in devising sound and contributed specific practical ideas about how to deal with low light on stage in specific scenes.[11] So while Collins usually manages the rehearsal room, organising, starting and stopping activities, Bodow hangs back, contributing text-editing, musical choices and larger-picture ideas ('what if this dance comes *after* that section' or 'why don't we use the off-stage area to solve the blocking problem').[12] His role can be seen as a fine dramaturgical complement to Collins' directorial position. Together, Collins and Bodow always explore musical impulses in the rehearsal room, allowing 'pacing, rhythm, dynamics, moods, and instrumentations' to organise material.[13] Exploring the theatricality inherent in a range of other media – television and film especially, but also pictures, texts, objects and everyday behaviours – remains fundamental to the devising process of all ERS shows.

Roles within the company generally remain fluid but defined and tend to develop organically. Certain members choose only to perform, while others double up on performing, technical and design aspects of the show. Long-time member Colleen Werthmann, for example, has focused on costume for most shows since 1998, while developing her career independently from the company as an actress and stand-up comedian. Katherine Profeta acts as choreographer for the company but also performed in *Room Tone* (2002). In this way, the open democratic ethos the company adopts encourages the professional development of its members which undoubtedly informs the work made together. This aspect aside, ERS follows a similar organisational model to other experimental theatre ensembles, most notably Goat Island, the Wooster Group and Radiohole in the US, but also Forced Entertainment, Shunt and, to a lesser extent, Complicite in the UK. All of these groups work collaboratively to develop models of collective decision-making in their processes. While making collectivity intrinsic to the process of generating material, each group nevertheless works under the discerning eye of a director who composes the work and takes greatest responsibility for major and minor artistic decisions.

Devising and rehearsing: beginnings

In the following section I identify approaches and practical stages the company go through when making work. As processes vary from show to show, and in order to draw upon a fuller history of their theatre-making, I refer to several shows throughout.[14] The first point to note is that ERS rehearsals take place in a number of different borrowed and/or rented spaces, and the locations in which work is made invariably contribute to the aesthetic and conceptual development of each show.

All devising periods begin in a certain amount of uncertainty, a necessary condition for a genuinely open process, and each starts by confronting the process of invention itself. The most difficult task can be figuring out *how* to begin, and in what direction to move. Very little is predetermined and the eclectic sources (see box 4.2) brought in during the first days will to some extent influence the direction activities take, though ideas and materials remain as disposable as the many cultural fields and situations they are drawn from, even very late into a process. Rehearsals usually unfold in relation to the following: 1) a series of clear but loosely defined interests and objectives, for example, a formal enquiry such as 'How do you put a novel on stage without turning it into a play?' as in the case of *Gatz*; 2) a range of 'found' materials and sources brought in during the first weeks that reflect current interests and leads to extensive discussion and watching video clips or films together, usually many times over; and 3) the use of practical tasks as a way of cutting into material, subverting it and/or beginning to generate new possibilities from it. Making a dance often provides a useful practical way of beginning to devise a world and mood for a piece; it also brings the company together in a shared activity and focuses them towards a concrete outcome that quickly gets them on their feet. Once made, a dance provides a block of material around which other sections expand in both a contrived and more *ad hoc* fashion.

Undoing dance

Observing ERS make the 'Mad Jack Dance' for *Room Tone,* I was able to follow a choreographic process from beginning through to production.[15] The techniques and

---

Box 4.2: Sources

ERS always work with multiple unrelated sources and influences, much like the Wooster Group, Goat Island, Richard Foreman and Forced Entertainment, though each group's method of application and treatment of their chosen materials invents a process and aesthetic quality unique to each company. Material sometimes congregates around a theme, such as haunting, spiritual transformation and possession in *Room Tone*. Often the original source is no longer present in the piece, though a response to it (in the form of performance material) becomes a constituent part of the performance. *Room Tone* used and drew upon the following in the creation of the piece:

- Literature: *The Turn of the Screw* (Henry James, 1898) and *The Varieties of Religious Experience* (William James, 1902)
- Film: *The Innocents* (Dir. Jack Clayton, 1961, based on James's above novel; *The Shining* (Dir. Stanley Kubrick, 1980)
- Music: *Jegog: 'The Bamboo Gamelan of Bali'* (performed by Werdi Santana); 'I See a Darkness' (version by Johnny Cash)
- Dance: A dance performed by James Brown and backing group, the Flames
- Sound effects used in the soundscape included: man grunting, groaning, horse chewing, slurping, sucking, a man breathing, ice in a glass, a doorbell, a door opening, a horse's neigh and an electric chair

It is important to remember that sources are also often *translated across media* in intentionally awkward ways for effect; a sequence of hand gestures from a film might become a dance; a dance informs the way characters speak; and so on. Shows become densely layered and detailed in this way.

---

activities the company has developed to isolate and then transform found gestures and movements into sequences of material were particularly interesting, a process that can be likened to translation, where material transposes from one language or state to another while retaining qualities from its origin.

'Mad Jack Dance' took almost two weeks to make and refine, though in the final piece its duration runs only minutes. This process began with learning and copying the face, arm and hand gestures from a sequence in Stanley Kubrick's classic cult horror film, *The Shining* (1980). In this climactic scene, actress Shelley Duvall as Wendy Torrance backs up the stairs swinging a baseball bat at her character's deranged husband, Jack (famously played by Jack Nicholson), who is coming to kill her in the film's terrifying climax. In this second block of rehearsals for *Room Tone* (April/May 2002), the number of performers working on the piece had expanded from three to five. *The Shining* provided a major breakthrough: the schizoid mania of Nicholson's performance and the concept of a building possessed within a repetitive cycle of haunting yielded a creepy ambience and provided a non-linear structure that helped contain the show. For much of the time, rehearsals took place in pitch-dark, performers (and observers) moving tentatively around the space with small Maglite flashlights. The darkness seemed to slow down all decision-making and subdued the performers' energy. This profoundly impacted upon the mood that shaped and then characterised the piece.

When beginning to make a dance, moves are usually taken out of sequence so that they can afterwards be composed in any order. In *Room Tone* rehearsals, up to two hours at a time were spent huddled around a video monitor, performers watching, copying and trying out the moves 'grabbed' from the Nicholson/Duvall sequence. To undercut this, Bodow wanted to set them to the offbeat tearaway counter-rhythm of gamelan music. Once moves are familiar enough to all members, the slower process of sequencing begins, and this is then drilled until it is learned. Performed only once in its entirety but recurring in abbreviated refrains so that the traces of movement vocabulary evoke the comings and goings of a ghostly presence, 'Mad Jack Dance' anchored the material that developed over the following weeks while providing an activity the group could practise together every day. In his role as artistic director, Collins refers to the importance of having something to surrender to when developing a nascent body of material:

> All I know I have to do is find a task for myself, something I can come into the room to 'do' for each piece, I need something to become a student of. I think as long as there's something to give over to – a book, a historical topic, even a strong formal challenge ('do a show in the dark') – and a fresh set of rules for making it into theater (the task part) then I'm okay. Unfortunately, those things don't always come easy.[16]

Tasks, rules and objects

Task-based activities or the tasks an activity can be broken down into – that is, the literal, functional demands it makes on a performer – often indicate not only a way to create material but an approach to refining detail and attitude in the work. In other words, by returning to think about the functional aspects of an action (what needs to be done here? what do the audience need to be able to 'read' from this? how do we make x appear at the back when we need her at the front?) the performers are encouraged to avoid searching for character motivation. This conscious move *away* from psychology and character is key to ERS's practice as it has been to the work of many theatre practitioners since the 1960s.

Once sources have been shared and discussed in terms of potential value (what do they bring, offer, suggest?), a rehearsal might proceed by taking two or three disparate things – an object, a piece of text, and an interesting sound, for example – to see what happens when they are placed together and what effects they produce as a result of such layering. This is how the large wooden box used in *Total Fictional Lie* (1998, *TFL*) became central to the piece. An indispensable prop but also a comic device used throughout the show, the box was originally found discarded in the rehearsal space.

In *TFL* each of the seven performers brought in documentary characters whose verbal and physical mannerisms they were interested in working on. These were sourced from a range of films and programmes watched independently prior to rehearsals. Rinne Groff brought in a piece of text from Nick Broomfield's 1994 documentary, *Aileen Wuornos: The Selling of a Serial Killer,* and had become particularly interested in Wuornos's verbal mannerisms when speaking to camera. Early on in rehearsals, Collins asked Groff to climb into the box and speak the text she had lifted from the documentary, while sound designer Blake Koh put together several disparate sounds and improvised with them over the top. As Groff is an advanced Ashtanga yoga practitioner she discovered she could fold her body easily inside the box and remain concealed for extended periods of time. But the box soon became key to the performance: it could hide/reveal performers, or be used as a table and a desk; at one moment its lid is even adopted as an oversized writing pad on which Susie Sokol, as a boyish 1950s pop teen-idol Paul Anka, scrawls an absurdly large autograph to give to another performer. Alongside Groff, Sokol appears and disappears into the box at different times during the show. In fact, Sokol's first appearance at the beginning of *TFL* comes when her feet and legs ascend from the box to the complete surprise of the audience (pre-show she is already concealed inside, upside down on her shoulders) balancing the removable wooden lid on her feet to perform a brilliant and bizarre comic routine (see figure 4.4). Her spindly legs and animated feet stand in for an ageing man whom the audience hears deliver a mumbling public speech that begins to break down into gibberish as the legs fall over the side of the box. The speech and audience response is delivered on a 'treated' audio track (words are edited out of the speech, glitches are amplified, and so on) while the performer's feet articulate the empty gestures of the bored speaker. In another routine reminiscent of the object-based physical wit of early slapstick gags, performer Leslie Buxbaum, who plays a meek Spanish-speaking housewife copied from a documentary about Bible salesmen, climbs in to share the box with Groff's brusque, antisocial Wuornos (see figure 4.5). Lodged together in what appears to be an impossible physical feat, both characters endeavour to tear open and share a packet of crisps using one hand each, the box lid becoming an umbrella they hold above them. Incongruent characters, situations and intentions are often spliced together in this concrete way, their unlikely conjunction in the world of a show determined by compositional and pragmatic rather than intellectually rationalised or emotionally coherent choices. Ultimately, meaning and logic remain as important in structuring work and making compositional choices as they do in theatre that strives to appear more 'natural' and linear, but the route taken here differs from more conventional approaches.

The *activity* of rehearsal is therefore often determined by attempting different possibilities that combine and displace the usual function of an object, character or spoken text without a predetermined outcome in mind. This allows for associative and unlikely connections to be incorporated into each new show, often stumbled across accidentally. The animated relationship between performer and object often guides this early exploration. Ultimately the response provoked by the physical humour of such scenes plays a significant role in the composition of the work, for, as Collins rightly observes, comedy enables sense and absurdity to coexist happily.[17]

4.5 *Total Fictional Lie* (1998), Leslie Buxbaum, Rinne Groff (feet).

Montage and mishap as methodology

In ERS performances, as in their disjunctive, associative making process, an interesting permutation of the principle of montage has developed over their sixteen years as a company honing methods for making theatre.[18] When treating material, words are often disengaged from actions, reactions are separated from characters, or actions are taken from one character/performer and distributed amongst several. The variety of miscomprehension this can produce often provides a basis for developing a scene. In 2000, during the second block of rehearsals for *Highway to Tomorrow* – a performance based on Euripides' *The Bacchae* but relocated from Thebes to modern-day St Louis, in which all of the characters are mischievously misnamed so that the original play is remoulded to a contemporary framework – the group worked on a dance they later called 'Impotence'. This was constructed from gestures performed by Tony Curtis in a scene from the 1976 film *The Last Tycoon,* based on F. Scott Fitzgerald's novel of the same title. (In the scene, Curtis explains to Robert de Niro that his character is impotent.) Curtis's movements, copied and transcribed in a similar way as described earlier for the 'Mad Jack Dance', retain nothing of the apparent meanings or intention of the original scene, but are used for the suggestive abstract visual language they provide the performers. This technique helps to distance performers from dialogue and the meanings that arise through verbal exchange. It builds on a device originally developed by

4.6 *Highway to Tomorrow* (1999), Randolph Curtis Rand, Paul Boocock and Susie Sokol 'copy' a sequence from *The Last Tycoon* in the dance 'Impotence'.

the Wooster Group, who use movement from films seen on video monitors which the performers watch and copy 'live' during performances while the video screen images are concealed from audience members (the video monitors are hung or positioned with the screens facing the performers rather than the audience). The spectator witnesses only the performers watching and copying, not the 'source' images. Gestures are played with as discreet units of material which, when combined with other materials, create a new combination of elements. In addition, the movements carry evocative traces of their former meanings liberated by the dislocated context in which they are resituated.

The labour of composition for each show demands that the company creates material that remains accessible even as it generates intrigue in the eyes of the observer. For while confusion can lead an audience member to retreat from a piece of work or lose patience with it, Collins argues that mystery is compelling despite the distance and/or difference it maintains as part of the spectator's comprehension.[19] In *Room Tone* rehearsals one afternoon, when the difficulties and challenges the piece had thrown up threatened to bring the process to a halt (which occurs often enough in the course of any devising process), Collins reminded the company of the importance of generating clarity in a production: 'It's our job to figure out what needs to be known to make things readable. And if you throw too many curves too far in, then people resent you.'[20] So while manufacturing material helps to make it stranger and less familiar, ultimately the logic each piece invents must enthral watchers enough that they want to figure out how to follow it through.

Awkwardness and misreading as generative states are structured into ERS shows in literal and sensory ways, such as the imposed difficulty of performing *Room Tone*

4.7 *Room Tone* (2002), Susie Sokol.

in near-darkness, a strategy which altered the behaviour of performers and audience members alike, intensifying the way the audience listened to the piece. In *TFL*, the documentary characters from disparate and ill-matched contexts coexist alongside one another and are forced to interact. In each situation, the strategies adopted prevent the performance from appearing 'natural'. In *Cab Legs*, paraphrasing the lines from a play each night kept the eight performers genuinely on edge, for the show had to be reinvented (within determined limits) each time it was performed. As audience members, we witnessed performers stuttering and stumbling across lines as they improvised sentences in real time, their objective to convey accurately the meaning of the lines in Tennessee Williams' play, *Summer and Smoke*, and in their original order. Focusing on agreed tasks, obstacles and impediments as a way of treating or preparing material (rather than on a psychological analysis of why a character might do what he or she does at any given moment) furnishes each show with an intensity of focus, though that focus might remain indecipherable to its audience whilst unifying the behaviour of the performers. This particular kind of energy and performance ecology – where things retain the process of their making, and demonstrate unpredictability through the (intentional) appearance of being underprepared, prone to collapse or determined by a cause that is no longer present – interests the company as a deliberate ethos applied to all of their formal experimentation. As performer Rinne Groff is careful to point out, however, 'by using precision too, we let the audience know it's okay, that we know what we're doing'.[21] This methodology works towards the invention of a hybrid delivery style, a kind of professional amateurism that enables the company to expand their audience's understanding of skill and theatrical virtuosity according to the group's revised engagement with theatre conventions.[22] The work is always in pursuit of non-traditional standards.

Playing with reality effects (that is, the staged contrivance of making things look or feel more real) and with notions of 'being real' on stage is another central concern in ERS shows (as with many contemporary performance groups since the 1960s), in part because it exposes a vulnerability and openness in performance that the group is interested to explore. This extends through their insistence upon working with the actual material conditions of the performance – the details of the space, the audience, 'found' set, props and costumes, the performers' abilities and limitations and so on. In an early conversation with Collins in 1999 in which we discussed making *Cab Legs* and *TFL*, he explained this in the following way:

> We work with the bottom-line truth of situations we are in, and we are often in small awkward spaces, where everything is imperfect. That's an inspiring place to be and we are always embracing that. If, for example, we stumble on some little illusion, we exaggerate the imperfection and the illusion of how it is being done. I guess we are always playing on the awareness of the audience and keeping it real.[23]

More recently, Susie Sokol expanded upon this notion, explaining how ERS members prefer to 'expose the problem of a situation' when making theatre.[24] An example of this might be observed in the case of the character 'Carl' in *Highway to Tomorrow (1999)*. Carl is represented not by a performer but by a column that sits obtrusively in the middle of the performance arena (this architectural 'blip' that obstructs viewing exists in both HERE arts space and PS122's downstairs space in New York). In part this decision is taken because the column cannot be avoided in any staging in the space; it also came about because the group needed an extra performer. An opportunity is made, therefore, of the substitutional inadequacy of (the) representation, which in turn draws attention to the fundamental ineptitude of theatre with its always-provisional system of stand-ins, copies, and poor imitations. The point is that in ERS's work, the inadequacies and misfortunes of theatre-making as an unsophisticated representational system are celebrated rather than concealed, and the coping mechanisms and solutions discovered incorporated into each production. This provides a constant source of creative discovery and play founded upon a philosophy of making-do.

Conclusion

It makes sense that ERS's members are usually drawn, therefore, towards sources that enable them to interrogate this self-reflexive interest in the theatre apparatus, so that they might expand the way audiences consider the relations between reality and fiction, actuality and pretence, and the attention staging can call to the mutable status of such couplings. Like other contemporary companies, members are drawn to the mechanical and practical inefficiencies of theatre machinery with its often-clumsy unsophisticated bag of tricks and manual effects in an age increasingly dominated by refined digital and portable technologies that mediate reproduction. Rather than compete with other media, the group might expose how something *doesn't* work, the ways in which theatre illusions *aren't* convincing, and instead focus upon the particular effectiveness of those inadequate means. ERS approach theatre-making with playful seriousness and laughter is prevalent in their rehearsal process. They also understand theatre as an arena in which one can productively trouble the lines of distinction drawn around certain categories of behaviour by allowing for the edges between things to remain unclear. To illustrate, I return for an instant to *Cab Legs*.

In an early sequence in *Cab Legs*, the half-broken loud squeaky chairs on which Sokol and Bodow (both performers in this piece) rehearsed a seated scene features in the final show, at one point upstaging an apparently intimate exchange by drowning it out. This example, where the inanimate overcomes the apparently animate, inverts the way the company constructed Carl, the 'deanimated' character played by an (inanimate) column in *Highway to Tomorrow*, who is positioned by Sokol's character, Teri the Seer, through the enactment of her relationship to the column.[25] In that exchange, Sokol nudges Carl (the column, whose representation is enhanced by a pair of stick-on plastic googly eyes), awaits a response, and then pulls out a script to show him where they are in the performance so as to prompt him into speaking. The scene imitates the behaviour of amateur actors or children who, when performing, seem blind to the fact that the audience witness their slips and prompts to each other. But while in this example Carl remains inanimate but rendered present by Sokol's 'acting', the chairs in *Cab Legs* become unusually animate objects, and the performers are forced to compete with their presence as they might do with puppets or other performers on stage. This child-like interplay between the three states – animate, inanimate and deanimate – reminds us of the continuum along which all theatre measures its aspirations which lie between illusion (hope) and dis-illusion (disappointment). In ERS rehearsals, the inadequacy of objects as props, and of acting as a way of approximating character, is confronted by the thwarted ambition of mimesis itself, the results of these various attempts mined for dramatic potential. The difficulties and mistakes encountered in making performance are therefore refashioned to craft skilful repeatable comedic incidents. Sokol points to the ambiguous status of the accident in relation to repetition in the company's process, remarking that 'The accident occurs and later you make it non-accidental so that you can use it.'[26] In a consideration of the uses of failure in the work of Forced Entertainment, Goat Island writer and

4.8 *Gatz* (2006), Jim Fletcher as Gatsby and Scott Shepherd as narrator Nick Carraway.

performer Matthew Goulish finesses this notion with the following observation: 'It is a common mistake of the artist to consider the unintentional more real than the intentional . . . Repeatability does not diminish reality.'[27] Nor does repeatability diminish the effect of an action in the so-called real world, long after the performance is over.

In these closing comments, both Sokol and Goulish indicate some of the lessons that might be learned from making theatre in ways that are less concerned with reproducing a world we imagine we know, or one that seems competent and logical. Instead, this insistently live art form might be allowed to elaborate upon the familiar in new and as-yet-unimagined ways that move us beyond representation. But also, these practitioners leave us with another useful demand: what can be learned from the unintended event, from accident itself as a critical, performative mode of enquiry? The accidental incident releases proofs of the unforeseeable effects latent within all processes of invention, that is, the uncontainable excess produced by invention and its renegade outcomes. As '"twice-behaved", not-for-the-first-time, behavior',[28] performance can 'capture' the accident and use it to build in alternative ways, so that ruin itself becomes a site of invention. And if ruin can be considered as productive, who is to say that it cannot teach us to better understand the generative potential of fallible acts, exchange and invention? Failure, as Paul Virilio observes in the opening epigraph to this chapter, 'reveals something important that we would not otherwise be able to perceive'.[29] In this respect, and when adopted as a tool for creative invention as in the work of Elevator Repair Service, the accident offers insight into the profane imperfection that inheres within all acts of discovery, real, fictional or otherwise.

Notes

1 The author gratefully acknowledges the support of the Arts and Humanities Research Council in completing this chapter. Thanks also to John Collins, Lucy Cassidy and Isabel Rocamora for useful comments in response to earlier drafts.

The phrase 'reversing the ruins' is borrowed from artist Robert Smithson (1938–73), whose art practice and writings investigated the development of form through entropy and the refocusing of formal construction through dilapidation. In particular, see *Hotel Palenque* (1969) in *Robert Smithson* (Los Angeles: The Museum of Contemporary Art, 2004). Together with Smithson's thinking, the title of this chapter acknowledges Jan Fabre's seminal 1984 theatre work *The Power of Theatrical Madness* which ghosts the development and working of so many contemporary theatre-makers.

2 Since *Cab Legs* I've watched six different shows (usually two to three times), and observed rehearsals for five pieces in various stages of devising, rehearsing and reworking.

3 Geographically, Broadway indicates the Theatre District of Manhattan near and north of Times Square.

4 These comments are collated from a wide range of critical reviews in journals/newspapers over the last ten or so years, including *Village Voice*, *New York Times*, *New York Magazine*, *The New Yorker* and *ARTFORUM*, and are often quoted by the company in publicity material.

5 Elevator Repair Service, publicity pack (2006).

6 For an in-depth discussion of the difficulties that have constrained touring and the production of *Gatz* in the US, involving the Fitzgerald Estate and a competitive commercial production of an adaptation of the novel into a musical, see Jason Zinoman, '*Gatz* and *The Great Gatsby* Vie for Broadway Stages', *New York Times* (16 July 2006), Section 2, 8; and John Collins' account of the history of making the show included on the company's website at www.elevator.org. The website provides a thorough resource and biography of the company's history and shows, including press and journal articles and extensive photos.

7 A group of founder members continues to carry the artistic vision and direction of the company, while others have left to pursue other objectives. Original members include: Steve Bodow, John Collins, Bradley Glenn, Rinne Groff, Susie Sokol, James Hannaham, Leo Marks, Katherine Profeta and Colleen Werthmann. In addition, the following have also been (or are currently) company members: Laurena Allan, Paul Boocock, Leslie Buxbaum, Bob Cucuzza, Jonathan Feinberg, Jim Fletcher, Ross Fletcher, Mike Iveson, Vin Knight, Michael Kraskin, Blake Koh, Aaron Landsman, Maggie McBrien, Joanna McFadden, Annie McNamara, Randolph Curtis Rand, Kate Scelsa, Charlie Schroeder, Heike Schuppelius, Scott Shepherd, Tory Vazquez and Ben Williams. This list is by no means comprehensive as membership alters with each show.

8 Email correspondence with Collins (July–August 2006).

9 Hans-Thies Lehmann, *Postdramatic Theatre*, trans. Karen Jürs-Munby (Abingdon: Routledge, 2006), p. 79.

10 The period also comes in the aftermath of the culture wars that seriously diminished American public, intellectual and artistic life throughout the 1980s, characterised by a homophobic right-wing sensibility intolerant of difference.

11 John Collins and Steve Bodow, email correspondence with author, July–August 2006.

12 Bodow, email correspondence with author, July–August 2006.

13 *Ibid.*

14 The material referred to draws on notes and reflections made while watching the following shows/rehearsals. Shows: *Cab Legs* (1997), *Total Fictional Lie* (1998), *Highway to*

Tomorrow (2001), *Language Instruction* (1999 production), *Room Tone* (2002). Devising process/rehearsals: *Total Fictional Lie, Highway to Tomorrow, Room Tone, No Great Society* (2006), *Gatz* (2006).

15 Dance names are not formally agreed. They are coined and used in rehearsals for referential and technical purposes.

16 John Collins, email correspondence with author, July–August 2006.

17 *Ibid.*

18 Here I refer to Russian film director Sergei Eisenstein's theory of montage developed through his ground-breaking films made during the 1920s, most notably *The Battleship Potemkin* (1925). To summarise briefly, *montage* – the juxtaposition of disparate images by strategic film editing – creates ideas not found in the individual images, so that the process of editing itself (not simply the materials) can inflect material with political vision and influence. This highly influential compositional technique has been taken up and adopted by many artists in a range of artistic disciplines since.

19 Sara Jane Bailes, rehearsal notes for *Room Tone*, April–May, 2002.

20 Sara Jane Bailes, interview and notes with John Collins, 2001.

21 In Coco Fusco, 'Elevator Repair Service: Interview with Steve Bodow, John Collins, Rinne Groff', *Bomb: the Arts and Culture Quarterly* (Spring 1999), 50–55.

22 For a more detailed discussion of the strategic development of 'professional amateurism' in the context of Forced Entertainment's theatre see Sara Jane Bailes, 'Struggling to Perform: Radical Amateurism and Forced Entertainment', *Theatreforum*, 26 (Winter/Spring 2005), 56–65.

23 John Collins, 'Re: Interview', email exchange with author (December 1999).

24 Susie Sokol, Interviews (notes and author's video recording), September 2005 and July 2006.

25 The term 'deanimated' is introduced by Julie Bleha in her insightful discussion about the company's working process when making *Highway to Tomorrow*. Julie Bleha, 'A God, a Thermos, a Play: Elevator Repair Service Tackles Euripides' *Bacchae*', *TheatreForum* 23 (Summer/Fall 2003), 79–88.

26 Sokol, Interview, 2006.

27 Matthew Goulish, 'A Consideration of Failure in Proximity of the Work of Forced Entertainment on the Occasion of the Company's 20th Birthday' (unpublished paper, draft), Lancaster University, Forced Entertainment 20th Anniversary Symposium (October 2004), 3.

28 Richard Schechner, 'What Is Performance Studies Anyway?' in Jill Lane and Peggy Phelan (eds), *The Ends of Performance* (New York: New York University Press, 1998), p. 361.

29 Paul Virilio in Sylvère Lotringer and Paul Virilio, *The Accident of Art*, trans. Michael Taormina (New York: Semiotext(e), 2005), p. 63.

5

Forced Entertainment – *The Travels* (2002) – The anti-theatrical director

Alex Mermikides

The company

The British company Forced Entertainment was formed in 1984 and still constitutes almost the same group of six artists, led by director and writer Tim Etchells.[1] This longevity and permanence is unique in British theatre. The group is based in Sheffield and regularly tours throughout Western Europe. Besides performances for theatre spaces, the company also creates durational shows, gallery installations, work for video and digital media and Etchells has written *Certain Fragments: Contemporary Performance and Forced Entertainment*, an introduction to the company's approach.[2] The recent collection *Not Even a Game Anymore*, edited by Judith Helmer and Florian Malzacher, testifies to the enduring interest the company attracts from audience members and scholars both in Britain and in continental Europe.[3]

The company's website describes its work as 'emphatically a group creation – made through improvisation and discussion and drawing on theatre itself as well as on cinema, music culture, literature and fine art'. The shows have a thrown-together quality: the sets and props seem to have been gathered at random and the performers (almost always including six members, occasionally with additional performers) adopt an almost casual mode of performance. The work alludes to contemporary urban experience with themes of identity, language, chaos and desire for order. Forced Entertainment's work continually challenges convention and is often surprising.

5.1 *The Travels.*

The Travels **and critical context**

The Travels, Forced Entertainment's 2002 show, begins. The performers Richard Lowdon, Claire Marshall, Cathy Naden, Terry O'Connor, John Rowley and Jerry Killick (in that order from stage right to left) face us across the long, gapped stretch of table on the stage of Kunstlerhaus Mosournturm, Frankfurt. Before each of them is a desk-top microphone, a well-thumbed copy of the script and a bottle of water. An overhead projector sits on a small table by Richard projecting a scrawled title on to the back wall 'part 1: tuning in'.[4] Jerry begins, telling us about his visit to Achilles Street and, in honour of Achilles' weak ankle, listing his own weak points (including inordinate rage at inanimate objects). The other performers address us in turn, describing where they were while Jerry sat on the curb on Achilles Street: Terry at a crossroads trying to decide which of the two country lanes before her was Rape Lane; Claire knocking back a mini bottle of wine on Bacchus Road, Birmingham; John being spat upon on Universal Road, Cardiff. Claire tells us that 'it starts with a list of street names – a list concocted from UK A–Zs and from internet map sites. These are streets with literal names. Streets that seem directly or indirectly to promise adventure, or at least metaphor and allegory.'[5]

Terry describes 'A lucky dip to determine who will go where'. Over the next

5.2 *The Travels.*

hour and a half we hear the performers' testimony of their visits to streets selected by name; descriptions of the UK's various cities, suburbs and rural areas; retellings of interactions with bemused, aggressive, friendly, indifferent locals; the performers' meditations on the conjunctions between name and street. The *set-up* (see box 5.4 for a description of key terms given here in italics) is defiantly banal, uneventful, unthe-atrical: just the performers speaking to us from across a table and the minute gestures of what they call the 'social business'; a silent chorus of five whose attention to the storyteller, and occasional nods or glances to each other or the audience, comment upon the action, a slow dance of hands reaching for water bottles or arranging papers. Richard rising from his chair to change the transparency on the overhead projector ('part 2: just girls/the futures', followed by a series of hand-drawn maps) becomes a grand event.

In its low-key, direct, almost mundane form of audience address *The Travels* exemplifies Forced Entertainment's preoccupation with the live encounter between performer and public – a concern particularly since the mid-1990s. The company's tenth anniversary in 1994 (when the Arts Council cut funding to the company) marks a watershed point between two styles in its work. Before 1994 it presented the experi-ence of living in urban England through a layering of fictions, broken and repeated narratives, artefacts of contemporary culture, and naive objects such as animal cos-tumes. In the second phase, shows like *Speak Bitterness* (1994), *Dirty Work* (1998) and *First Night* (2001) consist of a single, relatively static setting and activity that throw focus on the live encounter between audience and performer – the fact of one group of people in front of another. Tim Etchells' article 'Audience Tactics' is very much the company's manifesto: 'each project for us is an attempt to find new and appropriate solutions to the situation of standing up and trying to speak before a crowd of people whom one does not know and cannot trust'. The performers are enjoined to '[b]e "a group of people who are doing a job in front of another group of people". Think about task, about "work" (labour), about the strange yet simple situation of being paid by others so that they can watch you do things. Construct an onstage presence that is "human-scale", everyday.'[6]

The emphasis, then, is on the 'liveness' of the performance situation – defined by Peggy Phelan as 'representation without representation' – the 'reality' of audience, performer and their meeting in real time.[7] In Forced Entertainment's work, liveness is often manifested in a rejection of what the company calls the 'theatrical', a term used, as Etchells explains in an interview with Adrian Heathfield, 'in a derogatory sense: something that is trying too hard to affect you and is distorting itself by doing this'.[8] More generally, the company uses it to refer to the sort of theatre that Richard, loaded with fake explosives, ironically presents as 'good' at the opening of *Showtime* (1996): red curtains opening on to an impressive set, a good story with dramatic events. Yet although Forced Entertainment sets itself against the 'theatrical', its work never quite seems to let it go. This is most evident in a strand of its recent work that takes existing 'theatrical' forms and, through exaggeration and lampooning, over-loads them to breaking point: in *First Night* (2001) the welcoming grins of amateur popular entertainers twist into terrifying grimaces as the performers both welcome and insult the audience; and in *Quizoola!* (1996) the quiz show format becomes a sinister form of interrogation. But even in the more 'human-scale, everyday' shows like *Speak Bitterness* (1994), *A Decade of Forced Entertainment* (1995) and especially *The Travels* (2002) the cutting away of any 'theatricality' is so defiant as to be present in its absence.

This chapter argues that Forced Entertainment's preoccupation with 'theatrical-ity' echoes their proximity to a theatre tradition from which the company seeks to distinguish itself. While the company exemplifies live art in Britain, I will suggest that it shares characteristics with the post-war tradition of director's theatre, described by Arnold Hinchcliffe in the late 1970s as 'that significant part of recent theatre in which the producer [read "director"] plays a more than usually dominant role'.[9]

Forced Entertainment typifies the postmodern aesthetic and conceptual concerns of performance art and live art: their rejection of established conventions, blurring the boundaries between existing disciplines (for example, art and theatre) and mixing seemingly incompatible forms, styles, allusions and objects in a way that alludes to the Dadaist use of 'cut up' and 'found objects'. Performance art in particular is rooted in a rejection of artwork as a commodity and the notion that art can be posited as (in Tracey Warr's words) 'a fixed synopsis of the artist's intentions'.[10] The performance artist often seeks to create work that is outside of the conscious control of its partici-pants (or, any one of its participants), aiming, as John Cage suggests, to 'short-circuit human intentions'.[11] Composer Michael Nyman's description of experimental music – Cage is his illustrative example – provides a useful summary of the underlying principles:

Experimental composers are by and large not concerned with prescribing a defined *time-object* whose materials, structuring and relationships are calculated and arranged in advance, but are excited by the prospect of outlining a *situation* in which sounds [read 'actions'] may occur, a *process* of generating action (sounding or otherwise), a *field* delineated by certain compositional 'rules'.[12]

The use of 'compositional "rules"' which 'provide a bounded, limited range of possible events or actions' is a common creative strategy among performance and live artists.[13] This avoidance of 'calculated' and preconceived material and the locating of authorship outside of human intention represents a decisive split from the Romantic notion of the artist whose individual vision moulds the artwork into its particular form – the principle underlying director's theatre. Tim Etchells contrasts the company's approach to that of the American *auteur*-director Robert Wilson: 'We defer the authorship, the intention, the failure . . . Whereas when you look at Robert Wilson it looks like Robert Wilson, like he wanted. Robert Wilson signs it.'[14] While it could be argued that Forced Entertainment's work is as distinctly their own as Wilson's, the point is that the company sets itself apart from a 'theatrical' tradition associated with director's theatre, and with calculated intentionality, individual authorship and the display of artistic virtuosity – trappings of cultural elitism and hierarchy that sit uncomfortably with its ethos.

Performance/live art's avoidance of individual authority (and rejection of the director) reflects its roots in the political climate of the 1970s. The British alternative theatre movement of this period responded to the general mistrust of authority and hierarchy by forming democratic and collective creative strategies. True collectives, in which authorship is equally distributed among all company members, proved administratively clumsy, often creatively stunted and impossible to sustain, especially through the funding cuts of the late 1970s, but the spirit of collectivism lives on in a residual resistance to the directorial role. At the same time, recognition of the power of the individual director's vision in creating innovative theatre, as well as the practical advantages of leadership in making both administrative and creative decisions, ensure that the *auteur*-director never really goes away. Thus the role of director is often regarded with ambivalence in contemporary theatre.

This chapter sets Forced Entertainment's working practice in the context of two distinct models of theatre-making that have evolved in response to the opposing ambitions of performance/live art and director's theatre. These I call the system model and the ensemble model respectively. I will describe Forced Entertainment's process of making *The Travels* as an example of performance/live art's system model that nevertheless bears some of the hallmarks of the ensemble model, where a director works with a close-knit company. This is not simply an exercise in categorisation, locating the company's approach and work within one or the other traditions. Nor do I intend a critique of the company's apparently unconscious adoption of the trappings of a tradition (director's theatre), which its members regard as ideologically opposed to their own principles and practices. Rather I explore the way in which authorship – as I have suggested, an ideologically loaded concept that reflects a distinctly twentieth-century ambivalence that desires and opposes both hierarchy and equality, individualism and

---

Box 5.1: Models of theatre-making

Although it might be contentious to claim that theatre-making can be categorised in distinct models (particularly in the case of avant-garde practitioners with non-conformist methodologies), or that individual companies and practitioners can fit neatly into such models, my view is that shared traditions, influences, training systems, aesthetic concerns and socio-economic factors can lead to common creative strategies.

The system model: In order to avoid authorial intention, performance/live art companies create or adopt a 'system' of generating material (therefore the conception phase, and sometimes the fixing phase, may be truncated). Process participants tend to be compartmentalised so that they respond individually to the system, with little collaboration with each other. (This is not to be confused with Stanislavski's System.)

The ensemble model: This model is used by practitioners pioneering original performance styles and creative methodologies, as in the work of a number of celebrated directors (who may fall under the rubric of 'director's theatre'). They gather a group of practitioners who subscribe to the vision and are willing to dedicate themselves to its realisation. The group is a hierarchy centred on a charismatic director. While the material-generation phase of the process may involve the performers as authors, the fixing phase represents the reassertion of the director's authorship as she sculpts the material into shape.

---

collectivism – plays out in the day-to-day work of the rehearsal room, in particular through the role of the director. While we might question Etchells' perhaps idealised claims that the company avoids individual directorial authorship, analysing Forced Entertainment's working practice suggests that it is possible to achieve some resolution to our uneasy relationship with the director's role in contemporary theatre-making.

The process

20 March 2002: we are in the black-box studio of the Workstation, Forced Entertainment's base in Sheffield, UK, for the first day of work on what will eventually become *The Travels* (the working title is *In the Think-Tank at Dawn*). Etchells lounges on the empty tiers of the seating bank; the performers sprawl on chairs dotted around the performance area. I'm huddled over my notebook, pen hanging over a blank page, aware that my excitement at being here contrasts with the company's relaxed approach.

Etchells told me that they want to create a show that is 'more formal than *First Night*' and to 'put more pressure on themselves'.[15] The mood, however, is hardly

Box 5.2: Tim's dream

It was a great privilege to be invited to observe this creative process and I am deeply appreciative of the opportunity to gain an exclusive insight into Forced Entertainment's approach and to be the only outside audience to several unrepeatable proto-performances. I also became aware of the personal impact of the project upon the company – the pleasure of creative insight, the frustration of endless discussion, anxieties as first night approached – in a way that reminded me of Etchell's much-quoted description, in his introduction to *Certain Fragments*, of the audience as witness: 'to witness an event is to be present at it in some fundamentally ethical way, to feel the weight of things and one's place in them, even if that place is simply, for the moment, as an onlooker' (p. 17). On my last day of observation, Etchells tells me that he had a dream in which he finds, by his bedside, the notebook I had been using to document the process. It is a telling symbol of the extent to which, despite my efforts to be 'invisible' as an observer, my presence has indeed left its mark on at least one of the participants – I remember that being a witness is not just to feel 'the weight of things' but also 'one's place in them'.

5.3 The notebook.

pressurised: I discover over the next few days that Forced Entertainment do a lot of sitting, smoking, drinking coffee, talking and lapsing into extended silences during which the grumble of the cars in the garage next door is distinctly audible. What they are doing, to use Etchells' description in *Certain Fragments*, is 'waiting for something to happen'.[16] He describes the way in which the company find themselves 'anthropo-morphising the work as if it had desires of its own':

> Friends have sometimes reminded us that it is really our desires we ought to be consid-ering and not those of a dubious non-existent entity – and we laugh with them at our deferral/projection to this 'it' but at the same time we know there is also an 'it' . . . [which does] make demands, demands that have to be heeded if the work is to be worth making and sharing.[17]

This deferral of creative invention outside of the artists is typical of the system model, which is characterised by the use of an imposed mechanism or set of 'compositional rules' (the system) for the generation of material that will become the onstage actions of the performers. During the first phase of work on *The Travels* (from March to April 2002), Forced Entertainment engage in testing out a range of potential systems, what they call 'live games'. During the second phase, from August to opening night in Frankfurt in September 2002 (the company is away touring *First Night* and *Instructions for Forgetting* [2001] from May to the end of July 2002), the material that is generated by the system is *fixed* as aesthetic concerns determine how the material will be pre-sented to the audience. It is at this moment that the creative process deviates from the purest version of the system model (that traditionally used for Happenings, where the creators' desire to challenge the notion of artistic intention – and the perceived elitism of traditional art itself – leads to work composed almost entirely by chance or other 'outside' mechanisms) and the issue of directorial authorship comes into play.

The first potential system, which occupies the company only for the first day, is based on some pages of text that Etchells has prepared in imitation of the Readers Digest book of *Emergency What to Do*.[18] The performers gather around a long table with the task of posing absurd emergencies – for example, 'What to do if you can't stop crying' and 'What to do if you wake up dead' – and then offering 'bad advice' – stick splinters into the tear ducts in the first case. This *trial* is followed by a discussion. Robin Arthur is concerned that 'as a live game, it's not got a great deal of grace' and that it results in a 'semi-reasonable, slightly melancholic tone'. As Etchells observes, the group becomes 'tired of the condition of absurdity that is the bedrock of it' and eventually decides that it is 'boring'. We see from this that the concern is not so much with the material, but about the potential of the 'live game': assessing the mechanism by which material will be generated and the sort of material it is likely to produce. We then have an 'apology show', set up according to the following 'rules', outlined by Etchells: 'Terry comes on and starts and apologises that there's not a performance and explains why not; things that might have been in it, injuries, things that didn't arrive . . .. The rest of you in the chairs looking apologetic, including Rob in the gorilla [suit].' But on the following day this is abandoned for fear that it is too self-referential – as Etchells says, 'too Forced Entertainment'.

Over the next weeks, more ideas are tested, discussed (often at length) and then put to one side. An afternoon is spent exploring O'Connor's idea of telling 'really bad, sexist, racist jokes' into a stand-up microphone. One seam of work interests them for over a week: the performers, once again seated at the table, describe their purported actions in a range of imagined plays or films including an amateur dramatics farce, a murder mystery, a pornographic film and a slapstick clown comedy. Another week or so is spent on 'the gods' experiments: the table is now laid with a white cloth, a messy floral centrepiece and drink bottles. The performers, sometimes in deliberately bad toga costumes, each describe themselves as though they were a god in the act of creating the world and the creatures and objects on it. This idea is abandoned by 18 April after Etchells declares that the 'personal investment level' is showing 'no signs of getting hotter'. In the last trial of this phase Etchells asks the performers to line up in front of the closed front curtain and 'say who you are and then what you'd like me to be thinking about you. The formula could be: "I hope you're starting to notice I'm the pretty one" or something.' The resulting performance is the most sustained yet – we are surprised to look at our watches when it eventually peters out and find that an hour and forty minutes have gone by. Over the next two days Etchells transcribes the 'utterances' from the film recording of this trial to be used for the small-scale work-in-progress showing to the other members of staff at the Workstation (on 19 April, the last day of this phase of work). I am hopeful that, at last, they have reached some sort of end point, that they have something to go on, but when I bump into Etchells at the London premiére of *First Night* at The Place two weeks later he tells me that they had struggled to sustain the work-in-progress showing for more than thirty-five minutes, that they grew to dislike the way it 'skimmed the surface of the performance situation' and that they have abandoned this idea too.

Other companies might be concerned to have reached this halfway point with so little to show for it, but Forced Entertainment seems comfortable with this uncertainty. Its status means that individuals are not under outside pressure to make premature decisions (although they operate to pre-set deadlines). Most of the company's once-yearly shows are commissioned by overseas venues such as Frankfurt's Kunstlerhaus (which required little in the way of advance description of the developing show). This, together with restored support from the Arts Council and funding from Yorkshire Arts, Sheffield City Council and the National Lottery Fund, means that the group can continue to sustain a permanence that is unique in Britain. The company can afford relatively long rehearsals and, because it does not dissolve between productions, can continue discussion and development of new shows out of the studio. The group also has a reservoir of ideas that may be explored over several processes before these ideas surface, transformed, in the shows. The 'apology show', for example, is mentioned in Etchells' and Matthew Goulish's Institute of Failure website.[19] And the shows that followed *The Travels* develop some of the ideas I witnessed in its preparation: *Bloody Mess* (2004) includes a section derived from the 'I hope you're thinking' trial, and traces of 'the gods' experiment are evident in *The World in Pictures* (2006), in which, as the company describes on its website, 'an ill-advised version of the Story of Man proceeds to unravel amidst a storm of variably inaccurate advice and lewd interjections'.[20]

Thus, work on *The Travels* continued in on-the-road discussions during the touring break, resulting in two new directions that very quickly coalesced into the project's system on the company's return to the studio. A delay on the train from London to Sheffield means that I arrive late for the first day of the second phase of work, 22 July, and discover the company mid-trial. John Rowley has replaced Robin Arthur, who is on sabbatical. 'If a company member wants to pursue a particular project outside the company, we give them up to a year off,' explains general manager Matt Burman. This, he suggests, is positive for the company as well as the artist as it allows them to 'bring back something new'.[21] Decisions as to whether or not to grant a sabbatical are made collectively between the management and the creative team and the artist's pay is suspended for the sabbatical period. So far, Cathy Naden and Robin Arthur have taken advantage of the system.

In the rehearsal room, a familiar set-up: the performers are seated at a table that is strewn with notes, cups, cigarettes and ashtrays. Richard is describing the suburban home of a Tarot reader, John tells us about his experience on a psychic hotline, Jerry refuses to discuss what an African 'witch doctor' told him. I learn from Etchells that the company members have decided to set the performers 'projects' that put them in touch with the 'real world'. The earlier trials played with the notion of a 'virtual world' (the term was used by Etchells in the March rehearsals), where the performers refer to an event that they claim to have experienced – the fictitious theatrical performances and film genres, the 'what if' emergency scenarios, the gods' acts of creation – which are evoked through false memories, mock confession and competitive invention. Now Etchells wants to give them a real 'object' to describe – in this case their experiences of having their fortunes told. The particular choice of project relates to the second new direction that has emerged over the touring break. Etchells explains to the group that he has been dwelling on the notion of 'mapping and forecasting', exploring not only fortune-telling but weather forecasts, predictions for climate change, stock-market modelling – which is why we end up with what Etchells describes as 'six people sitting in semi-darkness, probing into the future'.

After the fortune-telling reports, the rest of this first afternoon is spent on a rather bitty series of prediction-based games in which the performers set each other or themselves instructions and give fictional accounts of how these are carried out. Somewhere in among these trials comes Etchells' instruction to 'make a list of UK towns and cities where you know the name and flavour of it, but you've not been there'. The task is for the performers to invent an account of their experiences in the cities (to be completed overnight). The following day these are read out. Etchells describes them as 'naked-making', rendering the performers 'quite vulnerable'. As O'Connor observes, the writing depicts each performer 'alone in a strange place'. The activity of 'verbalising your imaginings' seems to Etchells to be child-like. Although this constitutes a positive response, the fact that the towns and cities that they have been imagining also exist in the 'real world' means that the 'project' of visiting these places immediately suggests itself. 'One possible structure', says Etchells, 'is that you pick a place and then we'd pick a street from the A–Z and then you go to that street. A mission.' The project begins that very afternoon: the performers are asked to go away and select streets from maps of their destination towns and cities.

Once their choice has been approved by Etchells, they can visit the street. 'There's a debate of how much to force you to do more than just seeing the allocated street', says Etchells, but it is decided that for now their only instruction is to visit the street, take a photograph of its street sign and report back on the coming Friday (26 July).

The next week confirms that the 'street names project' is the process's system. At first it is assumed that the fortune-telling project will also feature in the show as well as additional projects (for example, sending Lowdon to Cairo on the basis that a Tarot reader told him he would find himself there), but by the following Monday (29 July) the group have dedicated themselves entirely to a routine of allocating streets to individual performers, giving themselves several days in which to visit them, then meeting in the studio once or twice a week to report back. As a system, the street names project quite clearly absolves Etchells from authorship over the material, opening the process up to the operations of chance. As Claire says in the show: 'So often the feeling that yesterday, even five minutes ago might have been a better time to arrive. That maybe yesterday there were lovers on Love Street where it cuts through the Science Park, but that for now there are only gardeners.'[22]

Artist Graeme Miller, who also works with mapping projects, suggests that such frameworks are a way to 'invite coincidence into the process'.[23] For Forced Entertainment the coincidence of street name and the street itself teases the performers' futile desire to make meaning out of the everyday. They engage in a 'reading', echoing the fortune-tellers' predictions. Claire continues: 'What to make of gardeners on Love Street? How to interpret? Is it nothing? Are they nurturing love? Or is "Gardeners on Love Street" also drawing a kind of blank?'[24] This becomes a literal process of fortune-telling when Claire, again, in the second section of the show, attempts to predict her own death by deciphering the 'clues' on her hand-drawn maps of the three 'Death' streets she visits.

Such reports illustrate ways in which the street names system gives authorship to each individual performer. Firstly, the performer has some choice of which streets or cities to visit (the 'lottery' of street allocation is partly fictionalised) and what task to perform on her street visit (the company's term was 'sub-project'), which will determine her experience there. These sub-projects included Cathy's Oracle Court cleansing ritual and Claire's listing of 'all the different kinds of drunk that I've been' on Bacchus Road. Secondly, the performers author their own accounts of their visit, either by writing a report (these take various forms including 'letters to Tim') or through improvising from memory and from their notes back in the studio (they are asked to write these up afterwards). While this evidently gives each performer a great deal of authorship over his or her particular contribution, it is also significant that, at this stage at least, there is no central author of the piece as a whole, no overview. In this aspect the street names project bears a key hallmark of the system-based creative approach, what Michael Kirby, in his definitions of the Happening, calls a 'compartmented' structure.[25] Each participant's creative input is self-determined, running in parallel with, but not affected by, the other participants' individual contributions. John Cage said of the Happenings form that 'if you have a number of people, then a nonknowledge on the part of each of what the other is going to do would be useful'.[26] This 'nonknowledge' allows performance/live artists

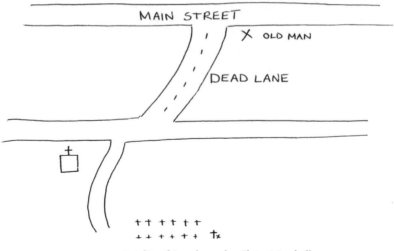

5.4 'Dead Lane' map by Claire Marshall.

deliberately to exploit what Etchells describes in *Certain Fragments* as 'a mis-seeing, a mis-hearing, a deliberate lack of unity' that comes about in group processes, allowing serendipity and distortion to produce possibilities that no one participant might have intended. [27] It produces work that bears the fragmentary, cut-up style of much postmodern performance.

Until the end of August, the street names project is the main activity. Etchells stays in Sheffield, collecting the performers' photographs and maps, together with the written reports which he compiles as what becomes known as the 'thirty-page document' (this categorises the reports as 'Love Lanes', 'Violent Places' and so on). From the beginning of September, the main drive becomes how to structure and stage this huge volume of reports, a task that, Etchells claims, causes him to 'despair'.[28]

The decisions about staging are shared between Etchells and Lowdon. A block of three days is dedicated to exploring a number of set-ups, particularly how to display the photographs and maps. In one version, the performers sit along the front of the stage (as in the apology show trial) with the photos projected on to the back wall. Another puts them in a semicircle of chairs facing a free-standing screen from which each performer in turn delivers her report. However, they soon decide to go back to the set-up they've been using so far: in almost every trial the performers are seated at a long table facing the audience. The final set-up is two tables, three performers at each, a microphone for each performer, and the overhead projector stage right. All attempts to show the photographs are abandoned when the company realise that they detract attention from the verbal descriptions of the streets. The final refinement is made the day before opening night, when Lowdon carefully angles the tables so they are about four inches shy of direct confrontation with the audience. It is a familiar set-up: Judith Helmer points out that in shows such as *Speak Bitterness* and *Instructions for Forgetting*, tables acted 'as a barrier that seemed to deny the possibility of intimacy

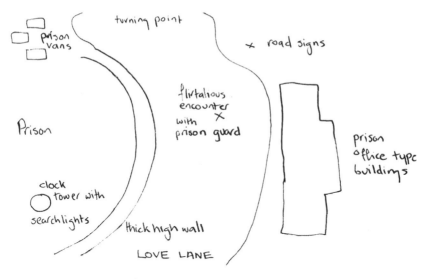

5.5 'Love Lane' map by Terry O'Connor.

even as it made it possible'.[29] Forced Entertainment tables are emphatically 'real world' and anti-theatrical. Their job is simply to put the performers face to face with the audience. At the same time, they create just a little distance both as a physical barrier and in the way that they serve the performers' 'task', whether this is to report, to confess or to show snippets of video. The tables often connote recognisably performative – but emphatically not performance – events suggestive of a 'panel of experts', an 'inquest', 'a press conference for a film', a 'lecture', a dinner party, anything but a theatre performance – in other words, 'an excuse for being in public'.[30]

The work on the set-up continues alongside the task of turning the thirty-page document into a 'script'. Etchells emails me the first version of this on 21 August, telling me that 'everything is provisional'. It consists of little more than a few reports (under the title 'Tuning in'), together with a note to say that there are 'No streets named after bad things. No death streets. No shadow streets. No confusion streets. No poison road'. This particular version is not performed, though it seems to have prompted a set of visits to 'bad things' streets. The first full version of the script is distributed to the performers on 13 September. As they begin to look at it, Etchells draws attention to the fact that there is 'an unevenness in terms of attribution'; in other words, that the person who originally contributed a report is not necessarily the one speaking it. We see that even at this stage there is a displacement of authorship (it is significant that neither the thirty-page document nor the first sketchy script indicate who visited which street).

The company flies to Frankfurt on 16 September and starts a pattern of intense work. There is a fairly formal full run each evening, often to a small audience of the venue's staff and visiting students who afterwards join the company for informal discussions in the Kunstlerhaus bar. Etchells makes revisions to the script or sections of it overnight in preparation for the following day's less formal runs and detailed

> **Box 5.3: The rules**
>
> *Forced Entertainment: The Rules*
> - Wait for something to happen, for a project (a system) to suggest itself.
> - When it does, subject it to thorough trial. Discuss its merit as a system, and the material it is likely to produce, at great length.
> - Don't commit too early; keep testing alternatives (save 'rejects' for future shows).
> - Once you've got a system, exploit it thoroughly.
> - Fix the material – but pretend you haven't.
>
> *Rules in the making of* The Travels
> - Stand at the microphone and tell a really bad joke, as racist or sexist as possible.
> - Explain what you'd do if you were invisible.
> - Describe how the world was created.
> - Apologise for a disastrous rehearsal process and announce that there is no show.
> - Visit a town; once there, ask locals where would be the best place for a love scene or a murder.
> - Stand in front of the audience and tell them what they are thinking about you.
> - Get your fortune told; do everything the fortune-teller tells you to in order to avoid bad luck.
> - Travel to any Story Street or Road in the UK and collect a story.

discussion, or the company breaks during the day to give him time to write. The group works through four versions of the script before the opening night on 27 September. The attention during this phase is on how to 'bunch' the street reports, how much contextual information to give (Naden volunteers to write the 'overview' description of the street names project), how to 'treat' each of the reports. A new vocabulary emerges as they discuss the various forms of report: 'raw' reports are delivered informally, as though from memory; 'boiled' reports are read out and are more poetic in tone. The 'utterances' may be 'short' as in the 'tennis match bit' of the final show, where quick 'one-liners' ('Friendship Way, Glasgow. 2 kids fighting with sticks') volley between performers. At times they may 'go long': one performer subverts the established pattern by speaking far longer than expected, often shifting into a more personal mode.

The show

The critical response to *The Travels*, in the UK at least, saw the show's apparent lack of 'theatricality' as a weakness. Jen Ogilvie described the show's 'deliberate mundanity' as a key 'problem' of the production.[31] Jackie Fletcher claims to have left the performance 'dissatisfied at being denied a performance'.[32] Even Joshua Sofaer, an advocate of live art, regarded not so much the set-up, but the stories themselves, as 'just a little too dull'.[33] These verdicts fail to appreciate the complexity of the live encounter that the show sets up. While there is little to see on stage, watching (and listening to) the show creates a sort of double vision as each of the stories told by the performers conjures images in our imagination – Jerry listening to a rude joke in a Muslim burial ground; Cathy sitting incongruously at a child-size fibreglass table in a Scottish theme park. Admittedly, the stories themselves veer between the banal (often the performers travelled miles just to stand on a deserted street) and the occasional sensationalised cliché of British parochialism (Cathy gets into trouble for photographing a child on an estate), but what keeps us hooked, and what continues to haunt us after the performance, is the experience of inhabiting what Anke Shleper describes as a 'poetic space'.[34] This, says Shleper, is a landscape that lies 'somewhere between documentation and fiction' and is constructed (and often deconstructed) entirely by the performers' interpenetrating and multilayered narratives. Its power, especially in *The Travels*, lies partly in its ability to conjure the details, atmosphere and emotional engagement with events that exist only in our imaginations. We experience a disconcerting alienation – we cannot, as Shleper suggests, locate ourselves within the conjured space; we can only see through each performer's subjective – possibly exaggerated, maybe even outright false – perspective. This gives the performers a strange sort of power over us – and the more 'banal' the performance and the stories, the more sinister is this power.

Authorship and vision

I have suggested that Forced Entertainment follow a model of theatre-making in which authorship is deferred and splintered through the use of a system. The street names project was used to generate a quantity of material, the content and form of which was determined partly by chance and each of the performers. While each 'report' has its individual author, the work as a whole is composite and fragmented. However, once Etchells begins to craft this material into a script, once dramaturgical and aesthetic criteria are applied, then we might ask whether this constitutes the imposition of individual authorship and, therefore, a transition into what I have described as the ensemble model of theatre-making. After all, the act of writing is the quintessential expression of authorship: a solitary creative act that commits to paper one vision of the show-to-be, excluding alternative visions. There is a limit to both the feasibility and value of tracing the author of each report through the various layers of re-writing and re-performance. However, it is important to consider how the particular creative strategies used by the company both serve and subvert Etchells' authorship and to ask, if not answer, the question of whether *The Travels* is an expression of its director's individual vision. Etchells himself would certainly object to the suggestion that any of Forced Entertainment's shows bears his own individual stamp. In his essay 'On Performance Writing' in *Certain Fragments* he dismisses the notion of an authorial '*voice* . . . that comes from *themselves*', claiming instead that Forced Entertainment's work is 'radio porridge', which he describes as the product of a 'gabbling voice composed of scraps and layers, fragments, quotations. No editorial, or at least no centre.' The result is 'writing that's more like sampling. Mixing, matching, cutting, pasting.'[35]

The sampling analogy is appropriate to the structure of *The Travels* but we should be aware that the performers' reports were not in themselves unchangeable samples. Even before Etchells incorporated them in the thirty-page document and the subsequent scripts, the reports underwent a series of 'treatments', as they were written and performed (not necessarily in that order), often more than once, by the performers. Once the selected reports were incorporated into the script, Etchells would himself clean up, expand and fillet them. Thus the 'scraps and layers' are not unambiguously outside of his control, but have been determined by him, at least partially, from the very outset of the street names project (remember, for example, that in their first expeditions the performers had to get Etchells' approval of their choice of streets).

Although the performers' comments were invited during the re-writing process, Etchells created each version of the script alone (they were not, for example, group-written); he made the major structural decisions. Performers offered suggestions as to the arrangement of the material, but their attention tended to be on the details – 'Love Street doesn't cut that well with Universal Street' (O'Connor), or (Lowdon) 'should Achilles Street go with his mythological friends?' I would argue, then, that what Etchells calls 'sampling' does constitute a form of individual authorship – though the question of whether the final script is an expression of Etchells' individual voice does not anticipate an objective answer. One possible guide is to compare the script with writing that Etchells is prepared to claim as his own: the essays in *Certain Fragments*. These certainly have a distinctive style, in particular in their use of a collage form which combines different tonal qualities and perspectives on a subject. 'On Performance Writing', for example, includes an 'official' voice, confession, lists (including 'A list of streets'), memories. Like the shows, it suggests a multiple voice with 'no centre'. The fact that these qualities are also evident in *The Travels* is one argument for suggesting that the show is an expression of his voice, though the extent to which this voice has been formed out of his long collaboration with the company puts this into question.

The fact that up until this point my examination of *The Travels*' authorship has centred on the script is, in itself, an indication of Forced Entertainment's originality of approach: more commonly the play text is the one aspect of performance that lies outside the director's authorship. It is in the interpretation of the written play text into stage form, in the 'writing' of performance rather than the literal writing of a script, that we conventionally locate the director's authorship. In fact, Etchells gave little explicit direction regarding the performance of the piece, the delivery of the reports or the social business. This, I suspect, is partly to do with the fact that Forced Entertainment's particular hyper-naturalistic performance style blurs the distinction between social and performance behaviour: the performers act as themselves, calling to mind Goffman's celebrated notion of the presentation of self.[36]

The resemblance between the performance and actual social behaviour is deceptive:

5.6 The Travels.

Box 5.4: Three terms

Trial: I share the company's reluctance (as mentioned by Etchells in 'Play on', p. 52) to use the word 'improvisation', perhaps because of its associations with performance traditions quite different to those of Forced Entertainment. Trial seems an appropriate alternative as its judicial connotations echo the thoroughness with which each of these provisional performances is examined.

Fixed/fixing: the phase of a creative process in which decisions are made as to what material will be incorporated into the performance score. This is often a relatively formal event, for example the creation of a script in devised theatre. The entire process, in my own terminology, consists of: conception, material generation, fixing, rehearsal and performance (though many instances of 'looping back' may occur in one process).

Set-up: Forced Entertainment's term for what others might call 'set design' or 'staging': basically, the arrangement of furniture and performers on stage.

Forced Entertainment's performance style can claim to be as sophisticated as that of the great directors, even if it does not seem to make the same demands of its performers in terms of physical training and the careful stage realisation of a director's vision. The demanding nature of a good many visionary directors is notorious. Etchells is evidently a long way from this sort of dictatorial director and, in its commitment to what Arthur describes as a sort of 'pragmatic socialism', Forced Entertainment is far from hierarchical in structure. [37] While the company has the ensemble's permanence and longevity, it is not dependent on the near-deification of its director. What makes *The Travels*' process less hierarchical and Etchells less of an *auteur* than we would expect in the ensemble model is a culture of transparency. Throughout the process, one of Etchells' most important roles was in making explicit the tacit aspects of the creative and decision-making process, speaking eloquently and at length about the effect of a particular trial or the reasons for a particular restructuring of the script.

What Forced Entertainment does share with director's theatre is a striving for a unique vision and, with this, a developed set of beliefs as to the company's place in the existing cultural climate and a distinctive aesthetic and performance style. Forced Entertainment's vision is manifested in several ways, not least its distinctive aesthetic: the seemingly amateur set-ups, the strict avoidance of theatrical flourish (unless it is there to be exposed for its ridiculousness), the performers' frontal arrangement. The company also shares with many of the directors' theatres a 'theory' that can be assigned to them in the way that Stanislavski is associated with his System, Grotowski his 'poor theatre' and Meyerhold his biomechanics. It even has a key text, *Certain Fragments*.

Forced Entertainment, then, operates through a hybrid model of theatre-making that crosses the distinct vision of director's theatre with the system model's short-circuiting of authorial intention. The group has an impressive ability to conceptualise their work, which seems somewhat at odds with the seemingly improvisational, almost meandering quality of their creative approach. Likewise, the productions have a thrown-together quality that belies the scrupulous attention to detail revealed in the company members' creative discussions. Each show is evidently the expression of a visionary sensibility, though the fact that this sensibility cannot comfortably be attributed to either Etchells as director or to the group as a whole is disconcerting. In coupling the director-led and the system models, Forced Entertainment has brought together two seemingly incompatible notions of creative authorship, pairing a commitment to anti-hierarchical group creation with the precision and rigour that comes from the clarity and uniqueness of an individual vision.

Notes

1 Etchells is described on the company website as the 'director and writer'. See www.forcedentertainment.com (accessed 6 July 2006).

2 Tim Etchells, *Certain Fragments: Contemporary Performance and Forced Entertainment* (London and New York: Routledge, 1999).

3 Judith Helmer and Florian Malzacher (eds), *Not Even a Game Anymore – The Theatre of Forced Entertainment* (Berlin: Alexander Verlag, 2004).

4 I use first names to refer to the onstage personas of the performers (both in trials and shows). This echoes the company's habit of referring to each other by their own first names in performance: the informality of first names, and the refusal to assume fictional identities chime with the company's anti-theatrical stance discussed in this chapter.

5 Forced Entertainment, *The Travels* (script), 2002, p. 5. See also Forced Entertainment, *The Travels* (video), 2002. Both are available from Forced Entertainment. A–Zs are city-based street maps, in book form, with an alphabetical index of streets.

6 Tim Etchells, 'Audience Tactics – Notes on *First Night*', in the *Forced Entertainment Educational Resource Pack* (2001) available from Forced Entertainment. See also Tim Etchells, 'A Six-Thousand-and-Forty-Seven-Word Manifesto on Liveness in Three Parts with Three Interludes', in Adrian Heathfield (ed.), *Live: Art and Performance* (London: Tate Publishing, 2004).

7 Peggy Phelan, *Unmarked: The Politics of Performance* (London and New York: Routledge, 1992), p. 3.

8 Adrian Heathfield, 'As if Things Got More Real – a Conversation with Tim Etchells', in Helmer and Malzacher (eds), *Not Even a Game Anymore*, p. 91.

9 Arnold P. Hinchcliffe, *British Theatre 1950/70* (Oxford: Basil Blackwell, 1974), p. 172.

10 Tracey Warr (ed.), *The Artist's Body* (London and New York: Phaidon, 2003), p. 12.

11 Michael Kirby and Richard Schechner, 'An Interview with John Cage', in Mariellen R. Sandford (ed.), *Happenings and Other Acts* (London and New York: Routledge, 1995), p. 56.

12 Michael Nyman, *Experimental Music: Cage and Beyond* (Cambridge: Cambridge University Press, 1999), p. 4. Italics original.

13 *Ibid.*, p. 21.

14 Etchells quoted in Heathfield, 'As if Things Got More Real', p. 92.

15 Unless otherwise stated, quotations from members of the company are from rehearsal observations that I undertook in March, April, July and September 2002.

16 Tim Etchells, 'Play on: Collaboration and Process', in Etchells, *Certain Fragments*, p. 51.

17 *Ibid.*, p. 62.

18 Readers Digest, *Emergency What to Do* (London: Random House, 1988).

19 See Tim Etchells, 'The Small Failures' (2002) at www.institute-of-failure.com (accessed 12 June 2004).
20 See www.forcedentertainment.com/current/currentWorldinPictures.html (accessed 3 July 2006).
21 Conversation with the author, 28 September 2007.
22 Forced Entertainment, *The Travels*, pp. 9–10.
23 Graeme Miller, untitled talk to postgraduate students at Goldsmiths College, University of London, 5 February 2003. Miller is a former member of Impact, one of Forced Entertainment's seminal influences. His work includes *Reconnaissance* (1998) and *Listening Ground, Lost Acres* (1994), both with Mary Lemley.
24 Forced Entertainment, *The Travels*, p.10.
25 Michael Kirby, 'Happenings, an Introduction', in Sandford, *Happenings and Other Acts*, p. 4.
26 Cage quoted in Kirby and Schechner, 'An Interview with John Cage', p. 57.
27 Etchells, *Certain Fragments*, p. 56.
28 Conversation with the author, 13 September 2002.
29 Judith Helmer, 'Always under Investigation: from *Speak Bitterness* to *Bloody Mess*', in Helmer and Malzacher (eds), *Not Even a Game Anymore*, p. 72.
30 Respectively, Etchells, Marshall and Killick in rehearsal; Anke Schleper, 'Off the Route: Strategies and Approaches to the Appropriation of Space', in Helmer and Malzacher (eds), *Not Even a Game Anymore*, p. 188; and Etchells, 'Audience Tactics', 2001.
31 Jen Ogilvie, 'NOW Festival 02: The Travels – Forced Entertainment' (at Sandfield Theatre) in You Are Here (visual arts resource for Nottingham and beyond) (2 November 2002); available from www.yah.org.uk/comments.php?id=57_0_1_0_C (accessed 30 June 2005).
32 Jackie Fletcher on the British Theatre Guide website (4 December 2002); www.britishtheatreguide.info/reviews/thetravels-rev.htm (accessed 30 June 2005).
33 Joshua Sofaer, 'Forced Entertainment – the Travels', review in *Live Art Magazine* (December 2002); www.liveartmagazine.com/core/reviews.php?action=show&key=139 (accessed 30 June 2005).
34 Schleper, 'Off the Route', p. 186.
35 Etchells, *Certain Fragments*, pp. 99 and 101.
36 Erving Goffman, *The Presentation of Self in Everyday Life* (London: Penguin Books, 1982).
37 Robin Arthur interviewed in Michelle McGuire, 'Forced Entertainment on Politics and Pleasure', *Variant* 2:5 (Spring 1998), p. 12.

6

Rodrigo García and La Carnicería Teatro – *Une façon d'aborder l'idée de méfiance (One Way to Approach the Idea of Mistrust)* **(2006)** – Approaching mistrust[1]

Lourdes Orozco

Introduction: the director and his work

Rodrigo García (b. 1964) founded La Carnicería Teatro (The Butcher's Theatre) in 1989, three years after moving to Madrid, Spain, from his Argentinian home city of Buenos Aires. As with a number of contemporary European directors and choreographers to whom García feels aesthetically and philosophically close, such as Tadeusz Kantor, Jan Fabre, Jan Lauwers and Romeo Castellucci, García's background is in the visual arts; he trained as a designer in advertising before entering the theatre professionally in 1989. García admits that his move to Europe was initially politically motivated; it was his incapacity to fight within Argentina's guerrilla movement that led him to explore other ways of releasing his anger towards his country's political situation. In a conversation in Brighton, England, in spring 2005, he told me, 'I write because I didn't kill' – a statement which could explain the underlying violence in his work.[2] Even in the aftermath of the fall of Argentina's military *junta* in 1983, the arrival of a new democratic government – led by the Socialist Workers' Party and involved in a series of corruption cases in its initial years in power – only served to consolidate his opposition to what was happening politically. García's concern for Argentina's political struggles triggered his writings and his emigration to Spain – his parents' homeland – in 1986, to pursue a career as a writer and theatre director.

After three years working successfully for various advertising agencies in Madrid, García created La Carnicería, which holds the name of the family business where he was forced to work for many of his teenage years. La Carnicería was primarily conceived as a means of staging García's own texts but, additionally, it staged works by other 'maverick' novelists, dramatists and visual artists such as Charles Baudelaire, Thomas Bernhard, Heiner Müller, Bruce Naumann and Fernando Arrabal. Since 2000, the company has focused solely on staging García's own work, at a time when other directors have also provided high-profile productions of García's plays in Europe.[3] The company's early years partly benefited from Spanish state support for new theatre in the 1980s, brought about by the cultural policy of the Spanish Socialist Party which sought to generate a network of small venues.

La Carnicería has always been highly productive. From 1987 to 1997 it devised eleven productions, most based on García's own writings.[4] This frantic level of creativity has not diminished since the company entered the international festival circuit in 2000 with *After Sun*. Commissioned by the European Cultural Centre of Delphi and premiered in the Delfos International Theatre Festival, *After Sun* then toured worldwide for three consecutive years, marking the beginning of the company's continuous cross-continental touring to date. *After Sun* gained García international recognition, placing him clearly within the international festival circuit beside other European *auteur*-directors mentioned above with whom he shares the ability to create visually striking performances which challenge text-based theatre within the festival context. *After Sun*, a fable about ambition based on the myth of Phaeton, proved that García was capable of inspiring disgust and admiration in equal measure by creating a poetic vision of contemporary consumer culture in which nudity, animal abuse and violence featured explicitly.

In a similar way to his compatriot Víctor García (1934–82), Rodrigo García has found a second artistic home in France, where he has been critically acclaimed and academically recognised as one of the most influential figures in contemporary European theatre. *La Historia de Ronald el Payaso de McDonald's* (*The Story of Ronald the Clown from McDonald's*) (2003), then produced at the 2004 Avignon Festival, and subsequently seen in Paris, consolidated his position in the country's network of national theatres where his works can regularly be seen. Furthermore, the French publisher Les Solitaires Intempestifs has produced translations of most of his works and their wide availability has encouraged not only productions, but also the author's inclusion in secondary school reading lists across France. In contrast, García's work has had difficulty finding a place within the Spanish theatre system and has only recently been welcomed in Barcelona's more progressive theatre landscape. Despite this belated progress in his reception in Spain, García still holds a degree of resentment that his adopted homeland has never been excessively welcoming: he states, 'sadly those who want to see my theatre have to travel outside Spain'.[5]

As demonstrated by the case study of this chapter, mobility is another of La Carnicería's defining features, facilitated by the company's structural flexibility. At the time of writing, the ensemble depends largely on casting that García carries out while touring, which means that La Carnicería has different actors performing in every production. However, in its technical staffing, the company presents a much more stable structure. Since 1986, García's collaborators have been Carlos Marquerie (lighting), Elena Córdoba (choreographer), Ramón Diago and Daniel Iturbe (video projections) and Fernando Esparza (sound). García insists that the company does not have big financial or structural ambitions and that comparatively little time or money is invested in marketing productions or publishing his texts.[6] Generally, La Carnicería devises small-scale productions with little scenography, contributing to the work's physical and symbolic transferability. Since its beginnings, the company has been greatly dependant on external funding. While government subsidies offered a degree of support in the late 1980s, in recent years financial stability has been secured through the support of both private and public – and mostly international – cultural institutions.

García's aesthetic and philosophical approach to theatre draws heavily from practitioners who are also visual artists. In a private conversation he mentioned the impact that seeing Tadeusz Kantor's work in Madrid had at the very early stages of his career. Furthermore, together with Calixto Bieito, he is Spain's clearest representative of the *auteur* tradition.[7] As early as 1994, García was explicit about his position within that tradition, declaring, 'I defend the work of the auteur, seeking alternative performance vocabularies which are extremely personal.'[8] However consistent his body of work might be perceived to be, a change of direction is patent from *After Sun*, when his preoccupations clearly moved towards issues surrounding globalisation. Since then, both his texts and productions have consistently denounced the exploitation carried out by the world's superpowers and the progressive disintegration of human values within the structures and beliefs of capitalism. The commoditisation of culture, the increasing mediatisation of society and the loss of idealism are the three major themes that inform his latest pieces. His texts, normally written in the first person, resemble pseudo-autobiographical diaries marked by an underlying anxiety about contemporary society. The collapse of value systems and principles, the death of ideology and the commercialisation and commoditisation of human relationships frame the actions of individuals who have been stripped bare by a consumer-driven society. García's theatre could be seen to be postmodern as it rejects the linear telling of a story, the use of characters, and the establishment of psychological relationships between word–action, presence–absence and audience–spectator. Halfway between performance actions and theatre pieces, García's work aims to disturb the audience by using all means of artistic expression which allow for the creation of loud, frantic, busy and aggressive spectacles. It usually revolves around issues of torture and exploitation, transforming current political issues – the recent Iraq and Afghanistan wars, Latin American dictatorships, the Israel and Palestine conflict – into reflections of personal and individualised processes. In many cases, these processes are embodied in animal abuse and rituals of submission between individuals, establishing an immediate link between public and private politics. While at first glance García's strategies for conveying meaning might appear to be amusing in their frenzied anti-establishment aesthetic, his work ultimately presents a profoundly disenchanted response to the traits of contemporary society.

The production: *Une façon d'aborder l'idée de méfiance*[9]

As in other works by García, *Une façon* did not feature characters or the linear development of a story; rather, it presented a series of unlinked situations in which the visual and sensorial prevailed over the psychological, seeking to create what Richard Foreman has called a theatre of 'situation and impulse'.[10] The bare and fully open stage, shared by four hens, a tortoise and three performers, was adorned only by the objects needed to carry out the piece's actions: a hammock, two bird cages, two tables, a fish tank, a water pipe, compost bags, milk cartons, honey jars, a salad bowl, sticky tape and two tables. The lighting, also a trademark of García's productions, consisted of projected frames of simple yellow, green and white light used to delineate the actions and their perpetrators over the blackness of the stage. Alongside the on-stage actions, García's texts were projected on the stage's back wall in the manner of a silent movie script. This technique, usually used to surtitle the actors' speeches when the company tours internationally, was the performance's only textual input, and another example of García's increasing mistrust of the spoken word.

However, in many ways *Une façon* demonstrates movement in a different direction within García's artistic career. In contrast to the usual overload of text and video projections, loud music and shouted speeches characteristic of La Carnicería, this piece advocated stylised audio minimalism, with a soundtrack made of the performers' movements and breathing and the sound of the hens eating corn. Crucially, *Une façon* was produced at a time when García felt disenchanted by contemporary production practices and an increasing mistrust in his ability to create. Thus, to an extent, the piece also acts as a symbolic gesture to protect his individual artistic voice from the categorising and commoditising structures of the international touring circuit. The production's scarce use of resources and its organic creative process are elements of García's tireless attempts to escape categorisation and commoditisation.[11]

The production's rhythm was established by a slow but constant stream of actions which was only interrupted twice; first, roughly twenty-five minutes into the performance, when a group of eighteen extras entered the stage to reproduce an iconic still image of the 1999 Columbine School massacre;[12] and second, at the end of the piece, when Jean Benoît Ugeux uttered a stoic complaint to the American multinational Dunkin' Donuts responsible for his persona's deadly cancer. Another trademark of La Carnicería, the video projections that feature as a backdrop to the actors' movements and speeches were this time replaced by the live feed of a mini-cam located first at stage level and, later, on the top of the tortoise's shell, offering an alternative perspective on what was happening on stage and producing close-ups of the tortoise's head. These images were projected in black and white, adding to the piece's slick visual composition and strengthening García's intention to produce what he called 'a classic piece, a Rembrandt'.[13]

For this work-in-process, García was accompanied by the above-mentioned group of usual collaborators with the addition of Alessandro Romano (assistant

6.1 Rehearsal day nine, 9 February 2006. Agnès Mateus during the talc scene and the projection from the tortoise's camera. The slow accumulation of dirt can be seen on stage where milk cartons, talcum powder and water help to create a lunar atmosphere.

director and stage manager), the Bonlieu's group of technicians, and performers Agnès Mateus, Juanjo de la Jara and Jean Benoît Ugeux, none of whom had previously worked with La Carnicería. The piece was commissioned by the Bonlieu Scène Nationale, a two-auditorium venue in France's network of national theatres, managed by the Franco-Spaniard Salvador García.[14]

In rehearsal with La Carnicería

I joined the company two days after the start of rehearsals on 3 February 2006 and was confronted with a very loose rehearsal schedule. The fact that the team was staying in two hotels only a few minutes' walk from each other allowed for rehearsal times to be decided on a daily basis depending on the needs of García and the technicians. However, during the first four days, the rehearsals followed a regular pattern. Starting with the performers' warm-up in the early afternoon (roughly two hours before García's arrival in the theatre), they continued with the official rehearsal involving the whole team (2.30 pm to 8 pm), followed by a post-rehearsal meeting (in which

Box 6.1: Director-performer dynamics: from fear to admiration

During rehearsals of *Une façon*, a shifting dynamic between performers and director was evident. On one hand, García established himself as a clear autocrat, claiming ownership of all the decisions taken in the creative process from the very beginning. On the other, this process was informed by an open dialogue between all the participants who were actively encouraged to express their opinions in the post-run discussions and who did so with varying levels of confidence. Indeed, marked differences between García's choice of performers stimulated productive on-stage and off-stage tensions which were essential in creating the underlying edginess that featured throughout the production. All three performers had a background in postmodern performance and shared an admiration for the director's work: Agnès Mateus is a regular performer on the Catalan fringe theatre scene and her collaborations with postmodern directors Roger Bernat and Simona Levi ensured that García's territory was familiar to her; Juanjo de la Jara is a Chilean actor and dancer, co-founder of the dance-theatre group Lengua Blanca, and performs regularly in Madrid's alternative theatre scene; Jean Benoît Ugeux is a Belgian actor and photographer who speaks Spanish fluently and whose first contact with La Carnicería was as spectator of *La Historia de Ronald el Payaso de McDonald's*. García's international success and cult status within Spain's alternative theatre scene mean that performers across the world are eager to collaborate with him. The performers' feelings of absolute respect towards the work of a genius-like figure visibly informed the whole creative journey of the piece. As a consequence, performers appeared to be juggling fear and admiration in their interaction with García which meant that only the stronger-minded were able to establish a clear position within the piece and the team, and secure their input into the production. One performer confessed to me that overcoming the anxiety arising from generating new material on stage had been the hardest part of the process due to the overwhelming fear that the director's negative responses produced in the performers. The shyness and courteousness tinting the performers' general behaviour in the rehearsal room made clear to me that not all of them overcame that fear.

everyone involved in that day's rehearsal was present) and dinner, which was attended by all of us and which, as the opening night approached, turned increasingly into an extension of the preceding discussion. Until day six, some structure was also visible in the order in which different elements of the piece were dealt with: days one to four were entirely dedicated to the generation of material and to editing and sequencing texts; days five and six focused on technology, lighting and sound design. The remaining days were extremely stressful and the team had to be on call at all times. During days seven and eight, large segments of rehearsal time involving the whole team were spent discussing the selection and linking of material; lighting and sound designs were only finalised one day before opening night. Contrary to what usually happens in La Carnicería's creative processes, *Une façon* had a complete run-through before opening night, mainly because of García's concern with the choreography involving

6.2 Team discussion at the end of day eight in the auditorium of the Annecy Scène Nationale. From left to right: Alessandro Romano, Agnès Mateus, Dani Iturbe, Rodrigo García (holding one of his drawings), Carlos Marquerie and Jean Benoît Ugeux.

the group of extras. During rehearsals, García told me that La Carnicería never do full runs before opening night, but a complete virtual performance emerges in the process where everything that will be in the final performance is latent.[15] In rehearsals the director clearly reiterated that changes within the piece could still be contemplated on the very day of the premiere, including the addition of material that had previously been dismissed.[16]

Already in the very early stages of production, and especially in the morning warm-ups (doing, for example, stretching and voice projection), significant differences between the three performers could be perceived. This was mainly a question of intensity: one performer was extremely dynamic and visceral, directing energy outwards; the other two tended to work inwards and with significantly lower levels of visible energy. This imbalance informed much of the rehearsal process and had a clear impact in the time that each of them spent on stage in the final performance. Performers who demonstrated an ability to generate material independently and to share its ownership were able to hold their place confidently in the performance. In contrast, performers whose style was more introverted struggled to please García's appeal for actions infused with high energy. García was callously intolerant of the performers' lack of assertiveness on stage and demanded conviction in all of their individual actions and interactions. This meant that those performers who were either

confident or dismissive of García's negative reactions were paradoxically most successful in securing their material in the performance. The director's strategies to attain
what he wanted from the performers proved to be highly productive albeit clearly
damaging the performers' relationships with each other. Thus, while the show offered
a critique of power relations in contemporary social structures, in many ways, such
relations were actually reproduced in the rehearsal room by the imposition of a very
clear hierarchy in which participants were encouraged to struggle with each other.

After spending the mornings working out a storyboard and drawing sketches for
the actions, García joined the group in the afternoon, bringing in ideas that had been
generated either prior to his arrival in Annecy – he started working on *Une façon*'s
texts in the summer of 2005 – or during rehearsals that week.[17] Writing and drawing
are part of what García sees as intimate creative processes, always preceding work in
the rehearsal room, and developed by him separately to the construction of the piece.
García generates work at home prior to joining the rest of the team in the rehearsal
room:

> I work at home a lot before starting the rehearsal process. It seems strange, because nor-
> mally theatre is made by a group of people. A director, a choreographer, has to spend
> much of his or her time working with a team. My case is different. I spend more hours at
> home or in my studio, on my own, and less time in the rehearsal room.[18]

In rehearsal, performers were constantly reminded of this distinction informing
the generation and delivery of material: 'we had agreed that texts and actions follow
separate paths', García said repeatedly. This was exemplified clearly in García's handling of written text. After working for over an hour on a set of physically draining
and emotionally challenging actions, Ugeux reached what he believed was the perfect
mood for delivering a text dealing with the recognition of his persona's imminent
death at the hands of an American multinational. The result was a highly emotional
reading that García dismissed immediately: 'I know what you are trying to do, but I
don't want it that way. Actions and texts have to be developed separately.'

On day four of the rehearsals, García stated ironically, 'today we'll do classic
theatre, proper theatre, text-based theatre', despite the fact that *Une façon* only featured one speech, Ugeux's Dunkin' Donut monologue (García's politically loaded
texts were intermittently projected on to the back wall). Throughout rehearsals,
García repeatedly stated his unwillingness to reduce or alter his literary material,
frequently reminding his team that 'the text is sacred'. Even when the texts had to be
shortened due to technical problems related to the size of the projector, wording was
kept intact. Despite the translator Vasserot not being present in rehearsals (she only
arrived in Annecy on the opening night), García insisted that the translations could
not be altered, even when it was obvious that the actors found them inadequate.

Furthermore, I would argue that the disturbing effect that García's works have
on many spectators is partly due to the clash between the texts' content and the way
they are delivered by the actors. Ugeux uttered the realisation of his persona's own
imminent death – the actor himself had recently had a very similar experience –
standing naked centre-stage, his thin body covered in honey, paint and compost,

6.3 Mateus on day eight and her scene with the hens, the third scene in the production. The hens were placed on Mateus by the other two performers and she had to slide across the stage trying to keep the animals on her. This was one of the most compelling images of the production, used also to create tension between the performer and the material, due to the difficulties involved in the delivery of the action.

humbly facing the audience as a sort of human dustbin. On opening night, after some initial laughs the auditorium fell into a deep and long silence. The ostensible lack of linkage between actions and texts within García's productions results in a palpable tension between provocative and emotionally discomforting images and the spoken or written word. García's reluctance to employ the pathetic and empathetic in performance is grounded in this clear division, which is as intrinsic to his creative process as it is to how his work is finally produced. This dichotomy – based, on one hand, on the material García produces privately (texts and drawings) and, on the other, on the work generated in the rehearsal room (actions) – provides the basis for both his processes, for generating material and the structure of his staged productions. In *Une façon*, the texts were an intimate reflection of García's experience as an artist and thus were to be treated with both respect and affection. Actions, on the other hand, are the performers' input into the piece and are to be energetic displays of exhibitionism such as de la Jara's compulsive dancing across the stage or Mateus' playful scene with the hens at the beginning of the production. Rhythm within the piece is achieved through alternating text and action, intimate and public processes of experience.

Most of the action-based material that was to be part of *Une façon* was generated in the first four days of rehearsal and subsequent rehearsals focused on working out the *mise en scène* and coordinating technical features. The team's initial frenzied levels of creativity – including those of García himself – meant that by day four he was struggling to select the actions he would include in the final production. García confessed to assistant Alessandro Romano, 'I have too much material rather than not enough.' At this point of crisis, where García was clearly struggling to structure the material,

Box 6.2: 'Authenticity' versus 'theatre'

In García's rehearsal vocabulary 'authenticity' was directly opposed with the 'theatrical'. On many occasions, this provoked him to state that the only good actor in the production was the tortoise, since she had no awareness of being onstage in front of an audience. García insisted that his performers had to reject the idea of re-enactment, disregarding any differences between the stage and real life. 'You have not come here to act, you are not making theatre. Who do you think you are? Marlon Brando?' His search for authenticity on stage is exemplified in early improvisation exercises for *Une façon*, where he established that there was no space for 'pretending to do things': 'if you are going to beat each other up, do it for real'.

his dependence on the team became evident; only the work in the rehearsal room enabled the physicality of his ideas to enter the stage. Nevertheless, García repeatedly expressed his frustration that he could no longer work on his own. After day four, long meetings were held in which the team discussed which physical material was essential to the piece. Actions' subject matter was never discussed; rather, individual actions were dismissed on the grounds of being too messy, long, loud or theatrical, meaning by this that they were too contrived and unreal.

Means for engendering actions roughly followed three different patterns. In the first, a performer would be asked to volunteer to carry out an action drafted by García on the storyboard. For instance, in the scene of the talc as drafted in one of García's drawings, one of the performers was to come on to centre stage wearing a hooded top in which a large amount of talc had been hidden previously. The powder was to come out slowly from the hooded actor as she/he moved her/his shoulders back and forth in compulsive outbursts, creating a surrounding cloud of smoke. It was Mateus who finally delivered the action because García preferred the effect her longer hair created.

Indeed, the production's driving force was a search for visual beauty that objects, animals and actors can craft on stage. 'Don't do this because it's ugly' and 'yes, that's beautiful' were regular directions given to actors during rehearsals, normally related to physical staging and colour composition. García consistently praised objects chosen for the scenography, all of which were brightly coloured to contrast with the blackness of the box. García especially liked the contrast produced by Agnès's black tracksuit and the whiteness of the talc. Equally, he reminded the team that the hammock (yellow against black), the bright green birdcages, the red couch brought in by the extras and the yellow water pipe were 'all beautiful objects that looked fantastic onstage and should always be included within the performance space so the audience could see them'. As rehearsals progressed, it became clear that the stage in García's creative process was an equivalent of the designer's studio and comparable to the meticulous arrangements on Robert Wilson's canvasses.[19] On the other hand, it was interesting to see how the performance's seemingly meaningless actions – another way of understanding *Une façon*'s beautiful stage pictures – were handed over to the audience in order to be interpreted and/or experienced. In rehearsal, the meaning of

6.4 García's storyboard on day five. The director would present different drawings to the team every day as guidance to the generation of actions.

the talc scene was never discussed; by placing it amidst the Columbine massacre scene in the final production it became an embodiment of death, as Mateus' black and white shadow spread her powder amongst the dead bodies scattered on the stage.

An alternative procedure employed to generate actions was improvisation, triggered by either an idea or a very specific sentence. For instance, performers were given a sentence out of context – 'I'll never do this again' – with which to create situations. On a different occasion, the performers were encouraged to play around with the hammock and sticky tape. In these cases, psychology was always neglected and no reference was made to the relationships the actors were to establish amongst themselves or with the material. These guided improvisations were driven by García's clarity in communicating what he liked or disliked to the performers who were then able to produce seemingly illogical chains of actions. These improvisations demonstrated that the ambiguous message intrinsic to all of La Carnicería's productions is achieved, paradoxically, by setting very specific practical ways of handling dramatic material. Once the improvisations had been set, long sections of time were then spent discussing how to reproduce spontaneous actions. Sometimes, however, actions were entirely created by the performers, as in the two opening scenes (Mateus aimlessly trying to find a comfortable position leaning against the wall, and the hens being placed on her back), both produced by the performers during warm-ups when García was not in the theatre.

6.5 Rehearsal day nine. Mateus, Ugeux and de la Jara 'unmake' a salad. After a lettuce, a sliced tomato, cucumber and carrot were individually recomposed with sticky tape, all four vegetables were returned to their natural habitat by being placed inside an opened bag of compost.

The specificity of the director's search was also seen in improvisation work for the scene of the deconstruction of the salad, for which a very strict set of parameters was established. This scene was to depict the return of a sliced cucumber, lettuce leaves and two sliced tomatoes to their original form and habitat. García considered this the central scene of the piece, conveying its philosophical and emotional meaning. However, he repeatedly failed to communicate this meaning to the performers, expecting them rather to realise his vision spontaneously. This demonstrated García's resistance to conventional theatrical blocking and his belief that actions would organically shape in his desired form. However, the director resorted to blocking at points when scenes were not gelling as he had predicted. The salad scene, for instance, was finally choreographed in great detail. It turned out to be a psychologically charged section within the performance and was executed rather automatically, exposing the performers' awkwardness since they were conscious of their incapacity to fulfil the director's ideal vision. The scene became also an example of how dramatic tension in La Carnicería's work is, in fact, achieved by generating a state of real tension on stage. In this particular case, a charged atmosphere was triggered by the director's constant reminder of the performers' incapability to succeed. Indeed, it became clear to me that the production's intrinsic violence – as is the case in general with La Carnicería's work – stems from the real psychological and physical violence that takes place in the rehearsal process and that is later reproduced in performance.

In Mateus' scene with the hens, another important element of the production came into play: the handling of animals. On numerous occasions García has stated that the pleasure in using animals arises from the ways their unpredictability adds tension to the performance. He is constantly seeking to surprise – and indeed shock – the spectator as he challenges audience preconceptions of what theatre is or should be. This is also why he rejects the validity of character within performance. In his view, decades of naturalistic performance have tried to lead us to believe that the stage mirrors society; but characters have lost their ability to convey meaning: 'a character appears onstage and the illusion is completely destroyed. We all know that is an actor pretending to be someone else . . . Watching people is much more fascinating.'[20] Hence, in marked contrast to the set score of a well-made piece, animals are totally unreliable, and able to change the production radically and unexpectedly. This anxiety that García is able to generate within his team – by constantly delegating responsibilities, introducing the unpredictable animals and not fixing the performance completely – is later felt by the spectator during the performance and is an important part of experiencing La Carnicería's theatrical journeys. Thus in describing the energy that informs his theatre, García uses the analogy of the boxer, whose body is in tension when executing the punch but also while waiting for his opponent to react, never allowing his body and mind to relax since relaxation could mean death.

As rehearsals developed, the processes through which ideas were fed into the show became increasingly apparent. García's intellectual curiosity and open disposition to popular culture revealed themselves as vital sources. The scene of the Columbine massacre and de la Jara's make-up were extracted almost directly from a photography book, a highly stylised exploration of radical youth movements in contemporary Western society.[21] The internet also generated ideas: images and videos were downloaded in order to produce actions or create particular atmospheres during rehearsal. La Carnicería's touring and, indeed, García's own nomadic lifestyle, provided another source of inspiration. The consequences of spending long periods away from home – in hotels, airports, restaurants and bars – contributed greatly to the feelings of displacement and mistrust produced by the piece. However, the way material such as the reconstruction of the Columbine massacre or de la Jara's make-up was used followed the same pragmatic instruction-based approach as discussed above. García could frequently be heard saying, 'this is what I want, just do it'. The choreography for the massacre image, for example, was staged twice before opening night with the teenage extras being given precise instructions of what to do when as well as a copy of the picture that they were trying to reproduce on stage.

The piece's technical side is devised from day five alongside the performers' material. Camera trials are set up and conversations happen about which cameras to use and how they affect the performance and its relationship with the audience. Although knowledgeable in this area, García is very ready to take advice from the technical members of his team, and prepared to make concessions and give up initial ideas. The fifth day of rehearsals was spent practically, testing all the technical elements of the piece except lighting. García is keen to spend time on this, making sure that every technical decision taken is coherent and consistent in relation to what has been generated by the performers. For instance, when faced with the option of using a hand-held camera with better image definition or a small static camera which could be camouflaged anywhere on the stage, García was very aware that his decision was going to be crucial in establishing the aesthetics of the piece. The technical aspect – what was or was not feasible – was crucial in constructing the final performance.

During the second day of technical rehearsals, three days before opening night,

Box 6.3: Animals on stage: can we eat them?

Since *After Sun*, the use of animals on stage has been a trademark of García's work, gaining him fierce criticism on the part of animal rights campaigners. However, García often uses animals as a way of highlighting contemporary society's hypocritical relationship with them. In *After Sun*, for instance, two rabbits were juggled in the air and made to dance and copulate onstage while Tom Jones's hit 'Sex Bomb' was played at high volume. While this scene caused many audience members to walk out of the theatre shouting at the actors and, on occasions, throwing chairs and other objects at them, García explained that other members of the audience would ask the team at the end of the piece if they could take the rabbits home to be cooked and eaten.

Likewise, the Madrid performance of *Accidens* (2005) scheduled for July 2006 was cancelled by the City Council due to the pressure of animal rights campaigners. In the piece, García presented an actor killing, cooking and eating a lobster with Louis Armstrong's 'It's a Wonderful World' as a soundtrack. Here again the director defended himself by saying that the performance contained an action which is carried out daily in restaurants across the globe.

Une façon used animals in a slightly different way. Their unpredictability served to increase tensions latent in the piece. As well as providing the production with striking images, animals were used by García to put pressure on the performers who were responsible for their behaviour on stage throughout the show. During the staging of the piece in Reus (near Barcelona) in June 2006, the difficulties of working with animals became visible. While the actors' interaction with both hens and tortoise had worked to perfection in France, it became a real problem on the opening night here. After the performance, the team assured me that during their short stay in Reus, where three of García's plays were being performed in three days, they had not had time to rehearse with the animals before this revival of *Une façon*. Consequently, the poetic opening scene in which the three performers hold the hens after they have been removed from Mateus' back became one of obvious stress as the hens behaved unpredictably and the actors had to struggle around the stage to catch them. Following this rather tense opening, halfway through the performance Ugeux forgot to keep an eye on the tortoise, which meant that the signal from the camera placed on her shell was completely lost; technician Fernando Esparza was forced to go on stage to find the tortoise and place it within the light frame.

the team had a discussion prompted by the director's acknowledgement that technology had added a large amount of material to the piece. As in previous cases during this process, there was a clear stress on the search for simplicity – 'I don't pretend to be cutting-edge,' García stated, insisting on the fact that he only wants a clean, simple image on which to project the texts. This meant that after two days spent generating images and projections the selection process needed to be initiated and, finally, only two images were chosen for the final piece: Ugeux's feet and the tortoise's head.

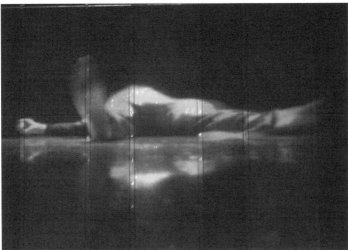

6.6 & 6.7 Real and projected images of Ugeux, the two different perspectives juggled in *Une façon*.

Lighting designer Carlos Marquerie and Mónica Giraldez, the company's manager at the time, arrived in Annecy on day seven. Marquerie's long experience in collaborating with García was visible in the director's complete confidence in his work, which meant that after exploring the resources available, *Une façon*'s lighting design was completed in one day. Furthermore, previous to Marquerie's arrival, García anticipated his influence by giving directions to the team that were conditioned by a not-yet-existent lighting design (for example, 'no don't go that way because Carlos will want to put a light here', 'don't worry about the colours because Carlos will give us simple, homogeneous lighting').

In the daily discussions that followed rehearsals, little or no attention was paid to the meaning of either individual actions or the piece overall. In fact, the piece was given a title two days before the premiere and only because of the venue's pressure to print programmes, posters and press releases. Indeed, no time was spent on analysing the piece, and nobody within the team posed any questions to the director about what the motivations behind the piece might be. The director's outspokenness ensured that his ideas were made available to the troupe at his discretion.

Instead of addressing abstract overarching themes, post-rehearsal discussions focused on recollecting the work undertaken during the day, with information provided mainly by Romano's notes and García's digital pictures. New storyboards were drawn, resources or techniques that had impeded actions were listed and responsibilities (re-)distributed. Generally, the conversations were pragmatic and the director insistently reminded everyone of their involvement in the whole piece as much as their individual scenes and/or responsibilities. As rehearsals unfolded, it became obvious that García had established an organic autocracy in which he was giving precise orders but was also ready to take on board advice on practical matters. However, there was a prevalent sense that the troupe was always ready to privilege the director's views, and that his role as the overall artistic engineer of the piece was respected by all.

The underlying sense of pragmatism behind rehearsal conversations also informed the sequencing of the piece, undertaken as a jigsaw reconstruction in which the various chronologies that had emerged in rehearsal were balanced against each other in very practical terms. Issues such as a performer having wet hair when it needed to be dry, being undressed when time was needed to dress again, crucially informed the piece's chronology, in which no attempt was seen to connect actions through meaning. Text and image projections on the back wall were also decisive in the construction of the *mise en scène*, the location of actions and the placing of objects on stage. For instance, the honey scene – in which Ugeux poured honey on de la Jara's and Mateus' naked bodies before joining them in a choreographed series of hugs – was delivered in close proximity to the audience and could be read both as a provocation or an invitation to the spectator to join the performers' act of love. However, the fact that the stage was already almost entirely covered with milk and water meant that, for the honey to stick, this action had to be performed down on the edge of the stage. By constructing *Une façon* through pragmatic reasoning, the piece encouraged 'free' interpretation, reinforcing García's belief in a theatre practice that goes beyond mere intellectual experience. With the performance, García was true to his aims to produce 'a clear and uncomfortable socio-political ideal: providing alternative viewpoints', liberating the theatre from constructing narratives in order to produce impulses rather than clear messages. However, this progressive approach to performance is achieved at the expense of challenging the liberties of everyone involved in the creative process. Thus the director's objective to denounce social injustice and encourage alternative viewpoints is frustrated in two ways; firstly, by employing a formula which repeatedly triggers the desired reaction from the audience and which satiates their liberal needs to feel socially aware; and secondly, his privileged position within the international festival circuit allows García to create, in the rehearsal room, a rigid regime which reproduces the same repressive structures that his theatre aims to expose.

6.8 Text and floating doughnut, images of devastation at the end of the piece. The text reads, '[The people] who should fulfil this task are the ones who are well-off. . .'

Reception

In France, the premiere's reception was cold. The performance had nearly sold out to a largely young audience and, as is common in response to García's work, some people left the theatre before the end of the piece, although in much smaller numbers than they did in La Carnicería's early days. No reviews were published in either the local or the national press and more programmers than journalists could be found amongst the audience. However, the performance secured a solid touring schedule and gained García a deal with Avignon to produce a new piece at that festival in 2007.[22]

At the Teatre Fortuny in Reus (June 2006), *Une façon* was appallingly marketed. No reviews were published in this case either and it could be said that the piece's reception was even colder here than in France. The team had not worked together for three months and little time was spent remounting the piece. The auditorium – a nineteenth-century proscenium arch theatre where metal seating had been placed over the stalls and part of the performance space – also added to the awkwardness of the performance. The fact that the latter theatre was significantly smaller than the one in Annecy transformed the piece's well-designed minimalism and elegant mess into an over-cluttered display of actions. My perception is that the performance never overcame the initial nervousness caused by the behaviour of the hens in the opening scenes and I spotted a few more instances in which it became clear that the piece had not been properly remounted. In contrast with Annecy, the performance was not very well attended, but my impression is that this was due to the Teatre Fortuny's poor marketing and a genuine lack of interest in García's work in this provincial and conservative town over one hundred kilometres south of Barcelona. I would even argue that tensions between the company and the theatre had permeated the performance and I was disappointed to see how the show had been used as a product to fulfil the political aspirations of a newly established production centre.

In Spain, as in France, García has actively fed his *enfant terrible* reputation, making sure that his artistic voice prevails over health and safety and other restrictive regulations. His works are classified as radical, innovative and socially committed, replete with angry criticisms of contemporary society. However, García's audiences have become largely immune to a critique that has turned into a spectacle and whose effectiveness is seriously challenged by the material conditions in which it is both produced and consumed.

Notes

1 I would like to thank Rodrigo García and La Carnicería's team for giving me full access to rehearsals during the time spent in Annecy. Equally, I am extremely grateful to Maria Delgado for her pertinent comments on this piece.

2 García, conversation with the author, 21 May 2005. All translations are the author's own.

3 Some examples are Matthias Langhoff's staging of *Borges* (2002), Arnaud Troalic's *Borges vs Goya* (2007), and two stagings – by Pascal Antonini (2004) and Christian Sterne (2004) – of *Haberos quedado en casa, capullos* (*You Should Have Stayed at Home, Dickheads*).

4 The director's CV can be found at www.theatre-contemporain.net/auteurs/garcia/pdgrgesp.htm although the page has not been updated since 2004 (accessed 7 January 2008).

5 García, online conversation with the author, 5 June 2005.

6 García, conversation with the author, Brighton, 21 May 2005.

7 See Gabrielle Cody, 'Introduction to Part III (Auteur Theatre)', in Rebecca Schneider and Gabrielle Cody (eds), *Re:Direction: A Theoretical and Practical Guide* (London and New York: Routledge, 2002), pp. 125–7, p. 125.

8 John P. Gabriele and Candyce Leonard, 'Entrevista: Rodrigo García', in Gabriele and Leonard (eds), *Teatro de la España demócrata: Los noventa* (Madrid: Fundamentos, 1996), pp. 39–46, p. 39.

9 *Une façon d'aborder l'idée de méfiance* was produced at the Bonlieu Scène Nationale, Théâtre d'Annecy, France, 1–10 February 2006. I shall subsequently refer to it in abbreviated form as *Une façon*.

10 Richard Foreman, 'Pearls for Pigs. Program notes' in Schneider and Cody (eds.), *Re:Direction*, pp. 172–4, p. 172.

11 The production was seen at the 2007 Avignon Festival and toured widely before that as part of the programme of 'experimental' theatre festivals across Europe.

12 The Columbine High School massacre (Colorado, USA, April 1999) was perpetrated by two students who shot dead twelve other students and a teacher before taking their own

lives. This massacre raised issues about the use and administration of guns in the USA and the impact of violent video games and films in youth culture, and it contributed to the rise of security in US schools and beyond. It inspired the work of American filmmakers Michael Moore (*Bowling for Columbine*, 2002) and Gus Van Sant (*Elephant*, 2003), amongst other cultural responses.

13 García in rehearsal. All subsequent unattributed references to García are to his comments in rehearsals.

14 See www.bonlieu-annecy.com (accessed 7 January 2008).

15 Significant parallels can be found between this and the way in which Susan Letzler Cole describes Robert Wilson's creative process. Susan Letzler Cole, *Directors in Rehearsal: A Hidden World* (London: Routledge, 1992), p. 161.

16 In a participatory talk (at Sadler's Wells, London, UK, on 29 September 2005), dancer Dana Caspersen explained that some of William Forsythe's choreographies were fully recomposed on the day of the premiere. Caspersen described Forsythe's method of rehearsal with words that resonate with García's own approach to the creative process: 'you plant a seed and you know that it is going to be a willow but you are not quite sure which direction it is going to take, how it is going to grow'.

17 This process recalls the methods used by the Wooster Group. Cole, *Directors in Rehearsal*, p. 105.

18 García, online conversation with the author, 5 June 2005.

19 Cole, *Directors in Rehearsal* , pp. 149–50.

20 José Henríquez and Juan Mayorga, 'Entrevista a dos bandas: "Yo no quiero ser un animal"', *Primer Acto*, 285 (2000), 15–22, 18. For other interviews with García see those carried out by Pablo Caruana: 'La Carnicería se abre al encuentro del público', *Primer Acto*, 294 (2002), 44–58; 'Se puede caminar . . . se puede sentir llover', 2005, available at www.ladinamo.org/ldnm1/rodrigo/rodrigo.html (accessed 26 October 2005); and 'De la acumulación y sus virtudes', *Primer Acto*, 294 (2002), 63–6; by Sharon Feldman, 'Rodrigo García's Ruins', *Estreno*, 31:1 (Spring 2005), 16–18; by José Antonio Sánchez, 'En un café de Ginebra: Diálogo entre Óskar Gómez y Rodrigo García (Coordinado por José Antonio Sánchez)', in *Ciudadan@s de Babel: Diálogos para otro mundo posible* (Madrid: Fundación Contamíname, 2002), pp. 387–414; and by Carlos Henderson, 'La gloria no cae del cielo: Rodrigo García en Aviñón', *Primer Acto*, 305 (2005), 72–5.

21 Francesco Bonami and Ralf Simons (eds), *The Fourth Sex: Adolescent Extremes* (New York: Charta, 2003).

22 The piece was presented in the 2007 Avignon Festival together with García's *Cruda. Vuelta y vuelta. Al punto. Chamuscada/Bleu. Saignant. A point. Carbonisée (Very Rare. Rare. Medium Rare. Charred)*.

7

Gekidan Kaitaisha – *Bye Bye: The New Primitive* (2001) – Theatre of the body and cultural deconstruction

Adam Broinowski

Bodies through *butoh*

Based in Tokyo, the performance company Gekidan Kaitaisha was formed in 1985 when Shimizu Shinjin, one of the actors of a loosely knit *shogekijô* (small theatre) group doing adaptations of Greek tragedies, volunteered to direct after their playwright had left. A new group of younger performers from the same university subsequently became the core of the company. Kaitaisha has come to concentrate on the condition of the body in relation to war and history, and its representation within globalised systems. Shimizu and performer-choreographer Hino Hiruko together continue the work of Hijikata Tatsumi's *ankoku butoh* (dance of darkness) which was rooted in an ethos and socio-political context of rebellion. Hijikata developed a series of intensely expressive performances, from his first *butoh* piece in 1959 through to work in the 1970s, that broached taboos and overturned conventional notions of dance. As Hijikata's youngest student, Hino had notated the dances Hijikata and his collaborators had created in a notation system called *butoh-fu*. Gekidan Kaitaisha's body-based practice loosely draws on the movement vocabulary and poetics of this tradition. It is designed to deconstruct 'what is', in order to reveal power – and in particular the structures that support it – and renew conditions for the body to become more itself.[1]

The basic premise of Kaitaisha's methodology is 'moving the inside out to allow the outside in'. Although Kaitaisha has consciously tried to avoid categories, I have found that the terms 'body theatre' or 'theatre of the body' best suit its style and approach. While the company's work displays elements of *butoh* and modern dance forms, Shimizu's approach is informed by the writings of critical theorists like Barthes, Derrida, Foucault, Giorgio Agamben and Deleuze and Guattari. The outcome is a corporeal theatre that stages cultural deconstruction.

Kaitaisha's productions include *De-control: Cell* (1999), *Bye Bye: Into the Century of Degeneration* (1999), *Bye Bye: The New Primitive* (2001-2), *Death is Living* (2002), *Bye Bye: Phantom* (2003), *Drifting View X: Bodies of War* (2003) and *Dream Regime* (2004-5). All the pieces have been shown in Tokyo, and touring includes Germany, the UK and the USA. Together they bear out a preoccupation with themes and movement vocabularies that have become more distilled over time.

I began participating in workshops with Kaitaisha in early 2001 and joined the company in May that year, at a stage where its process and theatre form were already developed. No longer engaged in simply creating something 'new', the company members were involved in a more intimate development of their art form, deepening their philosophical approach, their relationships with each other and with the structures supporting them.[2] The content for their productions is developed incrementally, so that body-phrases from workshops and previous productions are re-used in various configurations, with new ones introduced when they are formed. Consequently each production flows into the next, becoming an accumulating series. Rehearsals overlap with productions, with the performed outcomes dependent on factors including site-specificity, cultural context and reinterpretation of the evolving phases. It is as necessary to explicate phrases, images and concepts from past productions in order to write about the making of a Kaitaisha show, as it is to interview the director about his intent concerning the work in hand. As there is little discussion in rehearsal of the *meaning* of abstract images or movement, I have interpreted the artists' (mostly Shimizu's) intentions from conversation, and by tracing various sources of influence.[3]

Evolving *Bye Bye*: from body to scenography

Bye Bye: The New Primitive (*baibai* – 未開へ) opened at the Morishita Studios in Tokyo in 2001, then toured to five cities in the UK, three in Germany, played a season in New York in early October 2001 and a season in Singapore in 2002. Although the production had been prepared in Tokyo for an initial season at Morishita, the show evolved over time. Initially funded by the Saison Foundation, it was produced for touring by a combination of overseas theatres and organisations and the Japan Foundation.

When I first join Kaitaisha in 2001 it is with no premise other than to immerse myself in Tokyo life as much as possible during a six-month Japan Foundation artist's residency. The company knows me as the man-on-the-rings in a show by NYID, an Australian company Kaitaisha had collaborated with, where I used my experience as a theatre-maker, actor, dancer and former gymnast. In my adolescence, however, I had lived in Tokyo and I subsequently studied Japanese at university in Australia. I had also spent a year practising Noh theatre as an undergraduate in Shizuoka, and had

Box 7.1: An approach to making

While certainly not anti-rehearsal, Kaitaisha's approach is for the performers to meet regularly to maintain the condition of the body, irrespective of whether a show is looming, and to conduct a continuous practice based on set phrases. Productions are incrementally built based on the developments in these rehearsals, and on external sources such as cultural theory and current events that are discussed between members. Rather than an 'acquisitive' attitude, the artists work from the inside out, generating material in an evolving process of sensitising their bodies. The director Shimizu works in parallel, mindful of the performers while interpolating contemporary themes and materials into his particular sense of structure and image. For productions, rehearsals are intensified over short periods of time. Scenography is adapted according to the context of the audience and venue, and the cultural resonance in the particular scenes that are presented.

co-written and co-directed *Hell Bento!* (Tetrapod, 1995), a documentary exploring Japanese subcultures. Consequently it was with a deep interest in Japanese theatre in particular that I began to work with Kaitaisha.

Initially I am auditioned sitting on a chair in the middle of the studio that the company has converted from a car park. Shimizu, the director, wants to see what sort of presence I have on stage. He asks me to speak some text, a seemingly random list of words in English, open for me to interpret in the way that I choose. As a result of this 'audition' I find myself relegated to a small room adjacent to the stage, lit by the glow of a monitor, where I read the text over a microphone. As rehearsals continue, I commit to learning the company's particular movement patterns through dedicated practice, and am gradually initiated into the lengthy and demanding process of remaking my own body.

I agree with Tadeusz Kantor that the 'rehearsal is the art form'.[4] In this context, however, I am learning form and concepts the artists have developed over many years, rather than preparing anew for a single production. Desiring not to infringe upon the company's values and processes, from the outset I decide not to introduce styles from my own previous experience, although these will inevitably be present to some extent in my body. I discover that the concepts and forms are departure points for exploration through body and imagination, rather than embodiment being only a mimetic process. Understanding of meaning, which is implicit and abstracted, comes through practice and knowing the artists. Only when these first principles have been established do I look for ways to extend the work.

Following a series of workshops and studio performances – which follow Kaitaisha's usual pattern of intense exploration of movement forms and relationships on a smaller studio scale – the company invites me to perform in the production of *Bye-Bye* at Morishita Studios in Tokyo in June 2001. This is a daunting challenge considering my lack of familiarity with the intensity of the company's work, an audience new to me and the cultural differences that pertain. Over an intense two-week period, movement is rehearsed combining old phrases and new additions, and my role is adapted and integrated into the choreography, where sometimes I inherit an absent performer's part and sometimes make new material within the limits of the scene.

The approach is compartmentalised and modular. Rehearsal is divided into individual and partner scenes or group choreography, the latter entailing *mure-kehai* (a clumped grouping), crash (a dynamic hurling and catching), *rensa* (a chain-reaction-like grouping, connected but individualised), *gunji* (a coupling based on holding and releasing) and exile (a choreographed series of lines of flight and meeting points). Most time is spent on group choreography. In the studio, rehearsals are always framed in the language of 'pure movement' rather than by way of communicating particular emotions or intentions. At this stage, the structure of the work is fluid and depends on the performers' commitment and energy. Shimizu comes and goes as he preoccupies himself with scenographic ideas on paper, seeking stimulus from the performers in order to re-imagine scenes. In the studio, choreography predominantly remains the performers' responsibility (although underpinning principles have been carefully laid out) and in adapting it to different venues Shimizu is closely involved. As the informal choreographer, Hino gives advice on technique and approach. While all performers focus in greater detail on specific aspects of individual, partner or group movement, special attention is given to those whose form and presence needs refining. The group choreography is not principally geared to a particular production but becomes seamless through regular and continuous practice.[5]

About a week before *Bye Bye* opens, costumes are selected by trying different combinations from a sizeable collection kept in the tiny dressing room in the underground movement studio. Ultimately this is a subtle negotiation between the performer's desires, what suits the individual and the aesthetic range in relation to Shimizu's images. While all performers in the company have a base costume of lingerie (such as slips or corseted underwear), gauze head wrappings and black shorts, most have a 'suitcase' of costumes for other roles they regularly present. Nakajima Miyuki, for example, wears a schoolboy's shorts and hat. Both Hino and Nakajima might wear a *burqa*, *mino* (grass skirt) or *hanbok* (Korean traditional dress). Kumamoto Kenjiro wears a black suit or grey coat with a hood and Aota Reiko either shorts or a short dress and high heels. At this early stage I wear torn blue corduroy jeans, a long-sleeved collarless grey shirt and a coat, and carry a suitcase.

We then move to the venue where we have the luxury of rehearsing for many days in the space. Rehearsal begins once the tarquette, a linoleum flooring, is laid. Aside from Hino's opening scene, which is not rehearsed until other scenes are close to completion, the show is built in linear progression. As the scenography becomes more defined, sound (mostly electronic noise, sparsely used) and light are introduced to the movement, creating whole scenes that are energetically run then abruptly halted, and followed by long periods of silence in which Shimizu thinks through problems. Occasional passionate outbursts when something is not working are typical. In these periods, the performers repeat movement sequences in silence, maintaining concentration and warmth. The fact that there is little verbal communication helps to intensify the atmosphere in the space. Due to the emphasis on shadow in Kawai and

Ambiru's lighting design, when we gather for breaks the shock of daylight makes us wince.

With its long silences, stark, concentrated moods and serious themes, followed by intense bursts of energy, this production is not a light, happy experience. It's not that humour is lacking, but nor is it deliberately sought out in the scenes or the rehearsal process. Tension becomes a material substance, used to gauge the level the show has reached. The line of development from rehearsal to performance is almost seamless – exercises become sequences and these in turn are composited into the production. What follows, then, is a detailed summary of regularly practised exercises that moved from the rehearsal room to the stage in *Bye Bye*.

Body methods in rehearsal: the 'empty body'

The Kaitaisha rehearsal begins in the evening with light banter, stretching, and a group exercise to concentrate the use of the abdomen and balance, reinvigorating neglected parts of the body from quotidian stress. This is followed by *hassei* (発声), a routine of controlled breath and vocal exercises where air is slowly expressed in held poses that build in intensity and force until the body sweats from exertion. The body's condition is thereby prepared for *hakobi* (運び) or 'carrying', which is based on the *butoh* exercise of *hokô* (歩行) – walking up and down the rehearsal room in individual lines in a particular posture and concentrated state defined by a verbal scale called 'carrying'. This is similar to (but not the same as) the walks of the Suzuki method or the walking postures in Noh and Kabuki. The transformation of walking (an instinctive skill learned before memory) to 'carrying' (a constructed theatrical posture) is one of the more difficult aspects of the Kaitaisha performer's repertoire, and its principles are described in the following instruction from rehearsal:

> *Carrying*
> Push your soul out in front of you
> Let in the space around you
> Push the self outside to become empty space
> Follow your soul forwards
> Follow that energy
> Carry the space together with you
> Don't walk with your legs
> Be carried
> The space twists your body.[6]

This phrase enables the body consciously to sense the external atmosphere by becoming 'empty'. It is one of many exercises informed by *ankoku butoh* and devised by Kaitaisha to emphasise the progression of energy outwards from within the body. From my perspective, having become 'empty' after a period of 'carrying' the body becomes 'open'. Although often interpreted in psychological or confessional terms

Box 7.2: The practice of 'carrying'

For the performer in Kaitaisha, 'carrying' is a specific form of walking that places our accustomed form under consideration. Walking is considered a 'natural' skill learned before memory. 'Carrying', then, is a 'neutral' base and an ontological foundation, a way to move out into and perform the space (although ungrammatical, this choice of words is deliberate). Will is substituted by 'signs' from the space – 'you are moved', 'you are seen' – and the performer becomes less focused on self-expression or self-reification and more receptive to the body.

'Carrying' is therefore a practice – one that is also a positive act of resistance, if one considers the body to be 'full' with representational systems (subjectivity, community, identity) from which it is temporarily released. It entails a state of passivity that results from an active extraction of what we might call coercive encoding (the learned behaviours that condition our everyday bodily deportment). It creates an alert, fragile and vulnerable body, incompatible with the violence of everyday society. To varying degrees, in becoming space through 'carrying' the performer becomes object (客体) as well as subject (主体). From this basis, the performer 'transforms' through various solo and group sequences ('chimaera', 'pack', *suishô*, 'sea-dog') in relationship to space.

where the body describes an emotional transparency, this 'openness' connotes a bodily condition of awareness or greater sensitivity within changing conditions. There are specific aims and limits in exercises like 'carrying' – independence while following, solitariness without isolation, diminution while expanding, humble confidence or non-anxious alertness – but there is, too, a calm, centred quality that creates profound lightness. This is a development of the basic trust placed in the body as the source of inspiration – what Maria Pia D'Orazi calls an 'inner landscape', found throughout Hijikata's *butoh-fu*.[7] Within this condition an infinite amount of detail occurs to the body as it moves through decided positions. The lack of volition enables an ease in which unforced events are rediscovered. Will is not erased but used to create a state rather than, somewhat fleetingly, to occupy a space with self-expression.

During rehearsal for *Bye Bye*, as these ideas begin to manifest in their various forms, I am filled with conflicting thoughts concerning the positive and negative aspects of selflessness. The force of the will to open the body can inhibit the opening, and yet it is the responsibility of the individual to prepare to open. Needless to say, the performing body becomes object to itself as well as subject, and is also part of a larger subject/object. This is an important difference from Hijikata's 'become the object' (物になる), in which the subject is not acknowledged at all. The condition of blurred clarity that follows allows for possibilities of contact with the other performers in ways that cannot be choreographed. Ironically it is a selfless and embodied state that attributes most responsibility to the performer. Arrival at this state entails a process of bodily transformation that is also a change in the state of concentration. The performer's particular physical disposition contributes to her manifesting an inner quality that feeds back into the physical quality – there is a palpable atmospheric shift. This state is used in Kaitaisha both to support the performer's presence and quality and to convey events over time within a greater historical and cultural context.

Once the performers have begun to arrive at this condition of openness, how is it then applied to the production? I describe, below, a series of transformations that become sequences in *Bye Bye*. I apply Shimizu's terminology such as 'chimaera' or 'pack', and use terms such as 'skin' and 'medium' to describe the concepts in play. My observations regarding movement sequences and transformations are drawn from different stages of rehearsal, original production and subsequent touring productions.

Transformations (生成変化)

Be colours, be hybrids, be renewed slaves stripped of the ragged old skin and hold a new weapon.[8]

From monsters to avatars, clones to cyborgs, hybrid and transformed bodies are routinely put on display for visual consumption in contemporary culture. 'Chimaera', the opening scene from *Bye Bye*, creates a quality of space by way of Hino's transformation within it. I described this sequence in an article for the Japan Foundation:

> From the wings of the stage in Frankfurt I see Hino sitting on a stool thinly veiled in white powder and wearing a white corset and white swimming cap. She has sat for a while before the lights come up and will sit for a longer amount of time as the audience enters. An audible rumble plays under her and sidelights illuminate her lone figure in the black space. She falls forward from the stool. First slowly moving across the bare stage on all-fours then drawing herself up onto two legs, then to her toes, her arms raised and twitching in shocks and jolts, she appears to rise off the ground, phosphorescing in the pitch-black. I see Hino improvise with her senses. Although aware of the next movement in the sequence which she has practiced repetitively, I imagine that she is never certain whether that state will elude her or not, and that she is at once anxious and intensely concentrated. Each movement is more or less impulsive, as if surprising her. Gradually this anxiety gives way to an ease, a subtle confidence and eventual relief in near completion, arriving at a fluidity. I watch her progress through degrees of fixedness into a space outside subjecthood and security, into a place of flow and change. She seems to be the electrifying manifestation of thought in the dark cavity of the mind.[9]

In this instance, I see Hino's body become material 'energy' or actualities, redeveloping a consciousness undefined by a prescribed subjectivity (see figure 7.1). 'Energy' is a difficult term to define. Richard Moore's documentary *Piercing the Mask* (Sydney: AKA Productions 1992) shows performers from the *butoh* company Hakutôbô with radiating halos attached to their heads, their hands in a Buddhist *asana*. This interpretation of passivity is not the same as Kaitaisha's, nor does it depend upon the same kind of energy. Hino's transformation is a 'becoming space'; inhabiting and being inhabited rather than occupying, and informed by material complexity. The

7.1 *Bye Bye: The New Primitive*: Hino Hiruko in the scene 'Chimaera': 'the electrifying manifestation of thought'.

performer is object and subject, passive and active, going out into the body to allow space in. By not asserting an identity, the body's singularity emerges in mutable fluidity with the environment. It absorbs and exposes static systems of capture and commodification, becoming subtle in a controlled theatre environment.

In Kaitaisha, 'transformation' is a term used to articulate the progression towards becoming inhuman, something the body has not been; essences, colours, hybrids, objects, animals. Shimizu's reference is not celebratory, nor is it an expression of a core Japanese identity. It is closer to Deleuze and Guattari's notion of becoming 'inhumanity' than Schechner's universality of trance, Victor Turner's euphoric 'spontaneous *communitas*', Grotowski's 'holy body' or the culturally specific trance of religious ritual.[10] Shimizu contrasts the notion of 'becoming' to that of acting in order to describe the desired mode of transformation in Kaitaisha. He refers to Hijikata's philosophy of 'becoming something' (the object).[11] Hijikata writes, 'It is an improvisation to be born . . . many times I have been reincarnated. It is no longer enough only to be born from the womb. We will be born over and over again.'[12] In the way that Hijikata admired animals for their bodily perceptions and, in a different tradition, Artaud saw transformation as 'physiological revolution' – indeed, a 'revolution of the whole body without which nothing can be changed' – so Shimizu aims theoretically to deconstruct the 'human' body, contending that without such transformation 'we are not yet in possession of our bodies'.[13]

Shimizu regards the collective condition of the everyday 'mediated body' as trance-like. The 'human' is a double, subject to a narrative or programme that depends on and fills the body, informing its perception and unifying against possibilities of difference. In this Shimizu is informed not only by Artaud but also by Foucault's regard for the body as 'full' with representational systems – subjectivity, community, identity – imprinted by institutions of power. A pronounced valuation of individualism and a concomitant aversion to admitting personal limitations and dependencies; the repression of individuality for the sake of group harmony; the exploitation of either condition for profit – all are forces which Shimizu sees as besieging the body as part of a 'human' system. He regards the 'body as a battleground': 'everyone is digging holes in the hope of self-realization . . . but bodies will always be mediums or screens . . . power and force are the things that have been intentionally erased'.[14]

If the body is moved and constructed by this representational system of value, it follows that to 'empty' the body of these driving forces is to place them outside so they may be 'seen'. In doing so, the performer finds an opportunity to exist and move in a temporarily unidentifiable way. To see and be seen in every pore and follicle by all and everything, to be ever-present and over-exposed, all-conscious and un-self-conscious, and to fill and be filled by surrounding space – the pre-conditioned habitual form evaporates as the senses heighten. In this state, ideally the performers are able to perform with their senses; refracted, distorted, expanded or compressed, having neither origin nor telos (that which cannot be possessed). They are a 'polyphony' affecting and affected by transient media in space. The process entails the transformation or 'de-trancing' of the body from its mediated desires to a polyphonic state based on sensing.

Pack

Following the iridescent opening of Hino's scene in *Bye Bye*, the stage breaks open into a frenetic realm of shadow play. In a group choreography loosely called *mure-kehai* (群気配), a term denoting a sensation of the pack, bodies are acutely alive to space between each other (see figure 7.2). As I wrote in my journal:

> Bodies in black shorts and torn army jackets hurl themselves onto the stage. The pack moves in a mutating amorphous mass, twitching, crouching, throwing, catching, colliding into each other with the staccato of flesh meeting flesh in a phrase called 'crash'. At times it breaks into *rensa* (連鎖), a linked movement where performers respond in chain-like but relatively random reaction. Interacting with one another, we become each other, fusing if only for moments at a time, attentive to one another's movements as if we were

7.2 Group choreography: *mure-kehai* ('pack' sensation).

their own, emphasizing the material over the inter-subjective connection. Importantly, the bodies are aware, precise, unplanned, un-pressured, poised, balanced, trusting and independent.

Deleuze and Guattari refer to 'pack-like existence' as 'difference over uniformity, flows over unities, mobile arrangements over systems, seeing that what is productive is not sedentary but nomadic'. They articulate a body transformed from territorial identity into mobile anonymity, a 'becoming animal' belonging to a 'pack' whose uncivil existence undermines institutional power.[15] While Shimizu's terminology is influenced by his readings of these texts, and his production can be read as a Deleuzian 'war-machine', from the perspective of rehearsal I see the body's transformation as the removal of what Foucault describes as the 'slightest traces of (State) fascism' in the group-body.[16] The room created by the pack in this scene, along with the sound of animalistic howls, resembles a terrifying shadow-infested space. It reflects a wild, undomesticated world beyond familial, religious or State assemblages (see figure 7.3). Yet, compared to State power, it is not nearly as terrifying. The scene is interrupted:

An older man (Fueda Uichirô) intervenes in the pack's chaotic adventures, silently pushing a mirror on castors on stage, in front of which he places a live flame. Apprehending one body after another, he breaks the pack's connection. Individuated, each body disperses from the space. I am left standing facing the mirror with my back to the audience. (Author's journal)

7.3 The pack, wild and undomesticated.

Skin

Make your laws, disguise, reject, betray, destroy false consensus around diluted pleasures parasitized by all things.[17]

We have performed the alphabet sequence, described below, in the studio works leading up to this production, so no preparatory rehearsal of the following scene is necessary prior to entering the venue. Transformation takes place at the surface. (See figure 7.4.)

A man wearing an American army jacket stands with his back to the audience in front of a mirror. A flame flickers his reflection into the mirror.

From the back wall a woman wearing beige corseted underwear proceeds to walk along a narrow corridor of light lighting the centre of the stage.

The man speaks letters from the Greek alphabet, issued like bolts of electricity, and the woman begins to shake with increasing intensity as she progresses slowly along the path of light.

By the time he reaches 'omega' the woman has neared the edge of the stage and is shaking violently.

She speaks, 'Labour not, consume not, reproduce not,' and collapses to the floor. (Author's journal)

The scene typifies Kaitaisha's scenographic approach. It is constructed in rehearsal where certain movements are 'found' and text that Shimizu has written is added. The

7.4 From alpha to omega, the alphabet sequence. Adam Broinowski and Nakajima Miyuki.

movements along with the short, dense textual statements are refined to provide multiple or allegorical readings via an open, transforming body.

Nakajima is the woman. Her movement was created in rehearsal, conceptually informed by Hijikata's *butoh-fu*, and performed in 1999 in Kaitaisha's *Bye Bye: Into the Century of Degeneration* at the Setagaya Public Theatre. I am the figure speaking the alphabet. I notice that as Nakajima's shaking incrementally intensifies, her skin changes in infinitesimal gradations of colour and consistency. The evocative imagery and the ambiguity of the figures demand that an audience interprets the work in some way – although the meaning of the sequence is deliberately unfixed. Nonetheless, I spent a lot of time, mostly with Shimizu, informally discussing history and meaning with regard to Kaitaisha's work, and subsequently researching the texts that have informed his thinking. Here, then, is an observation of how the process of the body described above can be interpreted by way of its scenographic meaning. Nakajima's skin becomes the surface identity where a destabilizing conflict for territorial inscription takes place. The white male wearing a Second World War US army jacket and speaking the Greek alphabet represents the occupying culture's violence and symbolises the history of Western colonisation in Japan. At the local level, clad in the fraying garments from an old war, I could be the foreign teacher who 'enlightens' the local pupil in 'neutral' language, in the continued legacy of occupation. Logic, or physics, is the weapon/tool to humanise the Other in the victors' image. Clothed in the skin of war, the white man looks at his image speaking his own language, from the beginning to the end of 'history'. Yet the mirror occupies only a sliver of the theatre's dark space.

Box 7.3: Deconstructive scenography

Shimizu's way of thinking about scenography is exemplified by a Kaitaisha work-shop exercise for deconstructing language in the form of personal memories or narratives. In a manner similar to William Burroughs' cut-up approach to text, participants in this workshop write their stories on pieces of paper, make gestures or movements with regard to these narratives, tear up the pieces of paper and place the fragments in a pile. All the participants then read the words at the same time. In this way stories are recalled not through an identifiable narrative but through chance association. The exercise leads to specific embodiments and gives rise to multiple interpretations at any given moment.

Nakajima's corseted fragility shaking on a white highway of light is reminiscent of the famous photo, taken in 1972 by Huynh Cong Ut, of the naked girl screaming and running down the M1 highway having been drenched in napalm during the Vietnam War, and reminds us of Shimizu's interest in war photography. The staging awakens our collective memory of bodies sacrificed to a globalising free market, and suggests the white man's propensity to assimilate otherness through colonisation. That said, Japan does not lack its own history of colonial exploits (as, for example, the invasion of the Ainu land, the Ryukyus and Formosa during the Meiji era [1868-1912], and the invasion of Korea, Manchuria and China prior to the Second World War), and the Japanese body cannot be considered primitive. Yet, by internalising the language of the invader, we see Nakajima's body being cast in this 'primitive' role. In reaction, she self-destructively negates the prerequisites of survival in the imposed language. (This reading might be further developed in the light of the decreasing Japanese population and increasing suicide rate, both of which Shimizu has spoken about in post-performance talks.) Whether this is as an act of protest towards the larger nation-state, the result of the imposition of its structures, or even the consequence of collusion between states at the very apex of power is difficult to determine. Nakajima drags herself off, as if she were being dragged off, staring at the audience.

Medium (媒体)

Have no beginning, nor end, nor origin, nor telos, Have no concern with production or realization, Be barren.[18]

Another 'inhumanity' employed by Kaitaisha is 'the medium', which is regularly prac-tised by the performers in rehearsal. Formally, a 'medium' or 'prism' receives wave-forms, which it refracts and projects according to the quality of the medium itself. Where Hijikata refers to 'smoke condition' (煙状態) in the *butoh-fu*, in the movement phrase termed 'crystal discipline' (水晶) Shimizu refers to water 'passing through' the body, defining the movement quality. While the eyes 'screen' subjectivity, the body is both the subject and object of movement but not its source. This movement is at a dif-ferent speed, transforming into a different nature. Rather than a 'vessel' or container, the body becomes an opaque passageway affected by passing elements according to the body's singularity. Shimizu describes the process in *Tokyo Commands*:

> *Crystal Discipline* (水晶)
> Shoulders dropped, pulled up by the ears lengthening the back of the neck, drawn up from the pit of the stomach, knees slightly bent, feel the weight of your body sinking deep into the earth. 'Water' is sucked from the earth through the floor, into the soles of the feet, up into the legs, into the stomach, chest and shoulders flowing out through the top of the head. The 'water' draws the arm up in a straight-line in front of the body eventually raised above the head. With the quality of being passed-through, and the sensation of sinking or being drawn into the earth as you are soaring through the sky, the body moves through a number of image-forms; 'ghost', 'falling star', 'shifting sand' and 'execution'.[19]

If only for a moment, the release from the 'human' image delivers a delayed shock. What is 'de-controlled' is not only the body of the performer but the 'seeing system' of the audience. For example, when I witness this phrase in rehearsal at an early stage with the company, I respond in mild shock. As I noted in my journal: 'Kumamoto's dripping neck, his ambiguous face, translucent skin through which coloured veins pulse, the gloss of sweat-covered flesh, transform Kumamoto into a living, pulsing, sweating object. He becomes plant-like, an organism, something horrifyingly natural.'

In *Bye Bye*, crystal discipline is used as part of a scene called 'Family' (家族). Following the previous scene, the mirror is rolled off. The performers enter carrying stools and face the audience across the back of the stage in a V-formation. Kumamoto represents the salary-man, husband and father, Nakajima the office-lady, wife and mother. Both are wearing lingerie and bandages. Aota, the older daughter, is in shorts and a singlet and Ishii, the younger brother, in trousers. All garments are beige. At a given moment the nuclear family stand on the stools in unison and raise their arms as if saluting, or being saluted by, an external force. This straight, right-armed salute is potent and provocative, evoking a flat-palmed Nazi *Heil*, a hailing Mao statue, a Statue of Liberty pose or a salutary *banzai* to the Japanese Emperor when both arms are raised partway through the sequence. During the scene the lights become a star-studded constellation, at which this family-body gazes and salutes to one – or perhaps several – ideologies within a State economic system. And yet the body retains its ambiguity. The hidden particularity of each body, with its distinct experience, is drawn up through the repeating action. As the scene continues in silence, the weighty gestures gradually become absurd, then unrecognisable. We then see Kumamoto, in accordance with Shimizu's re-reading of 'the double', sensitise his body and emerge from and through concealing ideologies.

Downstage, Nomoto who is painted grey and wearing grey underwear, a Mars helmet and a tail, slowly walks across the front. I walk towards her from the other side. We meet in the downstage corner, a giant and a dwarf, our heights in stark contrast (see figure 7.5). Positioning myself at her side to face her, over a long period of time I proceed to raise my right arm and slap her on the shoulder blade. There is no other sound aside from these repeating impacts.

7.5 Moving from 'Family' to the slapping scene. Adam Broinowski walks towards Nomoto Ryôko.

I had seen a video recording of Kumamoto performing a similar scene in *Tokyo Ghetto* (1995). With little explanation in preparation for the rehearsal, however, my first slap is very tentative and produces much laughter. Shimizu tells me it sounds like I am hitting mosquitoes. Nomoto confirms that I should slap her harder. Determining that the emphasis is on sound, I find a practical way to produce the loudest noise with the least impact. As we continue, she begins to speak the names of the Japanese emperors. After this, we rehearse the scene only twice more before the performance to 'save her skin'. During the season she must ice her shoulder after every performance, although she observes that her skin becomes more resilient with repetition. As she is painted grey, each time her back is hit a plume of paint-dust rises. As I hit, the blood I spill from my mouth marks my body. At the agreed point, I stop the action, back away and say the phrase 'save our souls' (see figure 7.6). Nomoto resumes swinging her dagger and slow-marching around the stage, speaking the names of indigenous tribes, languages or peoples such as the Ainu, Chechen and Yorta Yorta, a text that she has performed in previous productions.[20] Following this:

> Hino drifts back on and towards the centre of the stage where she performs 'sea-dog' in a full-length slip of off-white lingerie. She faces the audience in this neutral mode, then suddenly begins hissing and spitting at the audience through snarling teeth. She moves forward and back as if hissing at the waves, like a dog on a beach. She points to the sky with a high-pitched whine. She then opens her mouth in a wide 'O' and her movement becomes more restricted. She falls silent. (Author's journal)

7.6 'Save our souls': the end of the slapping scene. Adam Broinowski and Nomoto Ryôko.

Hino's 'sea-dog' is another transformation. As often demonstrated during work-shops, this is based on similar principles to those of other transformations, although the intensities and movements differ according to the images informing them. 'Carrying' herself on, we see Hino then become a conflation of the sound and spray of waves breaking on a beach, a dog running back and forth at the water's edge, and the sea's limitless horizon reflected in her gaze. All performers then break into 'exile' at the end of this sequence.

Footage of the chaos rendered by carpet-bombing over Vietnam, fire-bombings of Tokyo and Okinawa and underwater detonations in the Pacific Ocean flickers across the back wall, accompanied by a rhythmic reverberation. The randomness of the pack straightens into a war apparatus of diagonal or parallel lines. As individual bodies are ordered into a fictive conglomerate, I speak Article IX from the Japanese Constitution, which starts by declaring: 'Aspiring to an international peace based on justice and order, the Japanese people forever renounce war as a sovereign right of the nation and the threat or use of force as a means of settling international disputes.' The constitution was promulgated in 1947 by SCAP (Supreme Commander of the Allied Powers), the US-led occupying administration, and at the time of writing is under government review. Its use here, then, begs questions about the status and logic of an institutionalised war-apparatus. As if rendered into statistics or propaganda, our bodies are disciplined; indistinguishable from our unit and indivisible from our nation, ready to be hurled at another such apparatus at any time. Harnessed into 'pro-ductive' force, these bodies then form three pairs across the space and perform '*gunji*'. Initially made for Kaitaisha's *De-control: Cell* (1999), this sequence explores the limits of two bodies, one that catches and restrains and one that is caught and seeks escape in a repeating series. The pairs mostly comprise combinations of male and female.

7.7 *Gunji* (holding and releasing): exploring 'the limits of two bodies, one that catches and restrains and one that is caught and seeks escape'. Hino Hiruko and Adam Broinowski.

Entwined and at times 'passing through' each other, these figures suggest the complexity and multiple meanings of the embrace (see figure 7.7).

Yet over the duration of the sequence the bodies become something else, reminiscent of Freud's case studies of soldiers in the First World War who 'after months at the front curl up and hide in deep trenches',[21] or indeed the *uluj* (the colloquial Arabic term means 'running animal' and is used to describe bodies during bombing raids). Reaching a limit, no longer able to tolerate the anxiety of their besieged senses, such bodies are shaken from the 'soldier-trance' ideals of manhood, fraternity and patriotism, from the sorts of illusions that, according to Foucault, serve to 'control, shape and valorise the individual body according to a particular system'.[22] All bodies burrow, clutch and hide in an abject state. A clump, having formed like a herd of sheep, breaks apart upon the proselytising call from my lone body on the floor. Then Kumamoto's wordless and random elegy, sung in a sustained agonistic cry, frames the event, wavers and gains in volume and tone as the shadowy bodies shrink from the stage.

Critical reception

Audience members responding to Kaitaisha's work frequently use words like 'intense', 'visceral', 'concentrated', 'absorbing', 'strong', 'weird', 'provocative', 'profound', 'beautiful' and 'ugly'. Given its references to violence and suffering, *Bye Bye* gained additional resonance by virtue of being staged around the time of the attacks on the

World Trade Center in New York and other US targets on 11 September 2001. The critic Klaus Wetzeling saw it in Hamburg and regarded it as a 'powerful theatre of war where the performers are war-machines whose bodies are battlefields', while Marga Wolffe saw the figures on stage as 'sick bodies carrying scars . . . male and female bodies that have been deeply stained by all of the century's wars'.[23] Conversely, Jack Anderson of the *New York Times* found that Kaitaisha's 'scenes of violence and terror provoked shudders . . . [but] cannot compete with real events'.[24] Referring to the attacks on the Twin Towers, two weeks after which *Bye Bye* was performed in New York City, this observation is irrefutable, and the events of 9/11 provided for a drastically different sort of representational engagement with geopolitics. Compressed into a screen and endlessly repeated as 'scenes' shown from different angles and at various speeds on media systems around the world, they made for an indisputable triumph of the real and its spectacle over any kind of theatrical representation.

Perhaps this goes some way to accounting for the New York critics' doubts about *Bye Bye*. Writing in the *Village Voice*, Alexis Soloski criticised the show for slowness ('glacial'), lack of purpose ('no organizing principle'), naivety (in presenting the message that 'war is bad'), lack of entertainment ('doesn't make for much theatre') and lack of reality ('failed to capture what war is like').[25] Despite the heady time in which they were written, both responses tend towards the assertion that theatre must somehow equal the 'real' with regard to the impact of its speed, scale and meaning on the viewer.

One sequence, 'a stretch in the play's middle', temporarily appeased Soloski: 'filmed explosions leap across the back wall, bright lights shine, actors writhe furiously, and loud electronic music assaults the ear. . . [the scene is] clear, cruel, alive'. The desire for theatre that warms the blood, however, went unsatisfied: 'if only the rest of *New Primitive* would climb up a few more steps on the evolutionary ladder', concluded this critic. In other times and places the response was different. Tokyo-based critic Nishidô Kôjin, reviewing the 1999 production *Bye Bye: Into the Century of Degeneration*, which contained elements that were reiterated in *Bye Bye: The New Primitive*, was not as perturbed by an apparent lack of thrilling spectacle and responded to the show's cultural resonances, not least in remarking upon Nakajima's 'tiny body exposed in the frontier of capitalism as the most fierce battlefield'.[26]

Opinion was also divided in relation to the slapping scene. One audience member complained of it being 'agonizing . . . seat-squirmingly nasty and dull', another saw the slapping as being 'like a heart-beat which makes any other thought irrelevant' and yet another, perhaps provocatively, spoke of the slapping scene as possessing the 'particular beauty of suicide and self-sacrifice'.[27] In each instance, fact and action are reconstructed into imagistic language that conveys fascination or revulsion in the face of pain.

Despite the reservations of some critics at Kaitaisha's refusal to engage in the ubiquitous conversion of violence into entertainment, paradoxically the full houses in New York so soon after 9/11 showed a public desire to engage with the production at this historic moment of crisis (for some audience members this was the first venture out of doors since the attacks). Many who remained in the auditorium of the Japan Society theatre for a post-performance discussion on 4 October 2001 related *Bye Bye* to the events of 9/11. One audience member asked, 'we know it's about us, but why us?' In treating the body as a confluence of cultural memory that extends beyond the personal, this production highlighted the connection of historical events with the present from a perspective not usually seen in a Western context. In Kaitaisha's works we see searingly concentrated bodies that do not represent essential truths but reflect many complexities. In *Bye Bye* and in subsequent work, Kaitaisha presents a theatre of deconstruction, founded on the highly sensitised presence of the performer.

Notes

1 I developed this line of analysis in my MA thesis, *Theatre of Body: Ankoku Butoh – Gekidan Kaitaisha* (University of Melbourne, 2003).
2 At the time of writing, the company comprises core artists Shimizu Shinjin, Hino Hiruko, Kumamoto Kenjiro, Nakajima Miyuki, Aota Reiko and Amemiya Shiro.
3 I am grateful to the members of Kaitaisha for allowing me to conduct research, and inviting me to perform and become a core member of the company. Their unconditional support, encouragement, generosity and expertise have been exemplary.
4 Tadeusz Kantor, *Wielopole, Wielopole*, trans. Mariusz Tchorek and G. M. Hyde (London and New York: Marion Boyars, 1990), p. 141.
5 This approach is distinct from when the company collaborates with international performers on a short-term basis, when those performer's personal stories are involved in the scenes. Peter Eckersall suggests that for Kaitaisha 'performance is a total reality and consuming life experience' (see Eckersall, *Theorizing the Angura Space: Avant-garde Performance and Politics in Japan 1960–2000* [Leiden: Brill, 2006], p. 164). The creations of scenes, however, do not arise from the lives of the company members *per se*, but are a creative amalgam of Shimizu's eclectic reading, current affairs, immediate context and the performers' creation of movement.
6 Translated by the author.
7 Maria Pia D'Orazi, 'Body of Light: The Way of the Butoh Performer', in Stanca Scholz-Cionca and Samuel L. Leiter (eds), *Japanese Theatre and the International Stage* (Leiden: Brill, 2000), p. 331.
8 Shimizu Shinjin, *Tokyo Commands* (unpublished 1999). *Tokyo Commands* features in several Kaitaisha productions since 1999.
9 Adam Broinowski, 'The Body in Avant-garde Theatre in Japan', *Japan Foundation Newsletter*, 29: 3–4 (April 2002), 13.
10 See Gilles Deleuze and Félix Guattari, *A Thousand Plateaus: Capitalism and Schizophrenia*, (vol. 2), trans. Brian Massumi (Minneapolis: University of Minnesota Press, 1987), p. 191; Richard Schechner, *Performance Studies: An Introduction* (London and New York: Routledge, 2002), p. 166; Victor Turner, *From Ritual to Theatre: The Human Seriousness of Play* (New York: Performing Arts Journal Publications, 1986); and Jerzy Grotowski, *Towards a Poor Theatre* (London: Methuen, 1968), p. 16.
11 Shimizu Shinjin in Gekidan Kaitaisha, *Dialogue with Otori Hidenaga and Shimizu Shinjin, Theatre of Deconstruction/Kaitaisha (1991–2001)*, trans. Maeshiba Naoko, Masuda Koji and Adam Broinowski (Tokyo: Gekidan Kaitaisha, 2001), p. 23.
12 Hijikata Tatsumi, in Asbestos-kan (ed.), *The Body on the Edge of Crisis*, trans. Adam Broinowski (Tokyo: Parco, 1987), pp. 50–1.
13 See Hijikata Tasumi, 'From the Jealousy for a Dog's Vein', in *Bibô no aozora* (美貌の青空) (*Handsome Blue Sky*) (Tokyo: Chikuma shobô, 1987), p. 35; Antonin Artaud, *Artaud*

Anthology (San Francisco: City Lights, 1965), pp. 171–3; see also Antonin Artaud, *Collected Works*, Vol. 1 (London: Calder, 1968), p. 22; Shimizu in Gekidan Kaitaisha, *Dialogue*, p. 87.

14   Shimizu in Gekidan Kaitaisha, *Dialogue*, p. 25.

15   Deleuze and Guattari *A Thousand Plateaus*, p. 233. See also Foucault on Deleuze and Guattari: Michel Foucault, *Power: Essential Works of Foucault 1954–1984* (Vol. 3), ed. Paul Rabinow (New York: The New Press, 2000), pp. 108–9.

16   Michel Foucault, *Power*, p.108. Eckersall describes Kaitaisha as 'an outlet for militant creative dissent' (*Theorizing the Angura Space*, p. 164). In person its members are adamantly peaceful. The group's objective is not reflexively to address theatre's role in social coercion but to deconstruct conditions at the site of the body, de-emphasising 'self'-expression while revealing particularities.

17   Shimizu, *Tokyo Commands*.

18   *Ibid.*

19   *Ibid.*

20   In my MA thesis (Broinowski, *Theatre of Body*, p. 55) I analyse the slapping scene used here and in *Tokyo Ghetto: Hard Core* (1995), in which it first appeared in a different context.

21   Otori and Shimizu in Gekidan Kaitaisha, *Dialogue*, p. 87.

22   Foucault, *Power*, p. 82.

23   Klaus Wetzeling, *Ballet Tanz* (October 2001), p. 49. Marga Wolffe, 'Within the Body Ruins', *Taz Hamburg* (3 September 2001).

24   Jack Anderson, 'An Experimental Work, Overwhelmed by Topicality', *New York Times* (9 October 2001).

25   Alexis Soloski, 'Bodies of Evidence', *Village Voice* (10 October 2001).

26   Nishidô Kojin, 'Bye Bye: Into the Century of Degeneration', *Theatre Arts* (June 1999), p. 118.

27   The first response is cited in Broinowski, 'The Body in Avant-garde Theatre in Japan', p. 18; the second was made during a post-performance discussion at Morishita Studios, Tokyo, June 2001; the third at the Storehouse Theatre, Tokyo, 31 January 2003.

8

Robert Lepage and Ex Machina – *Lipsynch* (2007) – Performance transformations and cycles

Aleksandar Saša Dundjerović

Robert Lepage (b. 1957) and his company Ex Machina are considered by theatre scholars and audiences alike to be amongst the leading exponents of experimental multimedia and international theatre.[1] Over the last three decades, Lepage has not only worked as a 'total theatre' author, being simultaneously actor, director and writer, he has also worked in different media – directing film, opera, installations, rock concerts and even a multi-million-dollar circus spectacle (*KÀ* for the Cirque du Soleil, 2005). His theatricality is founded on mixing live performance and multimedia, combining the actors' action on stage with visual projections (photography and film), sound and new technology (digital and robotics), creating stunning stage pictures and theatrical tricks. In 1982, Lepage joined Théâtre Repère and in 1993 he started his own company Ex Machina as a multimedia theatre group. In 1997 the company made their permanent base in a refurbished old fire station, La Caserne, in Quebec City.

Given Lepage's iconic status in international contemporary theatre and the critical acclaim his work receives, it is easy to overlook his origins which can be traced back to Quebec's collective creations in the alternative theatre milieu of the late 1970s. Lepage was not influenced by theatre but theatrical rock concerts and popular culture, mainly television and film. Though costly now, his theatre is a 'poor' theatre, driven by actors' improvisations and the necessity to overcome the obstacle of 'not having', made with whatever is available as a resource for playing – material objects, space, visual projections, live music and so on. In the 1970s, Quebec's culture of collective creation was based on a number of small theatre companies touring first locally and then nationally in search of new audiences and venues. They needed portable sets and very direct communication with a mostly non-theatre audience. This kind of theatre also implied performing outside Quebec, having to make a theatre language accessible to non-French-speaking audiences. Lepage's rehearsal process and theatrical style came as a result of overcoming these limitations of funding, language and venues.

Lepage gained recognition in the mid 1980s by going outside Canada and performing at major European theatre festivals. Lepage's theatre is a travelling one, made for international touring and the festival marketplace. It needs to communicate to global audiences who speak different languages. International festivals serve not only as the main performance venue, they are also business partners, commissioning and/or co-producing Lepage's projects. As he observes, it is due to the funding from these institutions that Ex Machina has been able to do its particular kind of touring theatre for so long.[2]

The globalisation of theatre and the presence of cosmopolitan audiences are also central to Lepage's way of making theatre; indeed, international audiences play a creative 'role' in Lepage's 'open rehearsals'. As Alison Oddey has observed, devising processes are 'able to define a relationship with an intended audience or community from the start, providing an opportunity for audience contribution or participation in the work'.[3] Lepage makes this relationship with the audience central, involving audiences (both local and global) in the developmental process of discovering the performance. The group uses the audience's presence and response in performances as open rehearsals to discover what is valuable in the devised and evolving *mise en scène*. The transformative quality of Lepage's *mise en scène* refers not only to the actor-authors' discovery of the performance in front of an audience, but also to the fact that change is visible on stage. It is a transformation of action and space that comes out of the performers' playfulness. Lepage points out that he is attracted to plays

> in which the characters are transformed, but also to plays in which the sets are transformed and matter is transcended . . . I think that if I remain fully aware of the stage as a place of physical transformation, I make it possible or can try to make it possible for the audience to really feel the direction in which the action and the characters are being hurtled.[4]

Further, Ex Machina's creative process takes up to three years and each culture to which the performances are presented (typically starting in Quebec and English Canada and progressing to the USA, Europe and Asia) leaves its imprint on the performance, influencing *mise en scène*.

This examination of Lepage's and Ex Machina's rehearsal process concentrates on the collaborative project *Lipsynch*, which opened on 19 February 2007 for six days at Northern Stage in Newcastle, England. From the beginning of the devising process in November 2005, without knowing what the story would be about, Lepage had nevertheless already decided that the final production would be nine hours long, made up of nine parts, and two to three years in development. In this chapter I look at the ways the material is devised, from working with initial resources – human voice and identity – in order to establish collaborators' individual reference points, to editing the material throughout the different cycles, and finally finding the version of the performance presented at Northern Stage. I examine Lepage's rehearsal process by looking at the three rehearsal cycles that took place over fifteen months through which four and a half hours of the first version of *Lipsynch* were developed. Lepage's

8.1 *Lipsynch's* Newcastle cycle, February 2007: Ricky Miller as Jeffrey is, as a teenager, a wannabe rock star playing guitar and singing in a rock gig. His character was central to the story for both Newcastle and Montreal cycles of *Lipsynch*, featuring in four out of Newcastle's seven parts and four out of nine in the Montreal cycle.

transformative process will continue well beyond the Newcastle cycle until the full performance is eventually invented or discovered. Once a story is 'discovered' the performance becomes fixed and is usually written down as a text. For Lepage the text is the end result – not the starting point – of the creative process; not a dramatic playtext but a recording of the performance *mise en scène*.

The company Ex Machina

Robert Lepage was trained as an actor in the Conservatoire d'art dramatique in Quebec City in a programme similar to any other major acting school based on the Stanislavskian tradition. When he finished the programme in 1978 he was among the few actors of his generation who could not get professional work in Quebec's French mainstream theatre and television industry. He was not a good student; he was rather considered by his tutors to be a 'Jack of all trades', someone who could not fully engage in realistic emotions and was always a bit detached from any scene he was doing.[5] His unusual abilities found expression when, in the summer of 1979, he attended a three-week workshop at Alain Knapp's Institut de la personnalité créatrice in Paris. Knapp's approach to the actor not as a mere interpreter but as a total

Box 8.1: The RSVP Cycles

Lepage's devising method originated from the RSVP Cycles. The Cycles were created by Anna Halprin, dancer, choreographer and director of the Dancers' Workshop in San Francisco, and her husband Lawrence Halprin, landscape architect and environmental planner. The emphasis of this method is on process (not product) and communication – the audience's response to what is presented to them. The RSVP's cyclical process can start from any one of its four parts, but usually the starting point is a resource. Resources (R) are the materials – emotional (stories) and physical (objects) – that serve as personal stimuli for the performers. As Lepage pointed out to me in interview, a resource must be relevant to the actor-author, 'an individual provocation rich in meaning' (Quebec City, December 1999). The scores (S) are a way of annotating the creative process, referring to action in space over time, and through them structure emerges. The third part is valuaction (V), a word coined to suggest a search for value in the action. It is a selection process, where various scores are synthesised based on what is valuable in them in terms of the development of future scores. The final part, 'performance' (P), refers to performing selected scores in front of others in the group and often an outside audience. Crucially, 'performance' is not a final product, it is not a performance that has to be prepared in order to become; it shows the process of becoming, it is an exploration through performing in front of someone who is there to observe.

The RSVP Cycles were redeveloped in the Repère Cycles by Jacques Lessard, who started Théâtre Repère in Quebec City. Lepage joined this company as an actor-creator in 1982. Although almost the same as the RSVP Cycles, the Repère Cycles centre on narrative development through synthesis of scores rather than on looking for images and physical actions, which are more relevant to dance theatre. In Lepage's theatre, actor-authors write their individual texts/scores from a collective starting point/resource that is embodied in a material object/space – a travel itinerary, a bridge, a wall, a parking lot covered in sand, tectonic plates, a pool of mud, a washing machine, architectural design, airports, personal diaries, and so on. Each actor brings personal material from which he or she can improvise, involving others in the group. Lepage relies on his intuition and the creative chaos he deliberately provokes to facilitate and sculpt collective discovery.

author – at once actor, writer and director – liberated Lepage's creative potential as a theatre-maker.[6]

Lepage was invited by Jacques Lessard, his former tutor from the Conservatoire, to join Théâtre Repère, an experimental theatre collective in Quebec City. In 1978, disillusioned by a lack of method in collective theatre, Lessard had gone to study with Anna Halprin in San Francisco. On his return to Quebec City, in 1979, Lessard translated and adapted Anna and Lawrence Halprin's RSVP Cycles[7] to create the Repère Cycles. Soon after Lepage joined Théâtre Repère, he became artistically responsible for directing new projects. At the centre of Lepage's creative process was a combination of the RSVP Cycles and Alain Knapp's actor-author approach.

> ### Box 8.2: Playing and accidental discovery
>
> Finding connections between various scores – disjointed segments of multiple narratives – is essential to Lepage's creative process. The material comes out of improvisations, brainstorming and free playing. Performance is discovered through coincidence and accident. Lepage believes that true creation is about not order and rigour, but the ability to invoke chaos and liberate the energy that comes from playfulness. In *Connecting Flights*, he argues, 'people want to regulate and tame the theatre. The theatre is something wild, without rules, that they want to prevent from growing naturally, organically' (p. 88).

Out of his experience with the collective Théâtre Repère, Lepage started a new company, Ex Machina. Set up as a meeting place between different arts and media, Ex Machina defines itself as 'a multidisciplinary company bringing together actors, writers, set designers, technicians, opera singers, puppeteers, computer graphic designers, video artists, film producers, contortionists and musicians',[8] as well as costume designers and computer animation experts. Ex Machina is intended to be a playground for all these collaborators to create through improvisation. Made up at first of former members of Théâtre Repère (including Marie Gignac and Michel Bernatchez amongst others), Ex Machina does not have a permanent ensemble; rather, there is a core group of collaborators who can come in or out of the long rehearsal–performance process. The company is mainly organised as a 'family' business: Lepage is artistic director; his sister Lynda Beaulieu is his personal agent at the core of operations; and Michel Bernatchez works as producer for Ex Machina as a company. In this way, Lepage has independence from Ex Machina to take on his own directing or solo projects while Ex Machina remains committed to his particular style of devising.

Lepage explains that Ex Machina aims to start work outside of the main centres, 'to move creative activity away from the production activities. Ex Machina is trying to find a way so that people can plug into different currents, modes, fashions, and trends: we want to be connected with what goes on in the world . . . That's why we wanted to be a company, and a space eventually, where people pass through.'[9] The objective is to separate the creative process from the market-oriented production process and its financial interests, which tend to put pressure on time and overshadow the artists' interests. The company's base, La Caserne, is a laboratory, offering an environment for exploration and serving as the meeting place for diverse arts, multiple media, and artists from around the world.[10]

The project

In 2003 John Cobb and Sarah Kemp, actors and artistic directors of the small UK touring company Théâtre Sans Frontières, visited Lepage in La Caserne. The idea to explore the relationship between voice and human memory was originally suggested to Lepage by Cobb, who had previously collaborated with Lepage in the 1989 production of *Tectonic Plates* and the infamous 1992 production of *A Midsummer Night's Dream* for the Royal National Theatre in London. This idea coincided with Lepage's own fascination with the human voice and his desire to use sound rather than visual images as a creative stimulus. After a few years of discussions involving Marie Gignac, Lepage's collaborator of more than twenty years, Lepage took on the project and extended the reach of its European collaboration. The project was joined by international collaborators from Spain (Carlos Belda, artistic director of the Teatro Tamaska in Tenerife, and the performer Nuria García); as well as by German actor Hans Piesbergen, who worked with Lepage in the 1993 Munich National Theatre Production *Map of Dreams*, based on a collage of Shakespearean texts. This group joined Ex Machina's actor-creators Frédérike Bédard, Rebecca Blankenship, Rick Miller and Lisa Castonguay, who all had experience of Lepage's creative process, having worked with him on a number of projects over the previous twenty years.

The company embarked on exploring the relationship between voice, speech and language, using four languages of performance: English, French, Spanish and German. The first phase began with a preliminary two-week rehearsal in late November 2005 at La Caserne. The subsequent rehearsal phases of three weeks each took place in March and October 2006. After each rehearsal cycle is completed, there is an open rehearsal with an invited audience who give feedback. The last three-week rehearsal cycle took place in Newcastle before the production officially opened, testing the production in English for an audience outside Quebec. By launching in a smaller venue in a city that is not a theatre centre, and by openly considering the performance as a work-in-progress, Lepage produces a much safer context for experimentation, controlling the audience's and critics' gradual access to performance. After Newcastle, *Lipsynch* went to Tenerife, where the performance was reworked and tested in front of a Spanish-speaking audience, before returning to La Caserne, where a new cycle was developed for Montreal's Festival de Trans Amériques in June 2007. This new cycle was five and a half hours long and made up of seven parts that lasted approximately forty-five minutes each, but there was an indication that two more parts were still to be developed. Even after two years of rehearsal development, the show was still raw and in fragments and did not reach its final developmental stage until the end of 2008.

Despite the ambition of initial plans for the project, little was defined before the Newcastle cycle; venues were guarded by the production team, touring plans depended on the process, and it was clearly indicated that Lepage was showing a work-in-progress. In the past, when showing at major international festivals while still in the early developmental phase, it had not been possible for Lepage and Ex Machina to manage the critics, who expect a finished product. All throughout 2007, the performances of *Lipsynch* were intended to be work-in-progress showings of the cycles, never a finished production. At the time of writing this chapter there were no official tours announced, and future plans for the production are kept secret. However, Marie Brassard (now in charge of dramaturgy on the performance) indicates that the plan is for the group to reconvene in December 2007 in Quebec City and re-work *Lipsynch* for the 2008 version, to achieve the full development of the nine parts, and to start a

8.2 Newcastle cycle: dubbing in a sound recording studio where a character, originally developed by Marie Gignac, is trying to find a voice for her father on a silent film. After a number of characters audition unsuccessfully for the voiceover part, Gignac accidentally discovers that her own voice when put through a synthesiser sounds just like her father's as she remembers it.

tour in 2008 with a scheduled possible opening in September 2008 at the Barbican in London.[11] (Ed. Note: the production did tour to London's Barbican in September 2008, then toured globally in 2008 and 2009, with touring scheduled into 2010.)

Lepage points out that he uses language as music and that Ex Machina has previously focused on 'telling stories using images, movement, space and music. Voice was rather an afterthought.'[12] However, using human voice, language and sound as a creative provocation for devising performance has been relevant to Lepage's theatricality for some time. His longstanding involvement with directing opera, and devised projects such as *Zulu Time* (2000) and *The Busker's Opera* (2003), point to his experimentation with voice and sound. The working title *Lipsynch* is a technical term used in film for voiceover, when the original actor's voice is dubbed using someone else's voice. This is a technique commonly used when translating films from a foreign language; it is also used in animations and documentaries. In a key scene in *Lipsynch* the actor-author Marie Gignac tries to find a voice for her father on homemade silent 16mm films (see figure 8.2). In the Newcastle cycle, Gignac became dramaturg of the project, overseeing connections of scores and further development of the performance narrative.

In *Lipsynch,* Lepage uses human voice and sound to explore memory and identity. His actor-creators play with voiceover, karaoke, synthetic language and computer-generated voice as metaphors for being removed from one's own identity and as tools for remembering. The themes of disempowerment through not having one's own voice, and empowerment through inflicting a voice on other people, are ones Lepage and the Quebec collaborators can relate to personally because the politics of language are closely related to Quebec's national identity. The province of Quebec has nine million francophone speakers, requiring all non-French language films for cinema and television to be dubbed into French. (Lepage points out that providing voiceovers is the biggest source of income for Quebec's actors.)[13] Protectionism of language is seen as an important aspect of Quebec's sovereignty. Lepage's theatricality was a response to the often claustrophobic cultural politics of Quebec in the 1970s and 1980s. He points out that 'Québeckers have that need to be understood, and to have access to the market, to be invited all over the world so that people follow you and don't say "Oh, it's not in English I don't want to see it." You have to do this extra effort to get the story clear, to illustrate it, to give another layer to it.'[14] This need to translate and the urgency to be understood forced theatre authors in Quebec to invent a theatricality, founded on visual images and the body, which was able to communicate beyond the constraints of localism and verbal language. Playing with language and using it as an element of theatrical expression – not only as a vehicle for meaning – is part of Lepage's signature. As Jeanne Bovet observes,

> In Lepage's plays, multilingual conversations are marred by misunderstandings and prove incapable of ensuring real communication. They are progressively and successfully replaced by other non-verbal languages: the language of the body and the language of art, which ultimately merge to allow not only communication but true communication between human beings in an altogether sensorial and spiritual process.[15]

Lepage's use of language also responds to his personal, family experience. He grew up in a bilingual family which was profoundly different from other 'typical' Quebecois households in 1950s-1960s Quebec City, where national identity was overwhelmingly defined as French, Catholic and white. Lepage's parents were initially unable to have children so they adopted two English-speaking children from English Canada. Some years after the adoption, Robert and Lynda were born. The household was a mixture of English and French.

The politics of language in *Lipsynch* respond to the tensions of communication in a multilingual context. Starting the devising process from the human voice opens up various other questions, concerns and provocations that each performer/writer can respond to by doing independent research and bringing in personal material. For Lepage the voice is 'the DNA of the soul, the unexplainable source of our being'.[16] For Scottish performer John Cobb, the provocation was in the relation of the human voice to memory, working from the audio recordings of elderly people remembering their lives. Miller had a personal dream of becoming a rock singer. Gignac was concerned with how the human voice – in particular, her father's – can be reproduced. Piesbergen came up with a computer voice for physicist Stephen Hawking. Each performer/writer engaged with his or her personal reference point that was in some way questioning the role of the human voice. Can the voice show who we really are? Is speech the same as voice? What is the relationship between memory and the human voice? This wide spectrum of starting points is personal and deliberately abstract, modelled through the performers' subjectivities and continuously shaped and crafted throughout different cycles of performance development.

The process

Lepage's rehearsals are in process, transforming through time, with fluid outcomes. Firstly, his rehearsal process is about actor-authors playing and improvising in space, with performances written on stage in front of an audience (what Roger Planchon calls *écriture scénique*).[17] Secondly, this work-in-progress develops through cycles, with the end performance of one cycle becoming the beginning resource for a new cycle. Finally, Lepage's theatre productions develop over years from a vast amount of improvised material that is constantly rehearsed/performed and in process with continuous feedback between actor-creators and the audience, following the pattern of the RSVP Cycles.

Lepage likes to sees his role not as a director in the traditional sense, but as a facilitator for actors to find their own texts, helping them to discover what is hidden and internal, and how to project it outside into the theatre space, establishing a response in the audience. Blankenship points out that what is important about this process of performing 'is that it is about persons who think about what they say, it is about a thought process behind the action and not only interpretation or application of acting technique'.[18] In the programme for his solo show *The Far Side of the Moon*, Lepage explains his role as a

> stage author, understanding the mise-en-scene as a way of writing. For example, in this work, the ideas from the mise-en-scene alternate with the actors' lines, one leads to the other ... What fascinates me about the act of creation is that you fill a space with objects that have no relation to each other, and because they are there, 'all piled up in the same box', there is a secret logic, a way of organising them. Each piece of the puzzle ends up finding its place.[19]

Lepage's rehearsal process begins from a personal reference point as a starting resource; in *Lipsynch*, the relation between voice and identity. Lepage stresses that sound is very important as a source of visual imagery, and that for him the radio is the 'real medium of the image because the listeners have to create their own pictures'.[20] The November 2005 and March 2006 first creative cycles in Quebec City started with each actor-author bringing individual material – their own reference points – into rehearsals and responding to these as a departure point for devising. The first cycle is usually characterised by long periods of individual and group research and free improvisation work. As though performers are working on solo shows, each brings a starting resource for discussions and collective group exploration.

Marie Gignac's personal reference point was to reconstruct her father's voice by dubbing silent family film reels. The group watched hours of homemade films that

8.3 The end of part one: Nuria García as Lupe (who has died during the flight) walks on top of the aeroplane.

Gignac brought in, brainstorming and playing with film dubbing as a group resource. Opera singer and actor Rebecca Blankenship started from her own voice as a personal resource and brought in a part of Gorecki's third symphony that she wanted to sing. Lepage liked this idea and wanted her to use the whole of the symphony throughout her part. Originally, Lepage made a drawing of an aeroplane showing a baby crying at the back and an opera singer at the front. This image made it to the Newcastle production where the whole first part was devised specifically around this image of an opera singer and a baby, with Blankenship's voice representing the cultured human voice in binary opposition to a baby's crying. Between these two extremes there were different versions of the human voice and sound, including technical manipulations of the human voice through recording, speech impediment, voiceover and computer-generation. Each of the seven parts performed in Newcastle had as its central theme one aspect of the human voice. Blankenship points out that 'this process is about finding out what you are passionate about and what empowers you. You start digging more and more, finding out new material, because the performer is personally interested in the subject and has the confidence to write their own lines.'[21] Two other members of the company, Kemp and Cobb, brought audiotapes of people remembering their past in different languages, looking for a link between voice and memory. Belda introduced the tape recording announcing the death of his father to his small town in Tenerife and inviting people to the funeral.

In addition to the starting resources, the rehearsal process is also defined by a set of self-imposed limitations. The overall structure of *Lipsynch* is not founded in the narrative but, like dance or performance art, relies on a combination of fixed and variable structures, where a few given elements are used to frame the flexible elements. The fixed structures include using nine actors to develop nine parts, with each actor creating a 'film reel' lasting one hour – making *Lipsynch* as a whole nine hours long. From the beginning, the lasting connecting element was to use four languages simultaneously, running parallel throughout the performance, deliberately dislocating language from the notion of cultural or national identity. Although chaos is important for Lepage's creative process, it is necessary to have a frame that can galvanise the creative potential, and keeps the chaos from exploding and becoming destructive.

Lepage does not believe in the boundaries and roles that separate artists in conventional theatre. Very often he shifts between being actor and director within the same production. This fluidity and deliberate resistance to committing to any single structure at the beginning of the process is hard to follow if one expects Lepage's theatre to build conventionally towards a final product. But the absence of structure and order is deliberate for Lepage. He explains: 'I believe that the only real invention comes out of chaos, so it is better not to know who you are, where you are when you start off if you want to accomplish something good.'[22] A typical frustration for the performers (resulting from what could be seen as Lepage's chaotic approach) is that conditions of uncertainty and lack of control over devised material often lead to the cancellation of productions, or frantic reworking before opening. For example, although *Elsinore* did open at the 1996 Edinburgh International Festival, Lepage subsequently stopped its run there, citing technical difficulties.

The idea that the creative process begins from chaos is not original to Lepage; it is a defining characteristic of most contemporary performance. In this context, chaos has both a stimulating and liberating role as well as problematic implications. As Blankenship observes, the work with Lepage can be both therapeutic and disturbing for performers, but it does allow space to investigate personal questions and to explore what draws individual performers to a particular theme.[23] This can be a volatile environment to work in, since the very personal becomes very public, and often material that may have been painfully introduced and worked on has to be abandoned. Although actors are asked to be authors, they do not have 'ownership' of the material. It is a collective work but Lepage is the one who assembles devised scores together and finds connections. More often than not, actors are immersed in the material and are lost in this process, unsure if what they are creating will make sense. For example, in the Newcastle cycle, the last part of *Lipsynch*, 'Elizabeth', was devised in forty-eight hours just before opening night. It was necessary to provide a unifying narrative framework for all the different parts in this cycle.

Lepage encourages performers to be spontaneous and to be aware of their immediate performance environment without thinking about the end result. Keeping an open mind, allowing the work to lead you and being ready to abandon ideas and accept new ones as they emerge is very important to this practice. Lepage points out that 'Theatre is an adventure that's bigger than we are; an adventure which we embark on with many questions, but virtually no answers.'[24] The performer has to eliminate self-imposed obstacles, break away from the idea that the work produced has to be consistently good, and accept that performance is a personal exploration where

Box 8.3: Open rehearsals

Open rehearsals are fundamental to Lepage's devising process and are about rehearsing while performing in front of an audience. His group starts from often ambiguous ideas that are translated into theatre through resources with which performers play and interact in order to communicate with the audience. It is in the process of communicating with audiences that actors discover what their performance is about. In the early cycles, unstructured and loose performance material is shown to the audience, using their feedback to help the performers shape the future process and discovery of a performance narrative. Lepage learned how to create in front of an audience while doing free improvisations for La Ligue Nationale D'improvisation (LNI) where he won an award in 1984 as rookie of the year. In the LNI's improvisation sessions, interaction with and transformation in front of the audience were crucial for shaping the process according to audience response.

mistakes are a vital element of learning. Although his final results are very structured and accomplished, Lepage refuses to work for the end result. He embraces the unknown, unpredictable and unstable. This leads to spontaneous creativity, emphasising liveness and connectivity with the audience.

Because the work is very subjective it is important to introduce the 'outside eye' to help shape the discovered material. Open rehearsals are positioned at the end of each cycle, and take place in front of an audience who is invited to observe the process. *Lipsynch's* March 2006 cycle had an open rehearsal where six hours of improvised material were shown to the audience. In October 2006, only two hours of that material were used as a starting point to devise the new cycle in a three-week rehearsal. By the time of the open rehearsal at the end of the October 2006 cycle, the group had so much material that, after seven hours of performing, one of the stage managers had to stop the show at 1 am because the invited audience had to go home.

Lepage believes that theatre is a meeting place, a venue for the integration of various art forms: 'you are a better director or actor if you are involved in writing, in poetry, lighting, if you are interested in architecture'.[25] His theatricality reinforces the idealised Renaissance concept of art, and the difficulty of differentiating between artist, engineer and architect. In La Caserne, Lepage uses both actors and engineers from his technical team to devise performance. Throughout the creative process actors and technicians are involved in the devising process so that action, scenographic space and technology evolve simultaneously. Members of Ex Machina's vast design, technical and production team collaborate on its shows but also work as independent artists, often running with their own companies and operating from the facilities in La Caserne. The *Lipsynch* production team is made up of longstanding collaborators, including Jacques Colin (visual images), Jean-Sébastien Côté (sound designer), Louise Roussel (production director) and Jean Hazel who is stage designing for Lepage for the first time but had worked as part of the technical team of *Polygraph* (1987) and *Tectonic Plates* (1988). Both actors and technicians are familiar with the evolutionary

8.4 Newcastle cycle: Nuria García.

nature of Lepage's work and the work schedule is arranged to accommodate the transformative nature of the creative process.

During the three-week rehearsal period in Newcastle, the whole team of collaborators works very intensely for up to twelve hours a day. The rehearsal day is divided
into three sections: the morning (10 am–2 pm), afternoon (2–6 pm) and evenings
(6–10 pm). In the morning, the rehearsal process starts with the technical team
working together with actors, not only as support, but bringing also their own ideas.
The computers are connected and video projectors are set up, ready to be used at a
moment's notice in order to explore ideas coming out of the rehearsal process. In the
afternoon, between rehearsal sessions with actors, the technical team comes up with
solutions for ideas discussed or explored during the morning session. In the evening,
the performers improvise with media and technology that will again be reworked as
the rehearsals develop.

In the March 2006 cycle the company set up an improvisation session in a
film voiceover studio, which came out of Gignac's personal resource. The technical
team transformed the whole of La Caserne's studio space into a film studio by using
cameras, projections and equipment. The performers then collectively played and
improvised with different aspects of voiceover work. Out of this resource, the whole
game of how to do dubbing was devised. The group of actors had to master dubbing
techniques and incorporate voiceover into the performance. Blankenship observes
that 'although this game was lots of fun for the group it was actually quite difficult to
learn how to match sound to the movement of the lips, but we played with lipsynch
doing voices for different characters from cartoon to popular films'.[26]

The group would sit around the table in the studio and listen to audiotapes, discussing issues such as how much of a person's character is conveyed through voice. Some actors would find a character from the tapes inspirational, do an improvisation about it or use the text, incorporating it into their own performance scores. Gignac's films and search for her father's voice became central to this cycle and played a key part in its open rehearsal. Subsequently, these scores influenced other parts of the performance and became a resource for other material developed for the October 2006 cycle. Both 2006 cycles emphasised developing scores from the starting resource of the human voice. Between cycles, performance research and work on characters continued; since actors are writers, the material develops with them and the creative process continues outside of group rehearsal time.

The extent to which cohesiveness and narrative structure is achieved is down to the third part of the cycle – the valuaction or synthesis phase. 'Valuaction' means looking for a value in action (in terms of its theatrical potential) and is fundamentally about editing scores together. In this period of rehearsals, the group members show improvisations to each other, discuss and look for dramaturgical connections. The audience's input to this stage is essential since Lepage is trying to find a story that will hold the production together. Lepage and the group use a storyboard throughout the creative process; however, in this phase it is used extensively to find the recurring themes and emerging dramaturgical connections between various scores.

The final part of the RSVP Cycles is the 'Performance' or representation phase where all the material is put together in front of an audience. It is where the narrative is found and the scores are connected. Performance is about doing a synthesised score publicly. It is important for the actors/writers as a way of finding out for themselves how the material that has been devised communicates and connects with the audience.

In Lepage's rehearsal process, there are long intervals between short, intense cycles. This requires strong commitment and focus from the actors. Being involved in a performance that is rehearsed over long periods of time requires actors to arrange their schedules and other commitments around rehearsal and performance dates with Lepage (and performers are only paid during rehearsals and performance dates). This can prove to be very strenuous and performers often leave the project at some phase in order to return to it later. Gignac was partially involved in the October 2006 rehearsal cycle, remaining as a script consultant on the project, and she was expected to come back to perform for the 2008 version. For the intervening cycles she was replaced by Frédérike Bédard, who worked with Lepage in *The Busker's Opera*. Bédard took Gignac's performance text as her own resource and developed it further for the cycle in February 2007. In the open rehearsal on 21 October 2006, Gignac's section of the performance remained the same as in March 2006, with everything else being transformed and developed in between the two cycles. Blankenship explains that, in the October 2006 cycle, the performance became 'like a web of interconnections between different personal material'.[27] She likened this process to a pot-luck dinner where individuals bring their own food and share it collectively.

8.5 Newcastle cycle: Nuria García as Lupe, dancing as a prostitute in a window in front of a faceless customer in Reepabahn, Hamburg.

Criticism and the audience

The audience's response as feedback that influences further exploration and development of the performance has an essential place in Lepage's creative process. However, the demands of the theatre industry for a final product that can be sold to an audience produce tension in relation to Lepage's approach to performance development. This point of tension relates to the critics' general complaint in the past that Lepage's performances are unfinished, often banal, and the storytelling amounts to a set of clichés taken from 'soap operas'. Lepage often justifies his work by arguing that his performances are not 'ready', meaning they are not in the right cycle and therefore not ready to be presented to audiences or critics expecting to see a finished product. Such tensions between open process and finished production were visible in the development of *The Seven Streams of the River Ota* in 1994 at the Edinburgh International Festival and *The Geometry of Miracles* in 1998 at the Du Maurier World Stage Festival in Toronto. Lepage has responded to these tensions by cancelling *Elsinore* in 1996 at the Edinburgh International Festival, banning some critics from productions (particularly Montreal critics), and making efforts to open productions as works-in-progress in places where there will not be mainstream critics (*Lipsynch* in Newcastle).

Managing the audience and critics is a necessary part of Lepage's work-in-process approach, making sure that there is an open rehearsal at the end of each cycle, but also ensuring that bad publicity does not damage the production's future development. Although Lepage would like to keep his laboratory approach, with controlled-access open rehearsals, financial restrictions define how far this can be taken. His producers and co-producers need to sell tickets. They must have the product by a certain time, show it to audiences and justify their fiscal year to sponsors. The more money spent on a production, the bigger the pressure to meet the deadline by which an end result must be produced. Therefore, the Newcastle version did not have a press night and was marketed as an opportunity for the audience to be part of the development of the performance. At the same time, audiences were charged £28 for tickets and the word 'work-in-progress' was not used in the promotional material. As Northern Stage's artistic director Erica Whyman pointed out, the idea was for the audience not to think that they were watching something unprofessional and incomplete, but to be aware that they were witnessing a process of creation where work was being shown to an (implicitly privileged) audience for the first time.[28]

But the main objective of the Newcastle rehearsals was to prepare the performance for a new audience in England. The company sought, from the various scores developed, the strongest emerging connections that could form a narrative throughline; for the Newcastle cycle, this was the story loosely centred on a musician and his biological parents, his adopted parents and the lives of people connected to them. However, though this broad outline was agreed, the company's thinking about how best to order its narration evolved even between late rehearsals (when the programme went to press) and the first performance. The programme published on Friday had already changed for Monday's opening. The programme listed the parts of *Lipsynch* using the names of characters that are central to the story in each part: 'Part 1 Ada, Part 2 Sebastian, Part 3 Jeremy, Part 4 Thomas, Part 5 Marie, Part 6 Lupe, Part 7 Elizabeth.'[29] However, on the first night, Thomas and Sebastian's parts were transposed in a run which started at 6 pm and finished around 11.30 pm, with two intervals.

The narrative connections established for Newcastle did not exist in Quebec City's October 2006 open rehearsal and were made prior to the Newcastle cycle. The

8.6 Newcastle cycle: Nuria García with projected images of a nude female body being touched by a number of hands representing sex trafficking.

narrative does not develop in sequence but focuses on fragments which are only linked together at the end of the cycle. It is also clear that the overall story is invented to pull together different parts, each with their own narrative. Structured overall like a musical video, each piece is independent. The stories told are full of television clichés and melodramatic and deliberately ironic moments that reflect on a fast and postmodern world where lives are globally interconnected. The composition period in Newcastle was also marked by extensive technical alterations. The production had very slow and laborious set changes, some of them lasting a few minutes and with a group of technicians (from Northern Stage, supervised by Ex Machina's production director and stage manager) openly setting up and even fixing loose parts in the movable set in front of the audience. For the Montreal cycle in June 2007, the technical aspects were further developed and scene changes were incorporated in the fictional *mise en scène*, making fragmented scores a part of the performance. In a typically Lepagean way, everything on stage became part of the spatial kinetics, where one event transformed into another. Despite the Newcastle performance's duration of almost five and a half hours (including intermissions), suspensions during set changes, and the undeveloped storyline, the performance was very engaging and immediately involved its audience in its world.

As with other Lepage work-in-progress performances the Newcastle audience were given comment cards during the interval. The cards explained the transformative and developmental nature of Lepage's production, stating that the final version of *Lipsynch* would develop over an eighteen-month period. The audience were asked to write comments on 'what you enjoyed, what confused you and any other comments you have about the show'.[30] These were the only UK performances in this

8.7 Montreal cycle, June 2007: this score in Montreal is the same as previously in Newcastle, however the relation between mother and adopted son has been textually developed from indication (illustration) to actualisation.

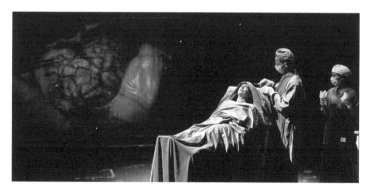

8.8 Montreal cycle: this scene was developed for Montreal, adding images of a brain being operated on into an existing score from Newcastle which had focused on the patient's examination before the operation.

phase, and the audience were told that they were part of the process of shaping the next phase.

In exposing the audience to a work-in-progress, Lepage builds spectators' interpretation and criticism into the devising process. By opening process to the audience, their feedback shapes the future narrative. Lepage's creative process exposes the audience to the unseen network of rehearsal exploration, opening up the process and allows the audience to see the making of art by people energised by discovery in front of the audience in that very moment. Lepage has compared his company's 'evolving artistic process to the image of a tree. The audience only sees the trunk, bark, branches and leaves. But the artist should be preoccupied by the growth happening underground, in that unseen network of roots digging erratically yet so expertly that it can hold, sustain and nurture the whole tree.'[31]

It is often implied that Lepage's theatricality is in a perpetual process of transition. Transformation and improvisations are ways of devising narratives, but once the performance is dramaturgically connected and the narrative is discovered the performance becomes fixed and stops evolving. However, it may take up to three years for the performance to develop and the audience is a necessary part of this process. As a result, there are tensions and conflicts between Lepage's process and his product, which needs to meet the criteria of a festival-ready performance. Lepage's theatre is improvisation theatre at its best, where live action is combined with media technology to create a distinct visual language, where the text does not pre-exist the process of development and the way it is performed results from the performers' immediate experience – depending on location, audience and, most importantly, the actors' personal material. But changes through time and different cultures also mean that the performance is unfixed, with actors often coming in and out of the project. The process is fluid and deliberately chaotic. The makers follow unknown directions through intuition and spontaneity, using elaborate media technology. Despite the emphasis on technological and digital apparatus, two simple principles are at the core of Lepage's work – the flexibility of improvisational theatre in the tradition of commedia dell'arte, and communication with audiences as in epic storytelling. It is a theatre that celebrates the moment of creation, liveness and performativity.

Notes

1 Although based in Quebec City, Lepage received the prestigious Prix Europe Award for Theatre in 2007 for his contribution to European theatre over the two previous decades. His extensive touring of European festivals and cultural venues was cited as a reason for the award.
2 Robert Lepage, interview by author, Quebec City, July 2005.
3 Alison Oddey, *Devising Theatre: A Practical and Theoretical Handbook* (London: Routledge, 1994), p. 20.
4 Robert Lepage and Remy Charest, *Connecting Flights*, trans. Wanda Romer Taylor (London: Methuen, 1998), p. 135.
5 Lepage, interview by author, Quebec City, January 2002.
6 For more on Knapp, see Josette Féral, 'Pour une autre pédagogie du théâtre: entretien avec Alain Knapp', *Jeu* 63 (1992): 56.
7 See Lawrence Halprin, *The RSVP Cycles: Creative Processes in the Human Environment* (New York: George Braziller, 1968).
8 Ex Machina website, www.exmachina.qc.ca/ENGLISH/ex.asp?page=Machina (accessed 17 February 2007).
9 Allison McAlpine, 'Robert Lepage', in Maria M. Delgado and Paul Heritage (eds), *In Contact with the Gods? Directors Talk Theatre* (Manchester: Manchester University Press, 1996), p. 154.

10 La Caserne serves as a rehearsal studio as well as a recording facility for video, film and sound. For example, the company shot most of the film *Nô* (1998) in this generic space, converting the whole building into a film studio. For *Lipsynch* the space was converted into a recording studio and film set location.

11 This is according to one of Lepage's close collaborators who did not want to be identified because of uncertainty where the production will go next.

12 Robert Lepage, Foreword to *Lipsynch* theatre programme, Northern Stage, Newcastle (19–24 February 2007).

13 Lepage, interview by author, July 2005.

14 McAlpine, 'Robert Lepage', pp. 150–1.

15 Jeanne Bovet, 'Identity and Universality: Multilingualism in Robert Lepage's Theatre', in Joseph I. Donohoe and Jane M. Koustas (eds), *Theater sans Frontières: Essays on the Dramatic Universe of Robert Lepage* (East Lansing: Michigan State University Press, 2000), p. 4.

16 Lyn Gardner, 'Mission Impossible', *Guardian* (UK) (19 February 2007), G2 p. 26.

17 David Bradby and Annie Sparks, *Mise en Scène: French Theatre Now* (London: Methuen, 1997), p. 41.

18 Rebecca Blankenship, interview by author, London, October 2006.

19 Lepage, theatre programme for *The Far Side of The Moon*, Royal National Theatre, London (July 2001).

20 Lepage and Charest, *Connecting Flights*, p. 126.

21 Blankenship, interview by author, October 2006.

22 Robert Lepage, interview by John Tusa, BBC Radio 3 (no date), available at www.bbc.co.uk/radio3/johntusainterview/lepage_transcript.shtml (accessed 11 September 2006).

23 Blankenship, interview by author, October 2006.

24 Lepage and Charest, *Connecting Flights*, p. 25.

25 Lepage, interview by author, January 2002.

26 Blankenship, interview by author, London, October 2006.

27 *Ibid.*

28 Erica Whyman in conversation with Robert Lepage, Northern Stage, Newcastle, 20 February 2007.

29 *Lipsynch* theatre programme, Northern Stage, Newcastle (February 2007).

30 *Lipsynch,* handout card, Northern Stage, Newcastle (February 2007).

31 Robert Lepage, *Lipsynch* theatre programme, Northern Stage, Newcastle (February 2007).

9

Richard Maxwell and the New York City Players
– *The End of Reality* (2006) – Exploring acting[1]

Sarah Gorman

The work of Richard Maxwell and the New York City Players (NYCP) is intriguing for its continued engagement with, and questioning of, theatrical realism. *The End of Reality*, one of two plays produced by the company in 2006, is particularly fascinating as it provides an opportunity to study Maxwell's preoccupation with capturing authentic North American dialogue alongside an apparent desire to experiment with new approaches to directing. This chapter is largely concerned with Maxwell's approach to acting, as his interventions into realistic modes of performance are one of the most striking, and often cited, aspects of his methodology. His approach to acting challenges the enduring dominance of Method-based acting in North American theatre training. By inviting his actors to approach acting as a task, rather than an invitation to draw upon internalised psychology, Maxwell foregrounds normalised assumptions about the relevance and efficacy of Method acting on the contemporary Western stage. By repeatedly altering the *mise en scène*, Maxwell creates a working environment that forces his actors to achieve – rather than imagine – spontaneity. In so doing, Maxwell indicates how the illusion of self-assurance and competence afforded by Method training can be seen to reinforce the putatively self-evident success and universality of the humanist subject. By casting actors unschooled in the Method approach and by inviting accomplished actors to reveal their shortcomings as performers, Maxwell draws attention to the system of training and labour which is required to uphold this illusion. Maxwell's textual concern for working-class characters in particular is reinforced formally through his interrogation of Method acting which demonstrates that this form of acting is not natural, but rather learned, through privilege.

Richard Maxwell founded the NYCP in 1996 to continue the experimental theatre work he had jointly produced with Cook County Theater Department in Chicago. His work has been received with critical acclaim on an international scale; the company was invited to perform as part of the Venice Biennale's thirty-seventh theatre festival (2005) and has received two Obies, for *House* (in 1999) and *Good Samaritans* (2005). Despite the popular reception and critical acclaim of his work Maxwell is reluctant to regard his directorial approach as established. He has stated that *The End of Reality* represents something of a departure in style; for example, he did away with the ballads of his previous pieces and invited his long-term collaborators to rethink their relationship to Method acting.[2]

Although Maxwell's approach is constantly changing, many of his productions continue to reveal an ambivalent relationship to theatrical realism. In contrast to much contemporary experimental theatre, Maxwell's theatre is peopled by characters who are psychologically complex and much of the on stage action is relayed through verbal interaction. Dialogue is well observed, inflected through a range of North American vernaculars. Terms such as 'dude' and 'whaddya think?' punctuate the speeches. Maxwell is concerned with storytelling, the structure of his work is predominantly linear and the plotlines work towards resolution. However, many of his plays can also be understood as 'musicals'; several of his plays feature narrative interruptions by earnest folk ballads. *House* (1998), for example, included four musical interludes and *Showy Lady Slipper* (1999), five. Consequently Maxwell's work is difficult to categorise: it incorporates aspects of both experimental and realist theatre. Spectators accustomed to the uninterrupted flow of a linear realist narrative may be surprised by the seemingly clumsy incorporation of fight sequences or songs; whilst those familiar with experimental theatre may be similarly surprised to see performers remaining in role for the duration of the performance. This tension between forms achieves a distancing effect, making the accepted contrivances, or conventional practices, of either form appear strange.

What is original and intriguing about Maxwell's work is its focus on a deliberate roughness or lack of finesse in some of the performances. For example, actors often appear to have difficulty suppressing the physiological signs of their nerves or find it difficult to forget their surroundings in order to immerse themselves in the world of the play. These lapses, however, do not appear so deliberate or consistent as to suggest that Maxwell is setting out to explore an aesthetics of failure. Furthermore, the lack of polish found in some performances actually succeeds in adding a dimension of believability to the characterisation. For me, these moments create a sense of uncertainty about the intentions of the director, and so present an intriguing and enjoyable dilemma.

Maxwell's work has consistently provoked interest because of this unusual mode of acting. Critics have described the actors' intonation as 'deadpan' (as detailed later in this chapter), but Maxwell feels it is more accurately described in terms of relieving the actors of the 'burden of emoting', an invitation which allows them to respond to the immediacy of the theatrical 'now'. For example, the actors avoid conventional patterns of conversational emphasis in favour of a more idiosyncratic rhythm; they frequently inflect the ends of sentences down rather than up, or flatten out the musicality customarily associated with recognisable turns of phrase. Erin, one of three female characters in *Showy Lady Slipper*, delivers the lines 'I love to drive long distances. It's the best' without observing the conventional emphasis one might expect upon 'love' or 'best'. The content of the speech testifies to a genuine enthusiasm, and yet the delivery does not; in performance the actor ran the sentences together and lowered the tone of delivery at the end of each clause. Despite Maxwell's ear for authentic dialogue, his direction invites actors to draw back from investing the lines with a performed sense of spontaneity. In questioning the need for the illusion of spontaneity he can be seen to be challenging what has become a conventional aspect of twentieth- and twenty-first-century modes of realist acting whereby the actor internalises an imagined psychology for each character.

In addition to drawing attention to established methods of performance, the adoption of contemporary patterns of North American speech also results in the conventional sounding unfamiliar; in the mouths of his actors, everyday patterns of speech appear mannered and strange. Although Maxwell's intention is not always this clearly defined, the contrast between realist dialogue and non-realist iteration works to invite a reappraisal or critique of culturally specific value-judgements embedded within conventional turns of phrase. So, when Frank in *Drummer Wanted* (2001) declares, 'I got balls, see?', it is possible to read his declaration as both an attempt to communicate a particular expression of working-class masculinity and a critique of the limited imagery and vocabulary at his disposal. By creating a theatre in which trained actors appear to act badly *'on purpose'* and untrained actors lend their voices to the complex thoughts and emotions of his characters, Maxwell draws attention to the learned, rather than innate, skills of communication which are highly valued throughout Western culture.[3] According to the dominant Western tradition of Method acting, the actor is customarily held to be an articulate, sensitive figure, whether animating a crude, thuggish character or a more sensitive, introspective figure. Several of the untrained actors chosen by Maxwell to perform in his plays bring his characters to life in a manner which draws attention to the spurious nature of this assumption. The hesitancy or awkwardness of their performances reveals the earnest self-possession of the Method actor to be both illusory and contrived. Asserting that 'in stage performance there are so many contrivances, [this] is why it's so hard to do or pull off', Brian Mendes, NYCP actor and Maxwell's close collaborator, indicates how the revelation of convention or 'contrivance' is a key motivating force in the work.[4]

Background to *The End of Reality*

NYCPs' 2006 piece, *The End of Reality*, developed from an interest in security-guard characters in popular Hollywood films; Mendes revealed how Maxwell noticed a pattern whereby security guards would momentarily appear on screen, only to be killed within seconds.[5] Maxwell began to wonder about the personal histories of these fictional guards, and this fed a desire to write a play exploring their day-to-day existence. Following on from this preoccupation, a security-guard scenario was realised in a NYCP film project, *The Darkness of this Reading* (2004). The film follows a security

9.1 The final scene of *The End of Reality* sees the entire cast involved in a choreographed fight sequence.

guard as he sets out to find the location of his latest job, and much of the action revolves around a series of encounters in a seedy bar, the security guard's arrest and the revelation that the building he has been commissioned to protect is already occupied by a malevolent criminal organisation. As with many characters in Maxwell's plays, the security guard represents a working-class or blue-collar worker with limited opportunities for promotion or upward mobility. Maxwell repeatedly represents characters whose destinies are somehow curtailed or hampered by their economic background, class, race or ethnicity. Although he writes dialogue which indicates that the characters believe otherwise, Maxwell demonstrates that the humanist illusion of autonomy and self-realisation upon which the American Dream relies is without substance or foundation.

This play also grew out of experiments Maxwell conducted with long-term actor-collaborators Jim Fletcher and Mendes, who took on the roles of 'criminal' and 'security guard' as they worked through material Maxwell had written for them. From these early exercises, the piece grew into a full-length play with six characters. However, rather than begin the rehearsal process with a complete script, in this instance Maxwell chose to audition and recruit the actors before finishing the script. Once the actors were in place, Maxwell produced a script written with these specific actors in mind.[6]

The play has a coherent narrative trajectory, and features psychologically complex characters who meditate upon the nature of their aspirations and fears in contemporary New York. The characters Tom and Brian are employed to protect an unspecified

9.2 The cast took responsibility for warming up both physically and vocally prior to rehearsal.

building, and as the play unfolds they are shown to enjoy a close friendship.[7] Tom and Brian recruit, and then lose, a number of new colleagues who are either abducted or realise they are not suited to the challenges of the job. One of the new recruits is Tom's god-daughter, Marcia. Brian develops feelings for Marcia, only to discover that

Tom is involved in a sexual relationship with her. The play's action revolves around mundane tasks associated with guarding a building and features prolonged discussion between characters as well as monologues by individual characters. The action of the piece is punctuated by two prolonged fight sequences. In the first, Alex, a junior guard, is abducted by an aggressive criminal whose sole motivation appears to be to harass those guarding the building. The second sequence features the return of Alex, now a criminal collaborator, who joins forces in ambushing the security team a second time round. The main body of the play deals with psychological revelation, as central characters confront their own sense of diminished self-esteem in response to their failure to protect their colleagues.

Sitting in on rehearsals for *The End of Reality*, I witnessed a number of very different tasks being undertaken. Over the last three days of rehearsal I saw the finishing touches being put to the set, lighting and costumes. The actors would often work together as a group, going over line-runs, rehearsing the fight sequences or doing speed runs of the entire show. Each evening ended with a run-through of the performance to a small audience made up of playwriting students, family, friends and colleagues. The company operate an 'open' rehearsal policy and, in this instance, discussed in detail how the presence of an audience altered the dynamic of the play. The structure of each rehearsal appeared fairly conventional insofar as the company conducted physical and vocal warm-ups, went over movement blocking and worked to learn last-minute changes to the script or fight choreography. Although any final conclusions about Maxwell's work risk, in Sara Ahmed's language, 'de-terming' its 'strangeness', and perhaps robbing it of radical potential, it is possible to deduce that there is no final point of closure in his rehearsal process and that change and constant revision feature as a crucial part of his methodology.[8]

Approaches to acting

In interview Maxwell has explained that he does not employ one fixed style when approaching the task of direction. He takes issue with the terms many critics have used to describe his actors' line delivery. In September 2003 he told Steve Moore of the *Austin Chronicle*:

> I get a little discouraged when I hear adjectives like 'robotic' or 'deadpan' applied to what I'm doing, because when I hear it described like that I almost feel like people think I start rehearsals by telling actors that this is the quality I'm going for. But that's not the case at all. That would be really easy, actually, to tell people to be deadpan and not emote, but that's not what it is at all. I'm telling them that I don't want them to pretend to feel anything. It's interesting that when people talk about the pressures of anything they apply words like 'dead' to it, which is a pretty pejorative view, I think.[9]

Maxwell experiments continuously in his work, and this may be partly why he resists attempts by critics and academics to name and fix his approach. He also takes issue with hasty summaries that represent a complex and intensive process as an imposed directorial style. Mendes stressed that Maxwell is reluctant to 'rest on his laurels' and will move away from proven artistic strategies in favour of new challenges and approaches to the work.[10] Illustrating this observation, at the end of the New York run Sibyl Kempson revealed how *The End of Reality* rehearsal differed from her previous New York City Players experience in 1999.

> In *Showy Lady Slipper* [Maxwell] was very stringent about the rule that we should not assign any particular interpretation, specifically in relation to emotional context, to the lines we were delivering. It was left for the audience to interpret – our job was to focus, deliver the text with all the energy and strength available to us physically, to commit fully, and allow for anything to happen . . . I was shocked when I came into *The End of Reality* rehearsals and there was so much emotional assignation going on, pretty much unchecked. I saw a lot of the performers just doing what they wanted with the text, assigning meaning and context left and right, and Rich was sitting there like he didn't mind at all . . . A big change over six years.[11]

Kempson's observation about 'emotional assignation' marks Maxwell's departure from a rehearsal model which called for the actor to resist interpreting the play script, and his move towards inviting actors to invest emotionally in realising a number of complex fictional scenarios. However, Kempson's description, written in hindsight, may give the illusion that this approach was deliberate and consistently applied, which contrasts with my own experience of watching the actors work with Maxwell in rehearsal. I monitored a number of discussions about the implication of 'committing' to performing on stage, about finding an appropriate 'ceiling' for emotional revelation, and about the nature of the task of acting itself. However, at no point did I get the sense that there was a pre-determined set of rules being applied, or that Maxwell wanted to communicate that he had an authoritative vision of how the play should be realised. Instead, the emphasis appeared to be on the actors taking responsibility for *committing to the task* of performing their role while leaving space to articulate a response to the immediacy of the present moment. This might involve thinking anew about how to respond to fellow actors in a certain scene, or how appropriate a previously successful interpretation (for example, appearing to cry) might be to the current performance. For example, Maxwell spent some time working with Mendes, Kempson and Marcia Hidalgo – as Brian, Shannon and Marcia – urging them to 'key into', or 'connect with', one another during their more intimate or confessional scenes. The actors experimented with physical proximity and eye contact, even turning their backs to the audience in order to heighten the intimacy of the verbal exchange between the characters. On one occasion, Maxwell told Mendes, 'Brian, if crying doesn't feel right, then don't do it . . . go with what feels right.' Mendes agreed that during some performances crying would feel like an appropriate response for his character, and on other occasions it would not. The actors' responses would ideally change from rehearsal to rehearsal and from night to night in order to capture some of the changes in real relationships as they developed between cast members and to retain genuine, rather than performed, spontaneity.

Although the language he uses in direction may correspond to that used by

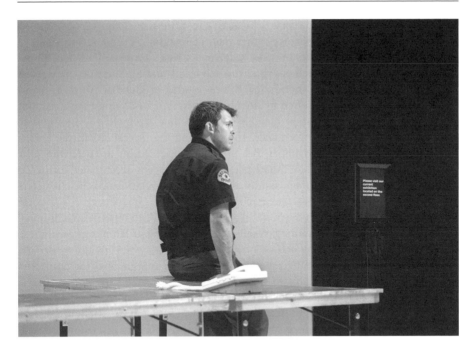

9.3 Mendes revealed that he would alter his performance of security guard 'Brian' from night to night.

9.4 Mendes restrains Kempson. Mendes told Kempson that it became increasingly difficult to restrain her as her strength grew during the run.

Method-driven directors, Maxwell asks actors to prioritise their response to the immediate context of performance rather than to imagine a response on behalf of the character. By asking actors to make judgements based on what they 'feel' in the present moment, the approach engages with the terms and philosophies of Method acting while resisting the assumption that this necessarily produces a natural or realist effect. The actors are not required to attempt to overcome or conquer the strenuous effects that nerves or exhaustion may have; instead they are invited to incorporate these elements into their performance. In witnessing the limitations of the actors, the audience is invited to remember that ability and opportunity are determined by context and training rather than innate talent. This message is accentuated further as the limitations of the performers signify alongside the limitations of the characters which come to light through each character's dialogue.

Maxwell's articulation of the Method actor's imperative to retrieve an emotional response as 'the burden of emoting' recalls the phrase 'the burden of representation' customarily attributed to gay actors, or actors of colour, when invited to occupy a role regarded as a metonymic representation of their marginalised or oppressed social group. In chronicling his experience of realising black characters on stage, David Wiles confesses that, despite his training, he felt ill-prepared for the feelings of ambivalence the portrayal of 'black characters' raised for him. 'Method asks me to forget the spectators. It simply doesn't offer tools for forging a relationship with them. It suggests instead that my relationship with the audience will be taken care of by immersing myself in the character's life. It will not.'[12] Both Maxwell and Wiles have articulated a sense that their training did not take account of the effect the presence of the audience has upon the experience of live performance for the actor, and that the pressure to continue to employ Method skills within this environment proved 'burden'-some. Failure to acknowledge the immediate performance environment troubles or encumbers the actor with complex emotional responses that are not resolved by retreating into the imaginary world of the character.

The desire to avoid pitfalls presented by the internalised 'burdens' of Method-trained actors appears to lie at the heart of Maxwell's direction and his decision to work with actors who have not necessarily been schooled according to the dominant Strasberg-influenced Method-driven technique. In considering the implications of the designation of his non-psychologically motivated performance as 'deadpan' he adds this qualification: 'yes, [in the context of theatre] it is perhaps deadpan; and yes, I can see that it can appear without effect, but not in comparison to real-life, only in relation to plays which the viewers have seen in the past; inconsistent not with reality but only in relation to a viewing history'.[13] Maxwell is at pains to point out that the incongruity of his performance style (if it can be termed as such) is that it disrupts established acting conventions employed in more traditional theatre contexts. His actors' 'inconsistent' acting style fails to repeat the conventions of realist theatre and Method-informed approaches to performance and, in so doing, encourages audiences to recognise how traits of realist performance have come to appear normal only through repetition and convention. This feature of Maxwell's work marks him as a contemporary of theatre companies such as the Wooster Group and Forced Entertainment, which have developed a self-reflexive, metatheatrical approach to theatre-making that might be more appropriately designated as making 'perform-ance' rather than 'theatre'. By drawing attention to the mechanisms and structures which allow the faultless realist production to emerge, metatheatrical techniques such as Maxwell's foregrounding of the nervous actor demonstrate how much labour, schooling and repetition goes into the preparation of a piece of theatre. Maxwell plays with the irony inherent in the realisation that verisimilitude relies upon anything but a natural or spontaneous performance.

Acting as a task

Having studied acting at Illinois State University, Maxwell is aware of the pressure actors feel to 'interpret' the text, or to 'emote'. These imperatives become problematic for Maxwell when they block awareness of the immediate context of performance. He does not, however, call for the actors to resist developing ideas about the emotional landscape of the play or the emotional preoccupations of the characters. A psychologi-cally driven mode of acting appears to become problematic for Maxwell only when it is fixed and unchanging, when the actor becomes over-reliant on a singular, inter-nalised response, and so cannot effectively respond to fellow actors or the changing context of each performance. Although Maxwell does not ask the actors to disinvest emotionally, he does ask them to keep their identity as 'actors' in the forefront of their minds during performance; for him, this is the actors' primary task.

For Maxwell, tasks associated with acting are identified as 'primary' and 'second-ary'; primary tasks relate to being responsive to the immediate material demands of the scene (fighting, delivering lines, following a sequence of movements); secondary tasks relate to psychological and content-based activities unfolding in the fictional world of the play. Reciting lines and repeating set manoeuvres are primary tasks, whereas pretending to survey the fictional location for signs of intrusion would be a secondary task. Kempson revealed that Maxwell would refocus the actors' attention during the fights by saying, 'remember your task' or 'return to your task'. He would also remind them that their primary task was to execute a learned pattern of choreo-graphed actions by reiterating 'sequence, sequence, sequence. Watch acting in lieu of sequence.' The performers' attempts to 'make [the fights] vicious through acting' were shown to appear 'ridiculous', whereas the level of focus and commitment they portrayed in attempting to execute their learned moves as efficiently as possible gave the fights a sense of believability.[14]

During a run-through of one of the fight sequences, Maxwell warned Bradshaw, 'Watch the acting Tom . . . The acting can't take the place of the action. Acting, that's a substitute for the words. Replace that with certainty and replace that with awareness.' Bradshaw replied, 'I'm not acting, I'm just concentrating . . . was I making faces?' Although it initially amused me that an actor should indignantly deny he was 'acting' in rehearsal, I then recognised the insight this exchange afforded into how acting was discussed in this rehearsal situation. 'Acting' stood for performance which relied upon

Box 9.1: Rehearsal tasks

In an email to the author (23 April 2006), Sibyl Kempson writes:

> I remember an exercise during rehearsals for *Showy Lady Slipper* long ago in 1999 that was great, and it had to do with finding neutrality as a performer. [Maxwell] gave us a task like walking into the room, looking around and moving a piece of paper from one side of the desk to the other, or something like that. After we would complete the task he would give the others who were watching a choice between two extremes – open or closed, happy or angry, corporate or domestic, giving or receiving, etc. according to what he saw in the execution of the task – and the idea was to repeat the task until the responses from the observers were more mixed, so that half the room would be seeing it one way and half the room would report to have seen it the other way. That was your goal. It was very empowering once you did it, and for me that had something to do with inscrutability, I think. I remember also being very impressed with the extremes he came up with to present to the observers (other cast members and the stage manager) – he was keeping them on their toes as well because one couldn't predict what he was going to say.

a level of pretence that was premeditated and perhaps fixed, a response which had become *conventional*, rather than spontaneous and responsive to the particular challenges that the run-through, at that particular moment, might offer.

In discussing his ambivalence about the term 'deadpan' to describe his actors' work,[15] Maxwell has stated that he encourages the actors to find a performance style that enables them to 'draw back from characterising emotion'. He points out that this does not equate to not 'emoting' or not 'revealing' on the part of the actors, but rather it gives the actors some freedom to 'think about what they *are* doing'. Again, the distinction revolves around the need to see the actors appreciating the pressures of the present theatrical moment rather than being preoccupied by an absent, fictional moment. This strikes me as quite a complex task for even the most experienced actor (especially an actor whose received notions of acting come via Method-based approaches). Hidalgo and Bradshaw, in particular, appeared to find difficulty with this aspect of the NYCP's work. During rehearsal Maxwell asked Bradshaw, 'What do you want when you're up there? Not to emote . . . not to betray emotions? Where does this "emote" come from?' Bradshaw asserted, 'I'm up there trying to fulfil the task', to which Maxwell responded, 'to go up there and fulfil the task is not enough. What do you *want*?' It became clear that being relieved of the 'burden' of emoting was not equivalent to avoiding emotion. Maxwell reminded Bradshaw, 'avoiding emotion – that's not the thing. It's not going to get you from A to B. It's not a binary thing. It's a paradox. You need to find *within yourself* what *I* need you to do.'

To my eyes, there was a marked difference between the ways the long-term Maxwell collaborators and the new recruits responded to the task-based approach to acting,[16] a difference manifested in the different levels of stillness and concentration the actors displayed. Mendes and Fletcher were highly economical with each gesture, appearing only to move in order deliberately to communicate an idea about their

9.5 Fletcher and Mendes each manifested a marked level of 'stillness' and focus during performance.

character's response to a particular situation. Hidalgo and Bradshaw, by contrast, struggled to maintain stillness on stage, their performances often shadowed by signs of nervousness. Hidalgo tended to purse and chew her lips, scratch her face and adjust clothing during scenes, while Bradshaw appeared to find solace in organising and reorganising the props on the table before him.

Although these gestures did not necessarily mar the performance, and could justifiably be incorporated into characterisation, the difference in levels of concentration and focus between cast members resulted in a curious tension on stage. In rehearsal, this difference in focus appeared to be discussed in terms of 'commitment', as if the stillness acquired by Mendes and Fletcher was the result of a heightened sense of investment in animating the scenario under way. On one occasion, Maxwell asked Hidalgo what she was intending to do when she flipped through the pages on her clip-pad; he stated that he had found the gesture to appear rather thoughtless. Her answer was vague, as if no clear objective had been in mind. As a result, Maxwell suggested she design a security questionnaire, or a set of forms to use, which could give her character something to focus on, an actual task to complete so that the gesture could be executed with a genuine, rather than performed, sense of purpose. As with Method techniques of actor training, motivation remains a key theme for Maxwell's cast; however, the emphasis on making actions believable does not rely upon the actor tracing a through-line to explain the character's psychological motivation, but rather on the actor genuinely investing in the task of turning the page, or reading the newspaper.

9.6 Maxwell gives notes after an evening run-through.

Hidalgo's approach, in particular, belied a desire to draw upon Method-based techniques to inform her approach to character. At various stages during rehearsal she would protest that she did not understand her 'motivation' for behaving in a certain way. The scenario transcribed in box 9.2, 'Brian and Marcia's kiss', illustrates

---

Box 9.2: Brian and Marcia's kiss

Richard: I have this idea this is where Brian goes to kiss Marcia. He goes to grab his coat – you grab him on the way past.

[They do a run-through of the scene. Marcia grabs Brian's head and plants an ostentatious kiss on his lips, then retreats.]

R: How old are you?

Marcia: 27 . . . I want to understand this kiss.

R: Funny that you're asking me about that one thing, and nothing running up to that. Why are you so afraid of the kiss? Why are you backing away from it?

Brian: You don't have to feel affectionate; you don't have to feel lust.

[They run the scene again. Marcia appears nervous. She moves around the stage, puffing out her cheeks and rolling her eyes. It appears that she is trying to find something for her character to do.]

R: I can't take it any more. I thought I could take notes and keep my mouth shut, but I can't. This is a really beautiful relationship, so I have very selfish reasons for wanting to keep it this way . . . You've got to key into him (remember that's something we talked about – primary and secondary motivation, we talked about that). The tasks you're doing remain secondary; what is primary is right there *[points both arms in Brian's direction]*. OK, so 'connect' is a good movement line for me.

[Marcia's demeanour on stage appears to be dominated by the physiological strain of remembering lines. She breaks eye contact with Brian, her eyes move across the space as if trying to recall something.]

R: We have to go back. . . *[pause]*. Let me just explain something to you. I can't do this stuff ahead of time, I have to see it. I need to do it again because . . . we need to do it again because . . . we're not there yet.

[Richard is quiet, thinking, He does not explicitly tell her what to do.]

R: Let's go back.

Marcia: To here?

R: Yes. Let's see how long we can keep you here. The meaning is in the text – you're not pausing enough to flesh the words out with meaning. *[Pause, drumming of feet.]* OK. Try this . . . cut 'for the record'. Cut 'hate is a strong word'. Try this. . . *[He walks across the front of the stage. M follows, exaggerating her steps.]*

R: Well . . . that was a lot better. Did it feel better? I'd like to see tongue in the kiss, but I don't want to push my luck.

---

an exchange between actors and director as they attempt to find their way through a potentially difficult scene. During rehearsal, three days before the opening, Maxwell called Mendes and Hidalgo together to work on a scene in which Marcia and Brian's mutual affection is made evident. Maxwell had written an embrace into the script, and during this rehearsal confessed that he was concerned that the 'connection' between these two characters was not emerging as clearly as he had hoped. He admitted to having 'selfish reasons' for wanting to ensure the audience could appreciate a kind of 'beauty' in the relationship. During run-throughs of the scene Hidalgo was clearly unnerved by the prospect of the embrace. One of her interpretations involved her character seizing Brian in quite an aggressive manner, planting a firm, but brief, kiss on his mouth, while holding either side of his head, and then releasing his head with a flourish. Maxwell responded initially by asking Marcia, in a firm but measured tone, 'Why are you so afraid of the kiss? Why are you backing away from it?' Mendes reassured her that she didn't have to draw upon her own emotions to inform the embrace; he said, 'You don't have to feel affectionate; you don't have to feel lust.' Hidalgo stated she 'want[ed] to understand the kiss', to which Maxwell replied, 'Funny that you're asking me about that one thing, and nothing running up to that.' After a second attempt at the kiss Maxwell asserted, 'You've got to key into him . . . what is primary is right there.' Maxwell's notes after early run-throughs would often express a concern that he wasn't 'feeling' what the actor 'wanted'. After a run-through on 9 January, Maxwell opened his feedback by revealing that:

> I'm left with a question about what you want. I'm left with a question about your being ready for the space. We spoke about forcing a kind of naturalism . . . and that's what I saw you do here. We spoke about this idea of filling the space and having the right presence and having the ability to fill it without pushing . . . It's about commitment.

Maxwell is clear that the forms of motivation relevant for him relate to short-term task-based activities linked to the exigencies of the script and the drive to create a performance, rather than the drive to facilitate the actor's ability to narrativise his or her character beyond the fictional world of the play. Hidalgo's experience serves as a reminder of how difficult it is for a newcomer to Maxwell's stage to abandon received Method-informed ideas about how to realise a 'believable' character.

Emotional valves

Reviewing the piece, Jesse McKinley drew comparisons with previous Maxwell plays. In relation to the style of performance, he observed that the NYCP actors appeared to have been 'let off the leash'. Indeed, Mendes and Kempson agreed that they had been encouraged to explore emotional revelation during rehearsals for *The End of Reality*. However, this 'freedom' was tempered by a desire to maintain some continued level of restraint in actors' 'emoting'. Maxwell's notes to the actors often referred to a 'forcing' of emotional response, which he found to be problematic because, in his view, the actors were expending so much energy in *forcing* emotion *into* their lines, there was no room to 'let anything else in'. From this, I inferred that an actor who concentrates too much upon imbuing lines with emotional energy becomes isolated from the possibility that something might be happening in the theatrical here and now which perhaps could, or ought to, affect how the line is delivered. A remarkable exchange took place between Maxwell and Kempson at the start of a run-through, in which

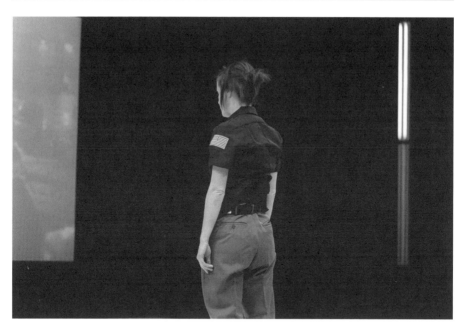

9.7 At Maxwell's suggestion, Kempson dropped the volume of her voice despite speaking with her back to the audience.

Maxwell quietly went to stand next to her as she delivered a speech about her ongoing sense of fear and apprehension. The speech began, 'I'm frozen with fear'. Kempson had been delivering her lines at a fairly high volume, as her back was to the audience, and her tone had been insistent and almost angry. Maxwell gave her a series of quiet instructions, and she resumed her speech, this time speaking in a more muted tone. Reflecting upon this exchange, Kempson related:

> This was a breakthrough for me in terms of understanding. What Rich said at that rehearsal was something like 'I want you to talk to Brian.' He was very quiet but very stern and it cut right through everything I was doing . . . It needed to be a give and take in order to accommodate a certain intimation of . . . proneness? (I hesitate to use the word 'passivity'!) but also a connecting to Brian, or a seeking of a connection with Brian. I was working according to old directives [used in *Showy Lady Slipper*] about filling the space and really of dominating, and wasn't letting or taking enough in as a result.[17]

The speech was transformed from a fairly aggressive, defensive one, which felt like a crude and inarticulate conveyance of the character's state of mind, to one which betrayed a sense of vulnerability and regret. Reviewing the piece, Ben Brantley wrote, '[The fact] that Ms Kempson speaks as if she were reading a bus schedule perversely makes the fear more credible – a fact of life instead of a moment of self-dramatization.'[18] Brantley's response suggests that Kempson's more muted delivery (and restrained emotion) indeed had a positive effect upon the efficacy of the line.

In a later rehearsal, Maxwell described the forcing of emotion in terms of a kind

---

Box 9.3: Finding a ceiling

Richard: Now this is specific, and leads into a general thing. When Alex gets abducted – we need to add a series of exclamation points. What's the ceiling? It's not about exclamation points (Brian, there are opportunities to blow it out of the water.) Marcia, what does that mean? How much you commit? This relates to your issue of your difficulty in connecting to the scene.

Brian: All I have to work with are 'no' and exclamation points?

R: Yes, let me worry about the text.

[They discuss cutting the fight. The actors ask if it is because they are not doing it 'right'.]

R: No, you guys are amazing. I'm not good at praising. I'm on the verge of being able to see what this might be. If I cut something it's not because of that. It's a brutal process.

[During a run-through of the scene R decides to re-introduce a previously cut scene. He says, 'I need to write you some new text.']

R: Take your time. Make sure that you're not pushing it out so hard that you're not letting anything in.

R: You know this conversation about 'ceiling' really applies here. There are bits in the text which indicate . . . 'I should be really angry here,' and that is a possibility . . . but I need to see what the ceiling is here (Tom, scale it back, bring it down). There are possibilities and you need to be in a situation where you're open to that. Why do I say that? Because I don't know where it's going to get to . . . I don't want to say you can't be angry . . . It's all possible. I don't want to see it happen if you're not seduced by that.

R: Alex, let Jim stand before you get up. *[To Tom]* Why the pause?

Tom: I'm trying to do what you want me to do.

R: Well, I'm trying to get you to do what you want to do *within what I want you to do* . . . so it's a constant struggle. It's a free world and everything . . . but it's not going to happen . . . it's a free country . . . but you have to do as I say.

---

of 'valve'. Discussing a later run-through he confessed that 'I guess tonight I felt like it wasn't enough from an energy standpoint. Where's that right place? You need to find it without obliterating everything else in the room. You need to find that place without it being like a valve – only letting things out, not letting anything in.' The metaphor of the 'valve' reiterates Maxwell's desire to see the actors continually acknowledging the reality of the theatrical present as one of performance-making rather than to suspend their disbelief in order to find themselves 'in character' but not in the theatrical space. It also articulates a sense of his view of the inadequacies of a Method-informed approach, which places an emphasis on the actor's emotional productivity, rather than the actors' emotional reciprocity.

Although no single, fixed methodology serves the NYCP's approach to rehearsal, a number of ideas were reiterated during the process. The key ideas appeared to relate to, firstly, the commitment of the actor to the task of participating in both rehearsal

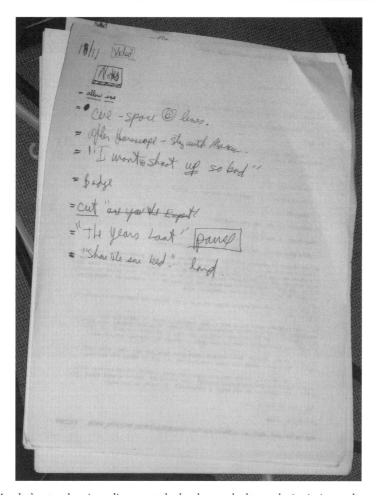

9.8 Mendes' notes showing adjustments he has been asked to make in timing and emphasis.

and performance, and secondly, as a development of this, the drive to acknowledge the significance of the collective experience of theatre-making and theatre-going. By doing away with the convention of the fourth wall, Maxwell ensures that audience and actors are united, rather than divided, by their mutual engagement in seeing the play through to its conclusion. Maxwell's insistence that the actors acknowledge the audience, by making regular eye contact and, on occasion, delivering lines directly to individuals, suggests that, for him, it is important to acknowledge the conceptual segregation of cast and audience as a theatrical contrivance. Although Maxwell rarely cites Brecht as an influence upon his work, his predilection for having actors deliver monologues directly to – and retain eye contact with – the audience is an example of a post-Brechtian application of *Verfremdungseffekt*. His refusal to allow actors to forget the presence of the audience suggests that Maxwell intends to retain the motivation, or rationale, for theatre-going as part of the evening's agenda. As discussed previously, the lack of the

9.9 The cast discuss the alterations they need to make to the blocking after the angle of the desk has been changed.

degree of polish, or finesse, in some of the actors' performances and in the blocking and set design, signifies for an audience adept at reading theatrical signs. As Brecht wanted objects on stage to exist as 'props', so Maxwell appears to want actors on stage to signify as animating, but not inhabiting, working-class characters. For me, this approach works to demystify the role of the actor because the labour involved in achieving the illusion of self-possession and spontaneity on stage makes itself felt through its absence from Maxwell's stage. The sense of self-assurance and composure associated with the Method-trained actor comes to appear mannered and contrived when placed alongside Maxwell's celebration of 'roughness' and, in turn, acts as a reminder of the way that theatrical conventions are learned, not innate, and change over time.

Reception

Reviews of *The End of Reality* in the New York press were generally favourable, although several critics described the piece as 'challenging',[19] and 'troubling, not gratifying'.[20] Many critics brought their awareness of previous NYCP plays to bear upon the work and reiterated the notion that Maxwell's work adheres to a 'trademark' style,[21] while also acknowledging that it demonstrated 'a wider range of emotions than in previous Maxwell productions'.[22] Critics described the piece as being about 'fear and faith in an uncertain time',[23] 'like a sustained cry of pain',[24] and 'a kind of surrender to the physical after emotional tension [has been] stretched to the limit'.[25] Analysing the fight sequences, many critics reflected my own perception that they had been 'slowed down' (although Maxwell denies doing this deliberately). Feingold suggests that the 'arbitrary biff-bangings' bring 'an eerily antiseptic, remote, almost dreamlike' quality. Along similar lines, Bacalzo recorded that 'the script is punctuated by several fight sequences that are both violent and hilarious. The action is slowed down, allowing for moments of humor, yet it's still raw and discomfiting.'[26]

Commenting upon the approach to acting and directing, Brantley describes a cast whose 'expressions rarely change', and whose 'voices remain calm and neutral with just a buzz of irritation at the edges'. However, he goes on to write that 'somehow, all that flatness starts to sound like a sustained cry of pain'.[27] Hidalgo was noted as having animated her character with 'a tough grace',[28] Mendes presents a 'cocky guard' and Bradshaw presented Tom as 'an avuncular type'.[29] Several critics emphasised the effectiveness of the actors' neutrality and, in addition to Brantley's commendation of Kempson's 'bus schedule' style of rendition, Bacalzo remarked, 'there is a quiet melancholy behind many of Hidalgo's speeches'.[30]

The alterations that Maxwell implements after each performance suggest he is striving to keep the process alive and stimulating, both for himself and for his collaborators. Similarly, his continued interest in working with and recruiting non-established actors manifests a desire to keep himself 'new' and to 'keep learning'.[31] *The End of Reality* represented a move away from a style of theatre-making that he felt had become recognisable. He confessed, 'I think I was seeing a pattern develop,'[32] so he chose to resist his customary theatrical impulses in order to work in a new way. Although the company could be seen to have a set stylistic approach, my observation of the rehearsal process revealed change to be central to the NYCP's concerns. Change enables the actors to retain a sense of apprehension about performance and to ensure that the signs of their labour remain visible. It enables them to avoid appearing 'at home' or at ease with their character. The heightened sense of risk which the cast retain creates an atmosphere of uncertainty and unease, which, in turn, invites spectators to address why they do not necessarily feel 'at home' in this particular theatre. These assumptions are worthy of investigation because once the Method actor's sense of accomplishment and self-possession can be associated with learned, rather than innate, behaviour, it is revealed to be accessible to those with the financial means to access the requisite training. Following this argument to its conclusion, I would assert that the cast's nervous performance works to critique the finesse of the Method actor, and this in turn serves as an allegory for a critique of the humanist subject. Those possessing a demeanour of self-possession and upward mobility do so because they have benefited from an education which teaches self-belief and provides social tools to enable the subject to overcome constraints presented by their social or economic background. Maxwell's actors avoid the veneer of professionalism associated with Method acting and instead draw upon a sense of apprehension to animate characters whose futures are affected by issues of access and opportunity.

Notes

1 Research for this chapter has been undertaken with the financial assistance of the British Academy.
2 Maxwell is self-reflexive about his changing attitude towards acting, stating that '[t]he conversations I have with [actor] Brian [Mendes] now are like "why are you *afraid* of Method?" you know, what's the matter with that, what's *wrong* with pretending?' Sarah Gorman, 'Refusing Shorthand: Interview with Richard Maxwell', *Contemporary Theatre Review*, 17:4 (2007), 242.
3 In his review of *Drummer Wanted* for the *Austin Chronicle*, Wayne Alan Brenner included an overheard snippet of conversation: '"It's kind of like", one student was heard to remark with much inflection, "really *bad* acting, but *on purpose*"'. Wayne Alan Brenner, 'Drummer Wanted: Richard Maxwell', *Austin Chronicle* (31 January 2003). Available online at www.austinchronicle.com/issues/dispach/2003-01-31/arts_exhibitionism5.html (accessed 15 July 2003).
4 Richard Maxwell and Brian Mendes, 'Talk Karaoke', *Contemporary Theatre Review*, 16:3 (2006), 350.
5 Author's interview with Mendes, 13 January 2006, New York.
6 With the exception of Sibyl Kempson's character, which had originally been created for Shannon Kennedy.
7 The characters appear in the script as '1', '2', '3', '4', '5' and '6', although they refer to one another as 'Marcia', 'Brian', 'Shannon' and 'Jake' in the play script. In some instances the character names correspond with the actors' names, although this is not consistent. When referring to the actors I use surnames and when referring to characters I use first names.
8 Ahmed provides a criticism of the ostensibly neutral writing-up of fieldwork observation used in anthropology and ethnography. She points to translation as 'one of the central models for the production of ethnographic knowledge' and argues that this approach is destructive and violent, as it 'produces knowledge . . . through a radical *de-terming* of the foreign'. Sara Ahmed, *Strange Encounters: Embodied Others in Post-Coloniality* (London and New York: Routledge, 2000), p. 58.
9 Steve Moore, 'Flicking the Switch: Toggling Between the Real and Artificial with Richard Maxwell', *Austin Chronicle* (19 September 2003). Available online at www.nycplayers.org (accessed 2 May 2004).
10 Author's interview with Mendes, 13 January 2006. Mendes revealed that the songs were dispensed with in *The End of Reality* 'because the songs *worked*'.
11 Author's email correspondence with Kempson, 23 April 2006.
12 David Wiles, 'Burdens of Representation: the Method and the Audience', in David Krasner (ed.), *Method Acting Reconsidered: Theory, Practice, Future* (Hampshire: Macmillan Press, 2000), p. 172.
13 Quoted in Lucia Mauro, 'Richard Maxwell, the Boxer', *Stage Persona: PerformInk Online*, 2002, at www.performink.com/Archives/stagepersonae/2002/MaxwellRichard.html (accessed 14 November 2003).
14 Quotations from author's email correspondence with Kempson, 23 April 2006.
15 Author's email correspondence with Maxwell, 19 May 2005.
16 For further exploration of acting as a task, see Philip Auslander's interviews with Willem Dafoe in *From Acting to Performance: Essays in Modernism and Postmodernism* (London and New York: Routledge, 1997) and Phillip B. Zarrilli (ed.), *Acting (Re)Considered: A Theoretical and Practical Guide* (London and New York: Routledge, 2nd revised edn, 2002).

17 Author's email correspondence with Kempson, 23 April 2006.

18 Ben Brantley, 'The Banality of Violence in a Willfully Numb Universe', *New York Times* (17 January 2006). Available online at http://theater2.nytimes.com/2006/01/17/theater/reviews/17bran.html

19 Lauren Marks, 'The End of Reality' *NY Theatre.com* (14 January 2006), at www.nytheater.com/nytheater/end2909.shtml (accessed 5 February 2006).

20 Michael Feingold, 'The Uninflected Life', *Village Voice* (24 January 2006). Available via *Village Voice* online at http://villagevoice.com/theater/0604,feingold,71911,11.html (accessed 5 February 2006).

21 Jesse McKinley, 'Playwright's Trademark is Deadpan. Now He Wants to Tweak It', *New York Times* (18 January 2006). Available at *New York Times* online at http://nytimes.com/2006/01/18/theater/newsandfeatures/18maxw.html?emc=etal (accessed 18 January 2006).

22 Dan Bacalzo, 'The End of Reality' (17 January 2006), *Theater Mania.com*, at www.theatermania.com/templates/printContent.cfm?strContentType=news&intTyp (accessed 5 February 2006).

23 Marks, 'The End of Reality'.

24 Brantley, 'The Banality of Violence'.

25 Feingold, 'The Uninflected Life'.

26 Bacalzo, 'The End of Reality'.

27 Brantley, 'The Banality of Violence'.

28 Marks, 'The End of Reality'.

29 Brantley, 'The Banality of Violence'.

30 Bacalzo, 'The End of Reality'.

31 Gorman, 'Refusing Shorthand', p. 243. Maxwell acknowledges that he has other creative outlets so that theatre can be put aside for a time, and his energies dedicated to producing work in alternative formats such as film or music.

32 In McKinley, 'Playwright's Trademark is Deadpan'.

10

Not Yet It's Difficult – *Blowback* (2004) – Unmaking *Blowback* – a visceral process for a political theatre

Peter Eckersall

Not Yet It's Difficult (NYID) relates arts practice to cultural activism. It aims to broaden connections between theatre aesthetics and politics by creating new forms of dramaturgical encounter. Artistic director David Pledger, technical manager and lighting designer Paul Jackson and myself, as dramaturg, established the company in 1995.[1] Based in Melbourne, Australia and with a floating membership of about twenty artistic associates, we make hybrid performance and multimedia artworks with an intertextual, montage approach to theatrical presentation. NYID's work combines aesthetic and political ideas: audiences are invited to experience performances intellectually, through engaging with discussions about politics, critical theory and reoccurring leitmotifs; and viscerally, through the intensity of images and overt use of bodies and media. Composite layers of dramaturgy that explore theatre as a medium of artistic expression work alongside contemporary narratives and socio-political content. NYID sees performance as a form of ongoing cultural investigation. As Edward Scheer observes, 'What matters in this is the production of ruptures, what Guattari calls "dissident vectors".'[2]

This chapter discusses NYID's rehearsal process with respect to *Blowback*, produced in 2004. *Blowback* is set in a future Australia occupied by US forces. Described in an NYID media release as 'agit-prop tele-theatre, part science fiction, part documentary and part absurdist metaphor',[3] the story follows an underground group of cultural activists who hack into the joint communications facilities of 'New Australia'. In the sections below I discuss key principles of NYID's approach to theatre-making and trace a developing aesthetic from the company's earliest work. I provide a synopsis of *Blowback* in order to contextualise subsequent discussion about the show's rehearsal process. I address the approach to developing ideas through dramaturgical workshopping with different participants; ways in which the company conceives of and utilises performance

---

Box 10.1: Body listening

NYID is recognised for its strong ensemble work and this is in part due to performers participating in Pledger's body-listening workshops. Body listening is Pledger's
training protocol that explores the body's relationship to performing spaces and
to other bodies. It includes developing movement patterns in relation to exploring the sense of actor presence in the space. It locates the performing body in a
combined cultural-aesthetic construction of space where bodies are not neutral
and their affective presence is explored. It is important to note that these are
political bodies, although not in a solo-performance-art sense where the singular
body is sometimes explored in role-play or as a form of self-revelation. Instead, a
possible new way of relating to the political substance of the body in performance
is proposed. In NYID, bodies signify power relations and are broadly signalling
didactic intentions, yet they are also dynamically expressive in unpredictable and
thrilling ways. The aim is to combine representational gestures with a substantial
reordering of the sensory experience of theatre to create political performance that
is substantive and simultaneously opens possibilities for the work to grow in the
minds of the audience.

---

space; modes of rehearsal for multimedia performance; and means by which director
David Pledger works with actors and performers in generating and rehearsing material.
Three aspects of NYID's approach to production are particularly important here: firstly,
the accumulation of physical and gestic performance vocabularies over time (see figure
10.1); secondly, the sense of 'disarticulation' and teasing apart of theatrical forms and
gestures; and thirdly, the notion of rehearsal as the culmination of devising processes.

The evolution of NYID's approach

Before 1995, David Pledger led a two-year research and development project from
which came NYID's early theatre vocabulary. This work was influenced in part by
Australian theatre's recent contact with Asian performance and new trends in the
European avant-garde of the late 1980s and early 1990s. Pledger worked with Tadashi
Suzuki[4] and saw performances by artists such as Pina Bausch. In this work, a new
kind of critical arts practice – characterised by systemic ideological mappings of the
body in space – seemed to offer aesthetic intensity coupled with political effect. Such
stringently intertextual approaches to performance lie between theatre and dance
and often incorporate new technologies. Pledger used these experiences as departure
points for his own postmodern and postcolonial project aiming to explore a nascent
creative and political understanding of an 'Australian sensibility' for the theatre. They
also informed his notion of 'body listening' (see box 10.1), which is both a training
protocol for performers and an approach to the presence and purpose of the actor.

10.1 *Blowback* interrogation scene: highly physical performance; Vivienne Walshe and
Luciano Martucci. Slamming bodies into walls was a motif first used by Pledger in a
development workshop for *K*. It figured centrally in *Journey to Con-fusion #3*, then in
Blowback and in NYID's *apoliticaldance* (2006).

Back in Australia in the early 1990s, Pledger drew on an eclectic mix of popular
culture, sources of which included comic book art, martial arts, music, films and sport,
as well as postdramatic styles of performance.[5] His development as a performance-
maker began with questioning established theatre practices and with experiments
that explore the sensory nature of theatre; in particular, the visceral and dynamic
experience of working with bodies in space. 'I was smelling my way through,' he says.
'Smelling, feeling, seeing, it's very sensorial; I think the process [of making theatre]
always needs to be.'[6]

NYID made over thirty original works between 1995 and 2008, including performances, film and television pieces, research and development programmes, art
installations and international collaborations. *Blowback* therefore comes at a point by
which the company had already consolidated its profile – as socially engaged, experimental and flexible in working across different media. By the time the production was
made, the company was well versed in a form of devising that entails ongoing creation
in and through rehearsal.

As theorist Gay McAuley suggests, 'the rehearsal process brings together a
number of people and materials, choices are made, and the performance is constructed
... In the theatre nothing exists in isolation.'[7] In broad terms, NYID rehearsals follow
this model, beginning with a lengthy period of cogitation and a formally constituted

dramaturgical element. Subsequent work with performers and the production team is followed by an intensive rehearsal and production period. David Pledger, supported by Paul Jackson and the production team, coordinates each phase. His role in NYID's creative process is pivotal. As he observes:

> I think you need to have someone with an overarching vision and I'm not interested in those environments where that is not the case. As an audience [member] I find them interesting, but as a maker, I'm not interested in them because I don't operate well in those circumstances. But I think if performance is essentially a social activity, then the social aspect of it needs to be incorporated in the dramaturgy. The social aspect is collaboration.[8]

A vital aspect of this collaborative approach is the accumulation of forms, techniques and ideas gleaned from earlier projects and reapplied to new contexts – thus, a sense of accumulation and disarticulation characterises NYID's rehearsal process. Analysing rehearsal techniques in *Blowback* therefore requires a wider discussion of the company, briefly to identify other works relevant to this particular production.

Early works

NYID's first production, in 1995, adapted *Taking Tiger Mountain by Strategy*, the Chinese cultural revolutionary play of the 1960s. This story of revolutionary heroism was reworked to explore questions of propaganda in contemporary Australia. The piece, which might be described as 'Foucault meets Mao', featured performance forms that were to become characteristic of NYID's work in subsequent years, including the use of song and music, dramatic group formations and marching, choreographed chorus routines supplementing and supporting monologue, martial arts and fighting, and interventions by the director playing a dramatic role. *Tiger Mountain* was at times humorous, confrontational, metatheatrical and intertextual. Various kinds of writing were used. For example, excerpts from Mao Tse Tung's *Little Red Book* of revolutionary dicta were contrasted with material from Kirk Denton's essay 'Model Drama as Myth: A Semiotic Analysis of *Taking Tiger Mountain by Strategy*'.[9] The performance used a mix of 'high' and popular culture forms.

Crucially, a kind of 'gestural choreography' was developed where actors, working in chorus, performed text with overt physical gestures. Moving in formations of complicated travel patterns, the text was gradually removed and replaced by a gestural semantics performed with great precision and intensity. By this means, a residue of language as performance transferred to bodily gestures offered a new mode of performative communication.[10] Methods of composition and rehearsal established in *Tiger Mountain* set in train patterns of work and creative relationships that continue to inform NYID's practice.

The following year, NYID performed *William Shakespeare: Hung, Drawn and Quartered* (*WSHDQ*). *WSHDQ* explored the political and artistic relevance of

10.2 Shakespeare invented violence; Paul Bongiovanni (right) beats Greg Ulfan with the collected works of Shakespeare in *WSHDQ*.

Shakespeare to Australian theatre where a lingering colonial mindset informs the history of Shakespearean production.

Adding to the company's performance vocabulary, one of the performers collected interviews with people about their connections to Shakespeare. These recordings were edited and used as material in the production. In later performances, notably *Sports Edition* (discussed below), interviews were filmed and projected on to screens and monitors in the space. They were an integral element of the early performance works from 1995 to 1998.

The technical scale of the company's projects greatly increased with the production of *The Australasian Post Cartoon Sports Edition* (1997), an arena-style, multimedia performance about sport and society, presented in a theatre converted into a large sports arena. *Sports Edition* featured high-energy combinations of dance, athletics, video art, music, fight sequences and excerpts from plays and films on sporting themes. It drew on interviews and archival materials, and combined live and pre-recorded video sequences. As the scholar Rachel Fensham comments, *Sports Edition* 'linked political rhetoric operating in the language of sport with physical action in order to illustrate well-established connections between concepts of nationalism and racial intolerance'.[11]

The devised productions described here go together with a cycle of play productions. In 1995 Pledger adapted and directed Stephen Sewell's *Dark Paths*, retitled as *Nil, Cat and Buried*, and in 1998 the company produced John Romeril's 1970 counter-culture play *Chicago Chicago* under the title *Chicago Chicago System 98*. In keeping

10.3 Interviews in *Journey to Con-fusion #2* (Tokyo 2000), NYID in collaboration with Gekidan Kaitaisha, Louise Taube on the screen. Interview sequences aimed to bring popular and diverse opinions into the theatre.

with NYID's metatheatrical attributes, these productions substantially rethought the contexts of the original works. More recently, *K* (2002) and *Blowback* explore issues of political complicity, the surveillance society, and a rising sense of military-style occupation in Australia. Pledger has also developed art installation and hybrid media productions including *Eavesdrop* (David Pledger and Jeffrey Shaw, 2004), *Walk-in Drive-in* (David Pledger and Callum Morton, 2006) and *The Meaning of Moorabbin is Open for Inspection* (David Pledger, 2008).

From 1999 to 2003, NYID collaborated with the Japanese company Gekidan Kaitaisha on *Journey to Con-fusion* (see figure 10.3). This project combined artistic practice with scholarship and resulted in three performance events and a volume of critical essays.[12] In 2005 NYID's bilingual production of *K*, in partnership with the Seoul Performing Arts Festival and Dolgoogi Theatre, gave another context for these investigations, exploring language and contrasting experiences of occupation and colonisation (political, cultural, military). This was followed in 2008 by *Strangeland*, a collaborative work for the Seoul Performing Arts Festival.

These collaborations are seen by the company as an evolving form of intercultural arts practice. In a fragmented globalised economy, they provide ways for artists to create new connections and production contexts, and to speak about the experience of globalisation to diverse audiences. Working in collaborative partnerships is a way of resisting the commodification of art in global tour networks where individual companies are marketed as the latest fashion or the most recent instance of exotic cultural production.

10.4 *The Australasian Post-cartoon Sports Edition*; Kha Viet Tran (right) teaches Katia Molino *Vovinam Viet Vo Dao* (a Vietnamese martial art).

Box 10.2: Process and the politics of performance

'"Natural" acting', writes the scholar Denis Salter, 'has tended to function . . . as a (mostly invisible) strategy of surveillance, designed to keep the unnatural – meaning, unregulated and potentially dissident – discursive formations securely in their place' (Salter, 'Acting Shakespeare in Postcolonial Space', in James Bulman [ed.], *Shakespeare, Theory, and Performance* [London and New York: Routledge, 1996], p. 117). NYID rehearsal processes developed from similar perspectives and aim to turn this situation around. Salter's postcolonial critique of the stage was an influence in making *William Shakespeare: Hung, Drawn and Quartered* (1996). His insights into the political nature of acting and theatre have, in some senses, given shape to NYID's approach overall. To borrow from Salter, NYID aims to make visible the act of theatre and to 'radically and continuously disarticulate' the theatre and its 'politics of location' (*ibid*, p. 129).

NYID's approach to rehearsal is performance-based. Pledger contends that the term 'performance' 'tends to be progressive, whereas theatre is often talked about as being in stasis. Performance has possibilities whereas theatre has closure' (Pledger in Peter Eckersall, 'On Physical Theatre: A Roundtable Discussion from NYID with Peter Eckersall, David Pledger, Paul Jackson, Greg Ulfan', *Australasian Drama Studies*, 41 [2002], p.18). The company continues to work in ways informed by these ideas. New work is devised from the 'ordering' of ideas, dramatic content, the careful organisation of bodies and space. The work is discussed, formalised, designed and then moved in space. These movements are practised and the team evaluates progress. The rehearsal concludes with performances but the process continues from one work to the next as an accumulation of forms and a renegotiation of context.

While NYID has worked in many fields over the past twelve years it is important to stress the sequential layering of forms evident in the work. As Paul Jackson notes: 'There is no one essential theatricality, there are just ways of interrupting various conventions . . . By being able to say this is a constructive process, then other possibilities could be constructed elsewhere.'[13]

Blowback's political context

Blowback responded to a particular view of Australia's relationship to the USA in the early years of the twenty-first century, and deals with questions of American interference in Australian political and cultural life. America has military bases in Australia and is an aggressively expanding source of cultural, media and economic power in the Pacific region. The play reimagines this reality in terms of an actual occupation of Australia, aiming to show some of the means and techniques of this prospective realisation of power and exploring possibilities for resisting its influence on Australian life.

Anthropologist Ghassan Hage contributed to the dramaturgical workshop for *Blowback*'s development. His writing on Australian culture helps explain *Blowback*'s depiction of occupation and authoritarianism. Hage coined the term 'paranoid nationalism'[14] to describe the tone of Australian politics and society in the years of the neo-conservative Howard government (1996–2007).[15] His work shows how cultural trends in Australia during this era manufactured a kind of border panic. Widespread fear of invasion was generated by conservative forces following the attacks on America in 2001. A key to understanding this mindset lies in the effects of a presumed American alliance with Australia over a longer period. Since 1945, Australia's foreign policy has broadly been linked to an American world-view in return for the perceived securities of an American military alliance. While a shared cultural idiom of freedom and democracy is assumed to underlie the alliance, America's presence as a colonising and imperial power that interferes in local economies, cultures and politics is also at issue for some. Critics of the alliance note how negative images of terrorism are used to reify feelings of anxiety in the community. Mirroring this is the fiction that Australia is a safe place protected for us by the alliance between our government and that of the US. As philosopher Tony Coady explains, 'Much of this combines exaggerated fear with extravagant attachment to a comforting fantasy of a stereotypical Australia. The fantasy is supposed to protect us from the fear.'[16] Paranoid nationalism, then, provides a social backdrop to *Blowback*.

Pledger's script also draws on state security terminology. As documented in Chalmers Johnson's *Blowback: The Costs and Consequences of American Empire*, 'blowback' is a term used by US security agencies to describe the situation where an apparently compliant and friendly régime funded by the security apparatus, turns rogue.[17] First used in a CIA report in 1954, blowback is, Johnson argues, 'a metaphor for the unintended consequences of the US government's international activities'.[18]

NYID's *Blowback* depicts such a system of occupation, exploring its social, psychological and physical consequences.

Media and information systems are primary sources of this 'invasion'. *Blowback* suggests how the tools of media/data can be reclaimed and turned against the colonising force. Thus, in the play, activists hack into the occupation's data operating system and, with a view to provoking a popular uprising, encrypt subversive visual information into the broadcast signal of a banned Australian soap opera called *A World of Our Own*. The implanted images are uncanny and amorphous, designed to haunt and ultimately awaken the Australian political psyche. As shown in the final scenes of the work, they are softly mutating black-and-white film images of sun shining through native Eucalyptus 'gum' trees. They convey a sense of phantasmic Australianness that helps to dramatise and problematise tensions around the paranoid nationalism identified above.

Blowback depicts the occupation as a panoptic world. While resistance is explored, the body politic is reoccupied by totalitarian forces signified by the intrusive mediatisation. In the show's final image, the cameras zoom into a close-up shot of a doll's house, a TV prop signifying the stereotypical soap opera world of occupied Australia. The image implies a pacified suburbia transformed by fears manufactured in the surveillance society. As Hardt and Negri argue in their attempt to theorise resistance in the postmodern space of empire: 'The multitude [of suburbia in this example] not only uses machines to produce, but also becomes increasingly machinic itself, as the means of production are increasingly integrated into the minds and bodies of the multitude.'[19] So too does occupation become a self-regulating experience.

Synopsis

Blowback begins with the presentation of a live taping of the last episode of a fictional soap opera. Scott and Charlene – named after much-loved characters from *Neighbours*, Australia's most successful soap opera – introduce themselves to the audience (see figure 10.5). They are played by ex-TV actors Todd MacDonald and Roslyn Oades. Their narrative journey takes them from the confines of their parochial *Neighbours* suburb, now a gated community, into the city and the countryside to see something of the outside world. As their travels unfold, the performers mark a path around the edges of the space. This is contrasted with the stories of three characters sitting at separate interrogation tables set among the audience.

At the first location, Australian military officer Colonel Tom Reeve, and US Military Intelligence Officer Jenny Ripper (Luciano Martucci and Vivienne Walshe), play scenes backwards: from the concluding scenes where Reeve is tortured (see figure 10.1) and his insurgent acts are discovered, to the arrival of Ripper on base to investigate the illegal images implanted in the digital broadcast network that the occupation forces now control. At the second location, in a Guantanamo Bay-style prison, the Australian officer's son Darko Reeve (Benjamin McNair) is interrogated by Military Intelligence Officer

10.5 *Blowback*'s Scott and Charlene. *World of Our Own* soap opera actors played by
Todd MacDonald and Roslyn Oades.

Casey James (Anita Hegh [Melbourne season, see figure 10.6], Rachael Gordon [Sydney
season]) from the Halliburton Corporation. The third location depicts a re-enactment of
a violent interrogation of one of the hackers as a weekly segment in the TV show *Military
Intelligence Abroad*. Hosted by two members of the American occupation forces media
division – Captain Mickey and Sargent-Sargent (Tom Considine and Natalie Cursio) –
Military Intelligence Abroad satirises free-to-air American armed forces network broadcasting as seen in occupied countries such as Korea. The hosts are cyborg-like media
cut-outs, although no less vicious for their two-dimensionality and bad TV production
skills (see figure 10.7). During the performance, events at each of the three interrogation
tables are transmitted to TV monitors via tiny surveillance cameras positioned above.
The soap opera scenes shot in multi-cam studio configuration in colour, contrast with
the gritty high-contrast, black-and-white look of surveillance footage.

The four parts of the story come together in the final scenes. Scott and Charlene
watch four minutes of film footage of gum trees projected by an old super-8 projector.
The clacking projector and the stilted film images are the very antithesis of the dys-
topic surveillance footage ceaselessly broadcasting to the four sides of the space. The
trees are random and beautiful; external forces cannot expropriate their phantasmic
low-tech recollection of the past. The sequence features antiquated fragile equipment
in the act of transmitting a sublime revolutionary image. It suggests that the shared
memory of gum trees – their sensory affect – opens a free mental space in the contemporary military dystopia. From this intervention, resistance to the cultural logic of the
occupation might begin.

10.6 *Blowback,* interrogation table. Military Intelligence Officer Casey James (Anita Hegh) interrogates Darko Reeve (Benjamin McNair).

The piece concludes in a pile-up of bodies, at first a sign of a reverent mourning of the Australian war dead, but soon transmogrifying into an image referencing the notorious mistreatment of prisoners at the Abu Ghraib prison complex in 2004 in Iraq.[20] To the strains of Australian folk-singing legends The Seekers' 'A World of Our Own' the cast retreat to banging their heads against the wall in an audio dystopia of paranoia and inertia. Pledger described this scene as a 'rendering of the political culture on middle Australia'.[21]

Dramaturgical development

Ideas for *Blowback* evolved over six years – from when Pledger first wanted to do a work on America – though the production process and rehearsal period stretched over five months in 2004. Discussions among the company identified themes to be explored in a dramaturgical workshop that, in turn, informed Pledger's writing of the performance text.

10.7 *Blowback*: American occupation forces' media division. Surveillance screen images contrast with live action. Tom Considine and Natalie Cursio.

10.8 *Blowback* space, reverse angle.

The NYID practice of involving members of the company in a discussion and development phase of rehearsal was extended in *Blowback* to include a two-week reading
and research project. Activities included pooling relevant texts on Australia–America
relations, gathering images and texts on the Iraq war and reading works for and against neo-
conservative politics. The group explored fundamentalist and cult religious practices and
modes of propaganda promoting them. We investigated techniques used in brainwash-
ing. We looked at aggressively marketed personal growth organisations and corporation
employee manuals. Both systematically remove people from their daily environment and
aim to 'reprogramme' their thoughts and behaviour. We approached people to speak to the
company about their beliefs and/or work. These included David Wright-Neville, a former
senior terrorism analyst for the Australian government and now academic; foreign policy
scholar Andrew Butfoy; religious scholar and Christian minister Dorothy Lees; Muslim
community members Asif Zaman and Rachel Butson; Tony Parkinson, prominent pro-
Iraq war journalist and foreign desk editor of the Melbourne broadsheet *The Age*; and
Ghassan Hage. Each speaker offered expertise and experiences that informed the project
in various ways. For example, Wright-Neville's insights into Australian and US security
organisations, Lees' observations on fundamentalism and Zaman and Butson's invitation
to attend prayers shaped material for the *Blowback* script and gave clues to performative
moments. Parkinson is an expert on Middle Eastern politics. His presentation in support of
the 'war on terror' gave insights into the mindset of dominant powers. Hage's contribution
was particularly important in outlining not only a political system, but a mindset or culture
of occupation – the central theme and metaphor for *Blowback*.

Ideas about the society under occupation informed the research process and a
play script was developed with the aim to show occupation as a psychic and physical
experience of total control. Likewise, while early NYID works connected external rep-
resentations of body images to political rhetoric, works such as *Journey to Con-fusion*,
K and *Blowback* began to explore questions of power from internalised perspectives.
As Pledger observes:

> One thing I became interested in was shifting from the gestural choreography to internalis-
> ing that gesture in a more realistic dramatic exchange. I also became very interested in the
> relationship between the body and a society of repression. Because I felt that over the last
> five years, there are many bodies in the world that live in systems of oppression. And that
> a country like Australia has profoundly contributed to those mechanisms of oppression.[22]

Working in the venue and with theatrical space

According to NYID's technical manager, Paul Jackson:

> Space is never virtual in NYID; space is concrete. Over the twentieth century, we learnt
> how to build theatres where the theatre does not exist. We build theatres that are the plat-
> forms for the work. NYID is the antithesis of this. Even when we work in a theatre space
> we think about the concreteness of that, not its virtuality.[23]

Box 10.3: The performance text

The performance script reflects the complexity of performance information that constitutes *Blowback* and is colour- and font-coded. Scene location information (for example, 'Scene two') is recorded in one colour and font. Indications of the pre-recorded video material (such as the soap opera credit sequence) are in a second colour. Musical cues and descriptions of live-camera shots (instructions to actors and camera operators about acting to specific cameras and shots required) are in a third format; and dialogue is in a fourth. In the excerpt below (rendered here only in different fonts), we see how this notation accounts for textual, performance and audiovisual elements of *Blowback*.

A World of Our Own

Scene 2

Video 6   Live-to-Air Multi-Cam Broadcast (All Monitors)

<u>Play in Music Theme.</u>

Scott and Charlene are in the same position. They turn to accommodate a better angle. They are in a close, medium two-shot.

Scott

I want to show you something, Charlene. Come with me. Please come with me. I've found a door, Charlene. To a new world. And a better place.

Pledger's polysemic script captures the diverse elements of the performance. Although a working document during rehearsal, the final script of *Blowback* presented in this manner was short-listed in the 2006 Victorian Premier's Literary Awards, one of Australia's main literature competitions. *Blowback* is a new kind of text for a mediatised theatrical environment.

Experimenting with theatrical space is an important aspect of the company's overall approach.[24] The location for *Blowback*, a run-down hall at the rear of the seedy poker-machine-infested St Kilda Army and Navy Club, was an appropriately *fin de siècle* location, evoking a dystopian ambience. The high ceiling and patched, paint-peeling walls gave a damp utilitarian feel. The set-up of fluorescent lighting bars, TV monitors and cables coiling everywhere suggested a military-style temporary occupation field post (see figure 10.8). As Jackson argues, this accords with 'a particular line about foregrounding technology and making it seamless that Pledger hovers on'.[25]

Pledger works architecturally to design the space and its dynamic flows. Processes of blocking – formal elements of most rehearsals – become an extended task in his overall visualisation of the performance. The question of moving the text through the space requires precise placement of not only actors and scenery (as is standard rehearsal procedure), but also camera operators and their movements, and the anticipated movements of the audience. Technical, media and audience effects are pre-planned by Pledger, in turn written into the script, and rehearsed as a kind of spatial choreography and media shot-board (see box 10.3).

In the eventual production of *Blowback*, the stage set-up – especially the placement of the audience – was visibly and dramatically significant. The venue was compact, with the audience and actors in close proximity. As Jackson argues, the organisation of space in this way aims to extend the expressive and interpretive possibilities of the performing body and is a hallmark of Pledger's design philosophy:

> Emptying the space around the performer is also about reopening the possibilities of the body to have agency. So much of stage design is actually about determining how the body can inhabit space by controlling the space. If you emptied the space, then all of a sudden the decisions and movements of the body become more apparent. The body is given a kind of agency that it cannot handle in a normal, traditional play production setting.[26]

During the performance, the audience watches a mix of live action and video transmissions. The spectators sit among the action and become in effect a socially representative group. So close were the bodies of audience and actors in the Melbourne season that the distinct boundaries of actor and viewer became blurred; each 'participated' in experiencing interrogation, torture, resistance. In this way, the play explored the sense of being 'embedded' like journalists in the Iraq war. It asked the audience to consider to what extent 'ordinary people' are explicitly authorising and authoring a mentality of occupation and are complicit in its acts of violence.

Rehearsing for mediatisation in performance

In *Blowback*, actors work both to camera and to the live audience simultaneously. Rehearsing the elements of performance requires thinking and planning in two and three dimensions of performative time and space. Theatrical images work in an epic mode and utilise, for example, dramatic dialogue, dance and direct address to the audience and also work as intimate scenes performed for transmission to the TV monitors (see figure 10.7). This generates great dramatic complexity for actors and crew, complexity that the rehearsal process must concentrate on.

Mediatised environments also require technical solutions that bear on questions of performance. As Jackson notes:

> A screen-based environment is very proscriptive . . . To make a screen read more legibly you have to create a high contrast environment . . . You need to ask what sort of environment do we need to be able to read a screen and what sort of environment makes camera operation possible. [In thinking about lighting] you need to think about the scene as an installation, as lighting bodies and as a [director of photography], for camera operation. From these interactions you arrive at 'the look'. And that [is] balanced against the very real limitations of what is [made] possible by the infrastructure.[27]

Pledger and Jackson must anticipate these factors. Pledger works his spatial and acting rehearsals to integrate with the televisual presence of the screens and their content. He usually brings to the rehearsal pre-mapped movements and a strong sense of what he aims to achieve on a visual and dramatic plane. Moving through

10.9 Televisual media in NYID performances. *Scenes from the Beginning of the End.*

and marking the space, testing these propositions on the floor, while keeping in mind camera shots and the effects of close-up images of actors' heads and surveillance footage, are key directorial tasks.

While the camera provides televisual layers to the performance experience, it also frames the stage. It picks out audience members, giving them a sense of intimacy and discomfort. It frames events in gestic detail (the cliché of the soap opera's close-up look past camera, surveillance images of beatings) while offering alternatives for reading the scene at hand (see figure 10.9).

The aim is to create interpretative possibilities for space. For Pledger, 'The minute you open up the space, the performer is more exposed . . . [I]f you are in an open space and the audience is always around you, every movement you make has meaning.'[28] Likewise, the use of television images in *Blowback* helps reinforce the point that different media play an important role in constructing our contemporary social reality.

Working with performers

NYID accumulate dramatic forms in making a new performance work. These are layered substrata that underpin the formal elements of performance and foster the interdisciplinary focus of the work overall. As I have argued, the principal aim is to create a dramaturgy that, in Baz Kershaw's description, is 'highly alert to the reflexive paradoxical principles of its own performative protocols and procedures'.[29] This makes for a metatheatrical frame. In the frame, however, performers often show fascination for detailing the work. For example, a performer can become exceptionally skilled in performing complex psycho-physical gestural choreography, another might handle intense dramatic moments while being very close to the audience, or they can work on a fragmented dramaturgical plane while making sense of the overall rhythm of the work. In Pledger's approach to collaboration, performers who have helped develop particular facets of the work can continue to work with these and even claim a certain iconic status. Their developed understanding of what NYID wants in performance terms is highly valued (see box 10.4).

In working with performers on *Blowback*, Pledger required differing approaches. Each of the four scenarios needed to be distinct and the audience had to grasp specific

> ## Box 10.4: Performers and the rehearsal process
>
> NYID prefers visual and physical forms of representation. However, trained actors in particular (in contrast to dance-trained performers who also work with NYID) are sometimes less enthused by this focus, perhaps feeling that work on character is downplayed for an overwhelming emphasis on *mise en scène*. NYID performers are required to be able to move and act – and their skills in combining these modes of expression are valued. Pledger himself trained as an actor and has knowledge of many working processes, not only from Australian training programmes but also from Asia and Europe.
>
> In pre-production, the overall dramatic effect of an NYID stage – the presence of bodies, the intertextuality, and interactions with space and audience – is strongly visualised; however, the processes of working with performers are not, at this stage, completely decided. Pledger is careful to support performers' individual needs and responds to their suggestions by modifying presentational forms. He sometimes rewrites dialogue to accommodate a performer's rhythm and readily includes their suggestions. Devising and adapting texts for performance is part of the rehearsal process, and workshops on dramaturgy ask for participation from the company as a whole. This sense of negotiation informing the writing process – one that invites feedback from actors and collaborating artists – continues during the rehearsal period.

gestic and genre forms. Scenes between Scott and Charlene played to cameras *and* live to the audience as the two actors marked the edges of the performance space in their 'journey' to the city. Intended signification was explicit: the actors playing Scott and Charlene were experienced television actors giving a sense of irony in their performances. These were actors playing in a soap opera with a sense of knowing the conventions and using them to deconstruct the form in a live performance context (see figure 10.5).

Contrasting this, the first two interrogation scenes were exceptionally psychologically internalised, required completely different actor sensibilities and were necessarily more realistic in style. As Pledger noted, *Blowback* 'was initially conceived in anger, after Abu Ghraib'.[30] In the torture scene between Darko and Casey James, we must believe the intensity and horror of this exchange (see figure 10.6). It is essential to the success of the work that a sense of injustice is communicated through realistic acting. And while the scenes between the two military officers Ripper and Reeve had a certain intentional 'Dr Strangelove' tone, they too needed to be rendered dramatically valid. Rehearsing both of these scenes, Pledger tended to apply more conventional actor-director techniques, wherein questions of emotional intensity and character were discussed and workshopped.

Finally, the actor playing Captain Mickey (Tom Considine) and the dancer playing Sargent-Sargent (Natalie Cursio) were required to develop their dance and acting skills (see figure 10.7). Their scenes began menacingly and were unresolved. In the second part of the performance, they transformed from playing a darker interrogation routine to giving a broadly satirical song and dance variety show performance directed for television. Rehearsal of this scene focused on choreography and shifting from dramatic to comic performance styles.[31]

Extremes of war produce a form of social reality that is distorted. In *Blowback,* the sense of a combined political-military psychosis was conveyed in the juxtaposition of the three interrogations. Each was a distorted image of reality coupled with a sense of *déjà vu* and hyperreality. This idea was key to the work as a whole and the rehearsal process facilitated the actors in discovering how to play this sort of reality.

Critical responses

Reviewers responded to *Blowback's* cultural and political agenda. Reviewing for the weekly arts zine *Inpress,* performance scholar Jonathan Marshall writes, 'Like Sartre, Godard and the Existentialists of the 1960s, *Blowback* suggests that, for such a fraught society, the rediscovery of the pointlessness of beauty, and of the individual's sublime pleasure in its rich yet simple ambiguities, will set free the shackles of such previously closed minds.'[32] Extrapolating from Marshall's review suggests that the Situationist-DIY aesthetic shown in the show's closing scenes, in which Scott and Charlene watch super-8 film of gum trees, helps to revive an indigenous memory of Australia.

Blowback aims to explore resistance to power by showing how power works. Members of the occupying force interrogate prisoners and officials about the images. In this way, the piece tries to depict an occupation mentality. In her broadsheet review of *Blowback,* Gabriella Coslovich writes:

> Actions are scrutinised and distorted; people are always at risk of being accused of treason or subversion. As is customary with Not Yet It's Difficult productions, the audience is immersed in the action. Seats are arranged in a circle and face the middle of the performance space. Camera operators film the actors and the images appear on the television screens lining the periphery of the theatre space. Reality is mediated through the television screen, and actions are under constant surveillance.[33]

The scholar Nikos Papastergiadis stated that *Blowback* 'proceeds by revealing the subtle and continuous process of colonisation of the imagination that is occurring under the banner of American hegemony'.[34] This continuum is mostly invisible, yet the outcomes are seen everywhere.

Like Brecht, NYID aims to 'show things as they are' – to focus attention on social problems and on the ways that power circulates and effects control. We recognise that to do this requires a substantial rethinking of theatre. Our rehearsal process is where this rethinking takes place. It is a process of development and preparation for performance. In linking politics, aesthetics and the history of the company's work we aim to make visible the invisible aspects of our world.

Notes

1   I would like to acknowledge contributions by David Pledger and Paul Jackson and thank them for interviews and feedback on this chapter.

2   Edward Scheer, 'Dissident Vectors: Surrealist Ethnography and Ecological Performance', in Peter Eckersall, Tadashi Uchino and Naoto Moriyama (eds), *Alternatives: Debating Theatre Culture in an Age of Con-fusion* (Brussels: Peter Lang, 2004), p. 60; Félix Guattari, *Les Trois Ecologies* (Paris: Galilée, 1989), p. 37.

3   NYID, 2006, Company website, www.notyet.com.au. Current projects, PDF download (accessed 8 January 2008).

4   Suzuki visited Australia in 1989 to give performances and workshops and in 1991 directed his work *The Chronicles of Macbeth* for Playbox Theatre in Melbourne using an Australian cast that included Pledger.

5   Hans-Thies Lehmann, *Postdramatic Theatre*, trans. Karen Jürs-Munby (Abingdon: Routledge, 2006).

6   David Pledger, interview with author, 1 September 2006.

7   Gay McAuley, *Space in Performance: Making Meaning in the Theatre* (Ann Arbor: University of Michigan Press, 2000), p. 16.

8   Pledger, interview with author.

9   Kirk Denton, 'Model Drama as Myth: A Semiotic Analysis of *Taking Tiger Mountain by Strategy*', in C. Tung and C. Mackerras (eds), *Drama in the People's Republic of China* (Buffalo: SUNY Press, 1987).

10   For further discussion of *Tiger Mountain*, see Peter Eckersall, 'Multiculturalism and Contemporary Theatre Art in Australia and Japan', *Poetica*, 50 (1998), pp. 155–64.

11   Rachel Fensham, 'Violence, Corporeality and Intercultural Theatre', in Eckersall, *et al.* (eds), *Alternatives*, p. 97.

12   See Eckersall et al. (eds), *Alternatives*.

13   Paul Jackson in Peter Eckersall, 'On Physical Theatre: A Roundtable Discussion from NYID with Peter Eckersall, David Pledger, Paul Jackson, Greg Ulfan', *Australasian Drama Studies*, 41 (2002), pp. 23, 26.

14   Ghassan Hage, *Against Paranoid Nationalism: Searching for Hope in a Shrinking Society* (Sydney: Pluto Press 2003).

15   The main conservative party in Australia is called the Liberal Party and was the ruling party led by Prime Minister John Howard from 1996 to 2007.

16   Tony Coady, 'The Folly of Dangerous and Foolish Patriotism,' *The Age* (7 October 2006), Insight, p. 7.

17   Chalmers Johnson, *Blowback: The Costs and Consequences of American Empire* (New York: Metropolitan Books, 2000).

18   Chalmers Johnson, 'Blowback,' *Nation* (15 October 2001), available at www.thenation. com/doc/20011015/johnson (accessed 8 January 2008).

19   Michael Hardt and Antonio Negri, *Empire* (Cambridge, MA: Harvard University Press, 2000), p. 406.

20   The scene draws on audience identification of a widely circulating image from the Abu Ghraib prison of a US female guard pointing to a pile of naked Iraqi male bodies.

21   Pledger, interview with author.

22   *Ibid.*

23   Paul Jackson, interview with author, 23 September 2006.

24   In past productions NYID performed in site-specific venues such as a public car park

(*Scenes of the Beginning from the End*, 2001), the public and private spaces of a museum (*K*) and a film studio (*Scenes* tour, 2004).

25 Jackson, interview with author.

26 *Ibid.*

27 *Ibid.*

28 David Pledger in Eckersall, 'On Physical Theatre', pp. 22–3.

29 Baz Kershaw, 'E-interview for Performance Paradigm: The End of Ethics', *Performance Paradigm* ejournal, 3 (2007), www.performanceparadigm.net (accessed 30 October 2007).

30 Pledger quoted in Stephen Dunne, 'Kylie Help Us', *Sydney Morning Herald* (21 April 2006), Metro section.

31 A dramaturgical subtext was also explored as the idea of the scene gave flesh to a dramaturgical thread in the story suggesting that, in the society of *Blowback*, TV is used as a form of social distraction, a way of escaping from the painful experience of living under occupation and of confronting the reality of one's situation.

32 Jonathan Marshall, '*Blowback* Review', *Inpress* (15 December 2004), n.p.

33 Gabriella Coslovich, 'Pledger's Dark Society,' *The Age* (3 December 2004), Arts section.

34 Nikos Papastergiadis, email communication with Pledger, in *Blowback* company brochure, 2004.

11

Luk Perceval – *Platonov* (2006) – Rules for a theatre of contemporary contemplation

Zoë Svendsen

Actors, who relate their woes in many clever sentences and with much waving of hands and rolling of eyes – they should be made to ride in the cars for passengers with heavy loads, to learn that a slightly bent hand can hold in it the misery of all time, and that the quiver of an eyelid can be more moving than a whole evening full of crocodile tears. Perhaps they shouldn't be trained in drama schools but sent to work in the forests, to understand that their work is not speech but silence. (Joseph Roth)[1]

From Belgium to Berlin

Luk Perceval's production of Chekhov's *Platonov* opened on 26 May 2006 at the Schaubühne am Lehninerplatz in Berlin. This is Perceval's second show at the theatre since being invited to become director-in-residence from autumn 2005. Perceval had originally trained and worked as an actor in Antwerp, Belgium, but in 1984, frustrated by what he regarded as an aesthetic ossification in the subsidised theatre, he co-founded an independent theatre outfit, Blauwe Maandag Compagnie, with fellow director Guy Joosten.[2] Their multi-prize-winning work was an influential part of the 1980s Flemish 'new wave'. In 1997 Perceval was invited to amalgamate Blauwe Maandag with Antwerp's main state-subsidised theatre, Koninklije Nederlandse Schouwburg. The new theatre, Het Toneelhuis, was established in 1998 with Perceval as its artistic director. This was an ensemble-oriented theatre that toured its award-winning productions across Europe. Perceval's breakthrough in the German-speaking world came in 1999, when the Schauspielhaus Hamburg, in co-production with the Salzburger Festspiele, invited him to restage Blauwe Maandag's highly successful production *Ten Oorlog* (1997). Known as *Schlachten!* in German, this was an extraordinary reworking of Shakespeare's history plays, stitched together in historical chronology and performed by a single ensemble of actors. Twelve hours long, *Schlachten!* staged the unfolding of history as a breakdown in language, from the classicism and relative textual fidelity of the company's *Richard II* to the iconoclastic, multilingual colloquialism of *Dirty Rich Modderfocker der Dritte* (*Richard III*), with Richard played by Thomas Thieme (Osip in *Platonov*, and more recently seen as Minister Hempf in the Oscar-winning film *The Lives of Others* [2006]). The production led to further invitations to Perceval to direct in German theatres, eventually resulting in the offer of the post of associate director at the Schaubühne.

Converted from a 1928 purpose-built cinema designed by Erich Mendelsohn, the Schaubühne was run by the celebrated German director Peter Stein from 1971 to 1985. During Stein's tenure it gained a reputation as a home to epic and extremely detailed versions of classic western drama. Since 1999, under the direction of Thomas Ostermeier, its mission has been to produce 'contemporary' (*zeitgenössich*) theatre, concentrating largely on international new writing, marking a break with Stein's legacy. Perceval's brief is to create versions of classics that re-imagine the text in a contemporary light, a process for which he had become known across Europe. His productions prior to *Platonov* include *Turista* by Marius von Mayenburg (2005, Wiener Festwochen), *Uncle Vanya* (2003, Het Toneelhuis), *Othello* (2003, Münchner Kammerspiele), *Andromache* (adapted from Racine, 2003, Schaubühne Berlin/Het Toneelhuis), *L. King of Pain*, adapted from Shakespeare's *King Lear* (2002, Stadsschouwburg Brugge/Het Toneelhuis) and Jon Fosse's *Autumn Dream* (2001, Münchner Kammerspiele, and 2002, Berlin Theatertreffen).

Perceval's recent work at the Schaubühne has explored crises of masculinity. In his production after *Platonov*, Arthur Miller's *Death of a Salesman* (2006), any capacity of the female to hold power relations in balance is voided by the sheer violence of masculine self-destruction. Thomas Thieme's Willy, large in body but little else, barely moves from his central position on the sofa as we watch him suck his whole family into the vortex of his despair. Perceval's subsequent project, *Molière: ein Passion* (2007, Salzburger Festspiele), amalgamates four plays by the seventeenth-century French dramatist Molière with dysfunctional male heroes at their centre: Don Juan, Tartuffe, Alceste (*The Misanthrope*) and Harpagon (*The Miser*). Retrospectively, *Platonov* can be seen as the first production in this trajectory of exploring male psychic and physical disintegration.

Authenticity and the classic text

Platonov, Chekhov's first surviving full-length play, was rejected by the Maly Theatre in 1882 and never produced in his lifetime. It deals with a disintegrating society in which monetary bonds masquerade as sociability; where, for want of any real escape

route, the figures play out their desires and frustrations on one another. The eponymous central character, once destined for great things, exercises his self-hatred by
destroying those around him. Perceval explains that his choice of the play was part
aesthetic and part practical. Interested in making work for the largest possible spaces
at the Schaubühne, he must choose from a repertoire 'which interests a large audience'. In Germany this tends to mean the production of classic texts. 'Then you have
the challenge – how do you surprise the audience, rather than serve them?'[3]

In addressing that challenge Perceval confronts not only the ghost of Chekhov
but also the luminous shadow of Stein, who created definitive productions at the
Schaubühne of Chekhov, Shakespeare and the classical Greek tragedians in the
1970s and early 1980s. As with Stein, Perceval's work with classic texts is the expressive outcome of a specialised rehearsal process, although neither the approach nor
the aesthetic are related. Perceval's focus is firmly on the contemporary moment:
'One can be just as contemporary with a play like *Maria Stuart* or *Platonov* as one
is with Sarah Kane', he suggests. 'It is a different dramaturgy, a different kind of
literature, but contemporaneity isn't about whether something is old or new.' His
own productions effect a different sort of engagement with the present than simply
the sprinkling of current references or fashions. They offer the increasingly cir-
cumscribed experience of *being there*. 'In our current culture of frenzied quick-fire
images everywhere', says Perceval, 'in the theatre I feel the need to listen, for it all
to come to a halt, a need for that which cannot be named and certainly cannot be
shown.'[4]

Perceval explains that his fascination with 'classic' plays derives from them being
'hieroglyphs, etched tablets from another planet, which nevertheless speak of the same
individual lack of direction. No answers, no results, just questions and much "I don't
know".'[5] The idea of not knowing, of 'nothingness' or 'emptiness', derived from Zen
Buddhism, is fundamental. Perceval describes the theatre as a 'ritual place where we
are able to acknowledge nothingness, to accept that we don't have any answers. Sadly
our society offers few alternatives [for such experience]'.[6] Theatre, then, becomes a
place of concentrated stillness, an engagement with humanity in which 'to see the
individual on stage, just as he is' (see figure 11.1).

Perceval's production of Chekhov's *Platonov* aims to train its spectators' eyes on
everyday life and the minutiae of human behaviour. Working against dramatic representation, it approaches a theatrical equivalent of the phenomenology of experience
so strongly advocated by Berlin writers of the 1920s such as Joseph Roth and Franz
Hessel, in their responses to the frenetic modernism of Weimar Germany. Meanwhile
the individual whom Perceval is interested to hold up to view has much in common
with the figure to whom the French philosopher Michel de Certeau dedicates his
exploration of tactical autonomy in human behaviour, *The Practice of Everyday Life*:

> He is the murmuring voice of societies. In all ages, he comes before texts. He does not
> expect representations. He squats now at the centre of our scientific stages. The flood-
> lights have moved away from the actors who possess proper names and social blazons,
> turning first towards the chorus of secondary characters, then settling on the mass of the
> audience.[7]

11.1 Luk Perceval's direction of *Platonov*: Anna Petrovna (Karin Neuhäuser) waiting for Platonov (Act 1). Still from rehearsal footage.

Perceval's enquiry into the everyday through performance operates with a de Certeau-like zoom lens. The work does not re-present a world elsewhere but systematically focuses attention on what is before us. Perceval observes that he is strongly drawn to Chekhov as a writer whose texts facilitate his own desire to strip away all that is unnecessary in theatrical presentation. 'He is an author who demands authenticity', he says, 'because when you read him, the figures are so genuine that as an actor – and also as a theatre-maker – you cannot reconstruct what is there, but rather must re-experience it, whereby the figure – and the actor – retains his humanity, his authenticity, his veracity.' The individual that emerges is certainly no hero, especially in the case of *Platonov*'s eponymous lead. 'Here we have a protagonist who in fact is no protagonist at all', says Perceval. Rather, he is 'a black hole' throughout, someone who 'completely refuses to play his role'[8] – whether that assigned to him by society or ostensibly by a conventional dramaturgy. This anti-dramatic characterisation sits comfortably within a postdramatic playing style. '*Platonov* is the ultimate attempt to see how far one can go with illustrating nothing on stage', says Perceval, 'so that one becomes fascinated simply by looking at people'.

First principles and prerequisites

In the read-through of *Platonov*, held a couple of weeks prior to the ten-week rehearsal period, Perceval neatly banishes the spectre of Stanislavski that inevitably haunts productions of Chekhov's plays with an apocryphal anecdote. He describes Chekhov's dismay at Stanislavski's 1904 production of *The Cherry Orchard* – full of detailed directorial extrusions – as being so great that he vanished for three days, apparently to walk off his horror. There is another sort of scepticism of Stanislavski at work in Perceval's production. 'If you follow Stanislavski', he argues, 'then you no longer react, you internalise everything, you've built up a whole framework just for yourself . . . you don't react, only pretend to act. Pretty quickly I discovered in rehearsals that every kind of illustration of the situation, or of psychology, or the one-to-one fulfilment of what the text says – that that doesn't actually interest me at all.'

By contrast, Perceval seeks to collapse the distance between the actor-as-person and actor-as-performer in the playing style. He requires the actors to come back to themselves – to 'be' rather than to 'act'. 'At the beginning I have to force the actors to stop "acting" [in the rhetorical, dramatic sense],' he says. This de-masking of the actor-as-person is a challenge to the performers, as Thomas Bading, who plays Platonov, observes:

> I have noticed that with Luk I can't take myself, personally, out of the equation, that is, me, myself. I am asked as Thomas Bading, with that which I have in me, and that's what I have to express, I have to affirm that, and I have to know myself, particularly here, as Platonov . . . Luk also watches very closely, and every attempt at escape . . . every time you seek a way out through a gesture, or what you say, and that forces you back onto yourself, and to really think the lines, to feel and then simply to speak. He won't allow any form of escape from that.[9]

In production, this paring down of action to everyday forms of behaviour has a powerful social dimension. Stripping away the dramatic agency of rhetorical performance reverses the power structures of the stage: rather than actors *playing*, the figures we see seem to be *played* – by their circumstances, those around them, their cultural location and historical moment. The characters' agency is demonstrated to be illusory.

Having produced an initial version of the text with Schaubühne dramaturg Maja Zade, Perceval uses the read-through to listen to the play and cut any lines that are repetitive or double the action. This process, embraced by the actors, who often suggest cuts or improvise alterations, continues throughout the rehearsal period. As the action develops to embody what was previously mediated through spoken dialogue, the text is cut further. An entire spoken scene at the start of Act 2, Scene 2, for example, is in the course of rehearsal concentrated to a kiss – one that takes place whilst the scene that follows is played. The starting point of the production, the spoken word, is no longer the primary motor of the action but is carried by it.

The first day of rehearsals proper begins with Perceval and then set designer Annette Kurz introducing the play and their ideas to date. We are at the Schaubühne's rehearsal rooms, on a nineteenth-century industrial estate to the north of Berlin, where we will be working Monday to Friday from 11.00 until 15.00, and occasionally in the evenings as well. The German repertory system entails that most of the actors in the ensemble perform in the evenings in productions at the Schaubühne or at other

> ### Box 11.1: Perceval's prerequisites for rehearsal
>
> 1. The actors learn the text by heart, prior to starting rehearsal.
> 2. The actors are present in all rehearsals.
> 3. The actors eat well in rehearsal. It is the task of the interns to ensure that there is healthy food available for people to munch on: not just tea and biscuits, but salad, fresh dips, cheese, water, vegetables, fruit, crispbreads.
>   Perceval: 'I don't like it when people sit around drinking coffee and smoking, and doing things that make you enervated. The energy is extremely important.'
> 4. Rehearsals last for three to four hours, but in that time there must be absolute concentration on the work.
>   Perceval: 'What matters is that in these three to four hours we have tried everything possible with the scene.'

theatres, sometimes involving long journeys to other German cities. Perceval makes it a condition, however, that the actors are continuously present in rehearsal. The rehearsal room is swarming with people: the fifteen actors in the cast, the designers and technicians, and myriad assistants to the creative team.

The actors spread out to occupy various seats around the stage, and attempt to run the lines of the first act from memory. 'First of all we work through the text, making sure that we can use it in any situation', says Perceval, 'and from the moment we've got that, then we can look and see what arises from the actors' encounter in the here and now'. From day one the actors are not permitted to read from a script in rehearsal. It quickly becomes clear that not all have the text at their fingertips. Perceval places great emphasis on line-learning, seeking to ensure the actors learn in such a way that they no longer appear to be 'quoting' a text: 'When a person speaks, it comes from another coordination centre [from the part of the brain that learns text] . . . The text needs to be transferred from one centre to the other. That's why I say when we do Italians [speed line runs], "don't give yourselves time to think".'

As well as continually returning to line-runs of scenes or whole acts throughout the rehearsal process, Perceval uses the game of badminton to achieve this shift. The aim is for the actors to speak fluently and on cue whilst concurrently having to react to what is happening around them – in this instance, the badminton game. The shuttlecock must be kept in the air without pausing or dropping a cue, and in this way it can be played by any number of actors, with one or more shuttlecocks. Perceval notes wryly that it has become a matter of competition between casts of actors on different productions to better the score of the last cast with which he has worked. Such attention to the moment includes the director's own relation to the playing rather than the play text. As Perceval notes:

> From the first day of rehearsals, when we really start rehearsing, I throw the text away, I don't look at it any more, even at home, because from that moment I am only interested in what happens in front of me, how do I get it such that I can watch for hours on end, like a cat, and remain in a state of heightened alertness.

11.2 Platonov dances himself to exhaustion (Act 2). Left to right: Osip (Thomas Thieme), Sascha (Christina Geisse), Jakow (Bernd Grawert), Platonov (Thomas Bading), Anna Petrovna (Karin Neuhäuser).

Design in process

The production's design elements are to some extent generated within the rehearsal process rather than being determined in advance as would usually be the case in large-scale repertory productions. Perceval sees an opportunity in his residency at the Schaubühne to escape from working with a proscenium arch and the theatricality that it infers. 'The architecture forces, when you build in a design, a reality all of its own,' he says. 'You have to work with the space, then it becomes an actor, then it becomes a location.' His production of *Platonov* marks the first time that the two largest of the Schaubühne's three studio spaces, usually partitioned, have been amalgamated for spoken-word theatre since the current administration arrived in 1999. This creates an enormous space seating six hundred, with a stage area 20 metres high and 50 metres wide, backed by an impressive concrete cyclorama that is part of the original building (see figures 11.2 and 11.3).

The design team comprises Perceval's regular collaborators: set designer Annette Kurz, costume designer Ursula Renzenbrink and lighting designer Mark Van Denesse. Kurz places a strong emphasis on the presence of the 'real', by way of objects or scenic

11.3 Triletsky: 'What's wrong with Anna Petrovna today? She laughs, she sighs, kisses everybody … You know, I think she may be in love!' (Act 2) Left to right: Glagolyev (Erhard Marggraf), Petrin (Michael Renzenbrink), Vengerovich Jr (David Ruland), Platonov (Thomas Bading), Anna Petrovna (Karin Neuhäuser), Triletsky (Felix Römer).

devices that are strikingly actual as well as figurative. In two recent productions with Perceval this has been taken to an extreme in the use of elements that ostensibly present a danger to the actors, from broken glass in *Andromache* (2003, Het Toneelhuis/Schaubühne) to live archery in *Maria Stuart* (2006, Schaubühne). Prior to production, Kurz begins with an array of images and an empty, proportional model box, in which stand miniature cut-outs of the actual actors in the piece. To this she adds a single point from which to begin – in the case of *Platonov*, a piano. A combination of the conceptual, pragmatic and aesthetic is at work.

'I asked Luk, "Give me a keyword for what the space should be for *Platonov*",' she recalls, 'and it was funny because then he said, "It should be cosy" – and here you are with the largest, hugest concrete hall'.[10] The final design for *Platonov* is a wooden floor, its boards criss-crossing in such a way as to imply the floor-plan of a large house (see figures 11.2 and 11.3). Ignoring boundaries, single railway lines litter the stage, alluding to a junction, while in their asymmetry denying the possibility of usage. The space rejects any illustration of actual place, serving to become whatever the figures indicate it to be: Anna Petrovna's drawing room, her garden, Platonov's front yard, or his schoolroom. Nevertheless, it resonates with de Certeau's definition of space as a 'practised place': the pianos are played, the rails are stepped or tripped over, or walked along. The relationship between playing space and visual aesthetic is symbiotic. By regularly visiting rehearsals and taking final decisions as late as possible, Kurz is able to fine-tune her design in response to the actors' use of the scenic starting points she provides. Whilst the rails exemplify an interpenetration of inside and outside, as well as alluding to a frustrated longing for escape, they also function to orientate the acting space. They provide boundaries and split the stage into distinct areas, offering actors routes and obstacles, and the production a physical means to express emotional turmoil.

Similarly, costume designer Renzenbrink's method is to develop the costumes through response to rehearsal. 'It is more or less about starting again from nothing,' she says. 'That is, searching anew, not repeating anything you've done before, but instead trying to look with fresh eyes in the new context and to think differently.'[11] She and her assistant provide the actors with rehearsal costumes at the start of rehearsals, which are replaced, altered or added to, several times over. Detailed changes such as the colour of a tie or jacket are made for formal reasons as much as those concerning individual character. As Renzenbrink observes:

> The most important decision happened one or two weeks into rehearsal. No more colourful costumes using the whole of the colour spectrum – instead we would largely use black and white, [alluding to] weddings, funerals. Above all it was to seem like an image in memory, like an old photo, where the colours have faded. In this way, the old red velvet armchair in the middle would become the only focal point of warmth . . . There were a few other points of colour dotted in the space: Karin's dark green military jacket [Anna Petrovna; see figure 11.1], the flowers on Lea's [Marja] skirt. In the end I swopped Felix's [Triletsky] red tie for a grey one, because I felt there were already enough points of colour in the room.[12]

The design process thereby takes place organically as a part of rehearsal practice – a myriad of decisions in response to what takes place on the floor.

Rules of engagement

From the very first day the actors run whole acts rather than rehearsing individual scenes or fragments of scenes. Having spoken through the dialogue of Act 1, Perceval arrests the actors' desire to get up and perform with the rule that no one is to leave their place. He reminds them of the situation of the beginning of the play, that it is terribly hot, and that they have all been drinking since early that morning – waiting for the arrival of Platonov. He gradually introduces further rules to shape the playing (see box 11.2).

How such rules are interpreted partly takes the form of a game of wills (conjoined or oppositional), provoking creativity in the rehearsal process. Another way of characterising these interactions – commonplace in ethnography since the work of Erving Goffman – is to use the paradigm of performance itself.[13] In the rehearsal

Box 11.2: Perceval's rules of engagement

Date	Rule
	Rules in italics were repeated with most frequency and applied throughout.
WEEK 1 (working on Act 1)	• It is even too warm to make theatre!
	• *Don't speak and move at the same time – or when anyone else is speaking or moving.*
	• Don't use any names except Platonov.
	• *Try using dialogue as you think it, not how it is written.*
	• (*Regarding music*) Whenever the silence goes on too long, start playing.
	• (*To Platonov*) Your hands never leave your pockets.

Perceval: 'I can see far too much "acting" on stage. Real people seek to keep themselves under control as long as they can.'

WEEK 2 (working on Act 2)	• *No one is to look at anyone else even (especially) when speaking.*
	• (*Regarding music*) Every time Platonov is about to leave, start playing.
	• Everyone is drunk.
	• (*To Platonov*) Just talk to your cock for the whole act!
	• (*To Platonov and Sascha*) Imagine that they haven't had sex for two years, and that she is completely uncertain of him and herself.
	• (*To Petrin*) Speak your text in made-up Russian.
	• (*To Osip*) He's [Platonov] fucking the love of your life!
	• (*To Platonov*) His favourite author is Strindberg . . .
	• (*To Anna Petrovna*) What she would really like to do is scream, but she represses the desire.

Perceval: 'The idea about not looking at each other came to me in the underground on the way back from rehearsals.'

WEEK 3 (working on Acts 2 and 3)	• Don't play the emotion.
	• Let silences happen.
	• *Don't answer to your cue, but answer the thought.*

Perceval: 'In life we don't wait for our cue to speak.'

	• Always break the others' rhythms.
	• Don't use the music to comment on or illustrate what is happening – let the music be an automatic character.
WEEK 4 (working on Acts 3 and 4)	• No holy atmosphere!
	• *Don't do anything with your body – just keep the energy in the words.*
	• (*To Anna Petrovna and Voynitsev, after they each find out that their beloved is sleeping with someone else*) No theatre, just think, don't try and demonstrate how you are feeling. No self-pity!
	• *The important thing is that all you really want to do is annihilate him [Platonov].*

room, then, there is a kind of *mise-en-abîme* effect, with the performer performing the practices associated with rehearsal by strict adherence to (or chafing against) the rules. Both in working as an actor and performing a character, the rules (as defined by the director) orientate one's interactions with others. In Perceval's process, the system of rules is explicit. It structures the work done in rehearsals and becomes ingrained in the production.

The framework provided is less a cage than an exoskeleton, as Bading describes. 'At first, I just fulfil the form . . . I torture myself for a while, and then I realise that this corset that he has given me, that I can serve it, that I do actually have room for manoeuvre within it.'[14] Indeed, within the restraints provided by the rules the actor can play with the lines and characterisation as appropriate. As Karin Neuhäuser (Anna Petrovna) explains, 'It is just a lot of fun when you can try out lots of things – I at any rate try out something new almost every time, because I want to fathom who in the end she is, this Anna. Finding life within this form is something I find a lot more exciting than leaving all possibilities open – then it is boring.'[15] In the course of rehearsals the work thereby acquires a richness that holds it open to multiple inter-pretations by an audience. The 'blank' memorising of text – independent from psy-chological inflection – means that the actors are sufficiently free to make changes right into performance, reacting in the present to what is happening around them on stage. Actors respond very differently to this possibility. Some improvise continually, others not at all. For an audience, however, it is impossible to distinguish these variations in technique, as they are held in balance by the form that governs the whole.

Over the course of the first week Perceval gradually introduces more rules to reduce activity in the room to what is essential. 'I try to get the lines as authentic as pos-sible', he explains, 'and seek a way that says, "don't speak at first, first of all look for the reason why you might say this sentence, at all, why you speak at all".' The rules generate an atmosphere in which every movement takes on significance. 'The idea was to split, as far as possible, the text being spoken and any movement, to separate out the music, to give everything its own place, and then to see how one can ultimately come gradually to a moment of truth, where every foot shuffle, every look becomes important.'

In the second week, rehearsing Act 2, Perceval adds the rule that no one is to look anyone else in the eye. This is a challenge for the actors, as Perceval explains:

> One prop for actors is to look at one another, because from the moment I look at you and, so to speak, connect with you, then I have something concrete to hold onto; as actor, I've got a direction, and then I know where my body should go. What I find much more interesting is how in everyday life, on the underground, we don't usually know where our bodies should go, lots of people don't have the confidence to look one another in the eye, we learnt how to do that in drama schools, but for many people it is unbelievably difficult.

The psychology of interpersonal relations on stage, grounded in dialogue and sup-ported by eye contact between actors, forms a web of gazes – a standard twentieth-century mode of capturing and sustaining audience attention in theatre. Here it is destroyed by the rule of no eye contact. Therefore the gaze of the audience is also less directed – there is no longer a 'centre' of action. Sometimes we do not quite know who is being spoken to – and therefore who will speak next. This both provides minute

11.4 Platonov: 'What did I do? Nothing good. When did I ever do anything that I didn't feel ashamed of afterwards?' (Act 2) Left to right: Platonov (Thomas Bading), Sascha (Christina Geisse). Still from rehearsal footage.

moments of suspense and brings the staging towards the authenticity that Perceval regards Chekhov as demanding. For eye contact is an essential part of sociability, so the impact of this simple instruction is the implication of a near-total breakdown of social cohesion in the world of the drama (see figure 11.4). In the eventual production this rule is not sustained rigidly – had it been, the form could well have overwhelmed the purpose it serves. Nonetheless, without the 'prop' of an alliance between conversation and eye contact, the gaze of the audience is less frequently specifically directed to any particular area on stage. A severance of the aural and visual takes place: listening to one conversation, I found myself observing another activity in a *mise en scène* that both evoked a Chekhovian dispersal of the centre and mirrored the increasing dislocations between time and place of our contemporary experience.

There is a risk in this approach, for the rules are not intended as a stylistic end in themselves. Perceval is concerned lest 'the actors think that it is a kind of formal theatre, that they should represent a kind of robot. And actually for me it is much more about delineating a heightened form of humanity.' Perceval's general practice is to offer such rules to explore what effects they produce in the acting. 'I start, the first four to five weeks, just to experiment quite roughly with the play,' he says. 'I try things out. Sometimes things that I don't use at all any more, later on, in order to develop – how shall I put it? – a fascination. Actually it doesn't matter what happens at all, the important thing is that the actors become fascinating.' Whilst Perceval insists that he has no preconceptions of what form rehearsals will take, it quickly becomes apparent that his rules will shape the underlying framework for the production. 'I just gave rough instructions', he says, 'not to move when you speak, don't look at one another – and this creates a huge loneliness [on stage].' When the text is played through this formal filter, we see characters incapable of sociability; a delineation of a broken society achieved without requiring the actors to retreat psychologically into themselves, to take themselves or their role too seriously. On the contrary, the form allows for absurdity, non sequiturs and the illogic of the everyday, giving room for abrupt and surprising changes in energy and direction.

Over the next few weeks, the rules become a mantra as each new act of the play is tackled. Some actors are quicker than others to follow this pattern of uncovering the psychological via physical form. For example, in their effort not to look at others, for a while some of the actors seem to be playing blind, unable to find their own focus. Therefore, according to Perceval, 'the closer we get to the premiere, the more I start to tell the actors about what I imagine to be the reasons why a person might just stare straight ahead [here, not look anyone in the eye]'. This might seem to entail coercive directorial imposition. Perceval insists, however, that he is after a fully lived and owned engagement with the character:

> I try to give reasons for [the form], so that the actor is able to develop this form out of his or her inner fantasy, from what he himself knows, whereby he immediately inhabits the form organically, rather than it being just an instruction imposed from outside. It is not meant purely as form, rather it is meant as something that arises out of a heightened form of being real, so that it is not a question of 'acting' but of 'being'.

'Less is more': an intermedial rehearsal process

On the third day of rehearsals Perceval and his camera assistant Nikolai Eberth start to film. Using digital video cameras, they step amongst the action as the actors play out the text, often filming from close up, seeking to capture both the detail of the acting and its spatial and emotional relation to what else is happening in the room (see figures 11.4 and 11.5).

This process has a number of significant effects. The very act of filming keeps the actors alert. 'They are much keener to act well for the camera [than if it were an ordinary rehearsal], because they know that I will show the film, and also that it is permanent,' explains Perceval. A director's attention in rehearsal is usually divided between the actors' work as it stands and creating an environment in which that work can develop in new directions. By means of the film, Perceval is able to some extent to separate these processes. It acts both as an aid to memory of what has worked in rehearsal and a means to explore where to take the work next. 'What I am actually experimenting with at the moment develops through the process of editing [the rehearsal films],' explains Perceval. 'When I'm at home in the evenings, and watch the rehearsal again, and choose the parts which I find interesting, then I always think "Okay, we can take this further, or that could become more sharp, that could be more extreme".'

At the start of most rehearsal days, especially during the first four weeks, the actors sit round a small TV to watch around twenty minutes of footage of the previous day's rehearsal, usually made up of a series of shots lasting a few minutes each edited by Perceval

11.5 Camera, action (Act 1). Left to right: Vengerovich Sr (Ulrich Voss), Vengerovich Jr (David Ruland), Benedict Haubrich (assistant director), Ivan Ivanovich (Horst Hiemer), Luk Perceval, Anna Petrovna (Karin Neuhäuser).

the night before. The shots are a mixture of work that he wants the actors to remember and reproduce, and places where he is unhappy with the acting. It is an extremely direct method of demonstrating his aim for the actors 'not to act'. 'What the camera immediately reveals is when the actors don't simply listen,' he says, 'when they don't simply watch what is happening, when they just aren't awake, and don't trust to their intuition, just to react to what is going on around them.' The playback enables Perceval to avoid a teacher–pupil relation with the actors, handing back to the actors responsibility for their performance. As David Ruland (Vengerovich Jr) observes, 'As soon as you see the film, then he [Perceval] barely has to give any criticism because you immediately see what's too much.'[16] The film is as useful to the group as it is to individuals. 'The advantage of the camera is that the actor suddenly gets a feeling for the whole,' says Perceval. 'It generates a collective consciousness, a collective responsibility.' This enables the actors themselves to take the work further with minimal interference. 'What I actually want to provoke with the camera is that the actors see the work as it is coming into being, step by step, and think for themselves about how it could be taken further, by which means they surprise me.'

If in the rehearsal room the camera becomes a kind of physical embodiment of the director's attention to the acting, it is also a means by which Perceval regulates his own responses. 'I try not to interrupt the actors' work straight away with comments, and the camera also forces me to be patient, to watch, and to wait', he says, 'until somehow a thread develops, which I would never myself before have thought of.' Such restraint is welcomed by the actors. As Horst Hiemer (Ivan Ivanovich) observes, 'What interests me most of all is that he lets the actor work freely, actually he only interrupts when necessary, sometimes I even have the impression that he holds himself back. As director, he'd like to do this or that, but says, "Hey! Better keep your

11.6 Anna Petrovna: 'It's simple: a woman has come to you who loves you, the weather is gorgeous, what's the problem?!' (Act 2) Left to right: Anna Petrovna (Karin Neuhäuser), Platonov (Thomas Bading). Still from rehearsal footage.

mouth shut!'"[17] The footage does not replicate theatrical presentation. Rather Perceval films the actors close up, from a metre or so away, picking out every detail. Nor is he interested in replicating a theatre audience's perspective, often filming from angles from which it would be impossible for an audience to view (see figures 11.1 and 11.6). By this means, Perceval 'collects' ideas and motifs from what the actors offer to him, in order to use this material to build the scaffolding of the final work.

Further, the process of filming in rehearsal permeates the aesthetics of the production as a whole. 'When I have time to watch people, then my mind starts to operate like a zoom,' says Perceval. 'I've arrived here in this huge space, and I feel the need to be able to watch [the stage] according to my own camera-eye-view, so that I myself choose where and what I will look at.' Perhaps surprisingly, given the enormous studio space created for *Platonov*, what Perceval describes is supported by my experience of watching the actors. The cinematically minute detail in the acting developed through the use of video in rehearsal is palpable even from a distance. This in turn encourages a visual concentration on the part of the spectator.

Scoring the performance

From week four of rehearsals onwards, once each act of the play has been worked through, Perceval starts to seek a rhythmic structure for the whole, focusing the actors' attention on the timing of exits and entrances, and showing on film the actors' interpretations of the text he finds most compelling. This is still a long way from the arranging of scene and movement described by the term 'blocking'; rather it provides a kind of performance score – what Perceval terms a 'scaffolding', an instinctive musicality informing the patterning of the *mise en scène*. This is not to say that the rhythmic pattern itself is comfortably harmonious. Discord and abrupt changes of tempo counterpoint the flow of speech or action, as it gradually becomes clear that Perceval's instruction to the actors not to take up the energy of others has paid off. Each figure has a unique rhythm and tempo, and each fresh entrance – or indeed exit – changes the balance of energy on the stage. The character Jakob (played by Bernd Grawert) provides a particularly strong example. An amalgamation of various characters in the text, he provides a background presence as a mysterious go-between, emerging in the finale as a Schadenfreude-filled victor. He also provides a live musical score to counterpoint events on stage, playing one or other of the three pianos placed at different intervals around the cyclorama. His slow, controlled tempo as he crosses the stage between Acts 3 and 4 operates as a direct counterpoint to the abject misery of Sergej (André Szymanski) just before, and the frantic despair of Sofia (Yvon Jansen) immediately afterwards.

The final two weeks of rehearsals take place on the stage at the Schaubühne with the set fully in place and with full technical support, giving Perceval time – 'a luxury' – to work with the actors in situ. The designers and their assistants tinker with details. The production is at a point where the work needs welding into a single performance flow. The warmth of the wooden floor lifts the space, making the curvature of the 20-metre-high concrete back wall seem like an embrace. Powerful footlights further lift the actors, picking them out against the space, and throwing shadows that echo and amplify their actions across the concrete walls on differing scales. The transition from rehearsal stage to the main stage is awkward in one respect. There is an acoustic problem: either the actors must resort to the very rhetorical mode Perceval seeks to avoid or will require amplification. The solution – microphones concealed at floor level around the stage – does not merely solve the problem technically. For the effect of hearing the actors as though in close proximity produces an intimacy of affect that belies the visual distance, acting as a kind of aural spotlight to focus the audience's attention on the action.

Over the penultimate week, the score is tightened, taking forty-five minutes off the running time, reducing the production to three hours in length. Each evening there is a run-through, while mornings are taken up with line-runs that concentrate on pushing the timing of entrances and exits, outbursts and silences – the performance score – into deep memory. On the third full run-through, a week before the premiere, Perceval asks the actors, who have been concentrating on erasing all longueurs from the production, to relax into its rhythm, and to breathe the stillness back into the work – the stillness with which the process began nine weeks earlier. Friday night's run-through remains the same length in real time, but in stage time a sense of infinite pause to observe the figures is brought to the fore. Cancelling Saturday's rehearsal, Perceval sends everyone home for a well-earned weekend off.

At Monday night's run, however, the performance score is hardening into the

> **Box 11.3: On giving notes**
>
> Without being overly secretive, the director tends to talk individually or in small
> groups with actors, often informally, almost never giving individual notes in front
> of a group, even in the last stages of rehearsal before the premiere. In this way, as
> Christine Geisse (Sascha) explained in a conversation with me, 'he makes everyone
> feel as though their role really matters to him, that he has really thought about it'
> (23 March 2007) (see figure 11.7).

sort of rigor mortis that might suggest over-rehearsal. Perceval's response is to discuss
with the actors the next day how it can be lifted. 'What's missing for me, is anger', he
says to his cast. '[Without it] it becomes a drawing room drama.'[18] He encourages
the company to free themselves: 'The form is there now, to be used, and as far as I'm
concerned, to be broken.'[19] His notes seek to re-collapse the distance between the
worlds of the play and the actor. Platonov, he suggests, is a figure who doesn't want to
play. 'What is it to perform alongside an actor who destroys the whole play?' Perceval
provocatively asks of his team.[20] His critique comes as a shock to the actors but it
works. Suddenly in the run that evening the production's edge is back, the figures have
regained the fascination so marked throughout the rehearsal process. The next day, to
disrupt the easy flow of scenes still further, Perceval asks Bading to interrupt whenever he 'gets bored' – indeed to disrupt the respect actors conventionally have for one
another on stage. 'Try and destroy every performance!' provokes Perceval.

'Like spying on your neighbours': the critical reception

The run-throughs leading up to the premiere are watched by an ever larger audience,
with the public dress rehearsal, premiere and subsequent performances fully sold out.
The challenge for the actors is now to sustain in audiences the state of heightened
alertness sought throughout the process. *Platonov* is Perceval's first production at the
Schaubühne to explore in depth the implosion of masculine identity that has become
a feature of his subsequent productions. As one critic noted, 'In the encyclopaedia of
contemporary life that Perceval shows writ large on the stage, the generation of men
now reaching middle-age is a disaster.'[21] The range of emotion in the production is vast,
from the suppressed tension of waiting that begins the performance, to the tenderness
between the horse thief Osip (Thomas Thieme) and Platonov's wife Sascha (Christina
Geisse) in their mutual loneliness, or from the cuckolded husband Sergej's (André
Szymanski) plaintive attempts at reconciliation with his wife, to Sascha's suicidal
despair. Yet there are few comic 'numbers' beloved of German actors and audiences.
An exception is the scene in which Sergej staggers drunkenly around shooting his
rifle, laughing uncontrollably and infectiously, failing dismally to cheer up Platonov
and utterly oblivious to his imminent cuckolding. This turn often received applause

11.7 Luk Perceval in conversation during rehearsal with Karin Neuhäuser and
Thomas Bading. Still from rehearsal footage.

from the audience. Despite the enormous range of styles of production in Berlin, the
tendency towards a postdramatic paradigm in performance has rendered set-piece
displays of actor virtuosity common, as part of an intended disruption of psychological flow. Examples from critically acclaimed productions by Perceval include a tap-
dancing Bellievre (Jean Chaize) in Schiller's *Maria Stuart* (2005, Schaubühne) and,
in Miller's *Death of A Salesman* (2006, Schaubühne), a fantasy sex object flashback
(Christine Geisse) and a fast-talking turn from Szymanski as Happy.

   Platonov, however, is not a production that seeks to befriend its audience. The
psychology of the characters is not displayed by the actors through a causal logic
that enables the audience to trace the 'why' of every action, hence the figures remain
intriguing and their actions inexplicable. In this lies the 'authenticity' that Perceval is
keen to pursue. Perhaps more significantly, the dramaturgical effect in watching this
mode of performance is that it directs us towards the future, to what will happen next
rather than the 'why' of what has already taken place.

   The critical reception for *Platonov* was mixed, betraying a profound ambivalence about the subject matter. This production does not yield easily analysable
representation. Instead you are confronted with an experience that throws you back
on your own subjectivity. As one critic noted, 'at the beginning, Perceval's *Platonov*
provides a lesson in the art of listening'.[22] Nor does it often provide comic release
from the bleak depiction of a culture – and a man – in freefall. For several critics,
this rendered the production 'boring', although for the listings magazine *Tip*, which
highly commended the production, it was, 'a long evening – and at the same time
like a highly concentrated single moment'.[23] Others felt it an impertinence that
the production appeared actively to refuse to 'entertain'. For example, the *Berliner*

11.8 Ivan Ivanovich: 'God has lost patience with us and has unleashed his might.' Left to right: Marja (Lea Draeger), Platonov (Thomas Bading), Anna Petrovna (Karin Neuhäuser).

Zeitung complained that 'Perceval, with his arty refusal of theatricality, robs the eponymous hero of what's left of his drive – his aggressive, sexual rage – leaving behind a self-pitying sleeping pill, who flails around lamenting . . . Boredom and depression – doubtless important themes of the bourgeois stage – are paradoxically employed as a means of active audience participation, in that the audience does not have anything to do and ends up listlessly impassive.'[24] *Die Zeit* pinpointed the aim of the characterisation of Platonov as a descent into the abyss, an implosion not only of a person but the centre of a world. However, this was regarded as a theatrical mistake: 'This Thomas Bading [Platonov] is even more crumpled up than the play already is in itself, he loses himself in pale moroseness, he lacks the magnetism to rock this world and its women.'[25] Nevertheless, Perceval's *Platonov* has continued to attract good-sized audiences, although it is increasingly infrequently played at the Schaubühne.

These responses are testimony to the fragility of the balance Perceval perceives to be at the heart of theatre, 'Disgust and fascination: that is the dichotomy in how we regard the stage. It's like spying on your neighbours. People doing what's forbidden. It's from this tension that theatre derives its life.'[26] Steeped in the tradition of 'director's theatre', German theatre critics often seek the explicit 'signature' of the director. While Perceval's aesthetic is recognisable, it is less due to a trademark style than to the capacities he develops in his actors both for great stillness and sudden violence (see figure 11.8). He does not pre-impose a style but excavates the text anew with the input of his actors and design team. Perceval's production of *Platonov* was one of his most radical to date, eschewing 'star' performance to focus on theatre as a space of silence, emptiness and contemplation.

Notes

1 Joseph Roth, 'Passengers with Heavy Loads', in Michael Bienert (ed.), *What I Saw: Reports from Berlin 1920–1933*, trans. Michael Hoffmann (New York: Norton, 2004), pp. 95–6.

2 See Hans van Dam, 'Ohne Scheu erzählten alle, was sie zu sagen hatten: ein Essay über Luk Perceval', in Thomas Irmer (ed.), *Luk Perceval: Theater und Ritual* (Berlin: Alexander Verlag, 2005), pp. 79–117.

3 Unless otherwise stated, all quotations from Perceval are taken from recorded conversations between Perceval and the author conducted on 28 February, 28 March, 27 April and 28 May 2006. Translations from German are by the author.

4 Luk Perceval, 'Alles ist möglich', speech given at the Schauspielhaus Hamburg, 9 April 2000. www.lukperceval.be, p. 10.

5 *Ibid.*

6 *Ibid.*, p. 9.

7 Michel de Certeau, Dedication, *The Practice of Everyday Life*, trans. Steven Rendall (Berkeley, CA: University of California Press, 1984), n.p.

8 Perceval's note to actors in rehearsal, 23 May 2006.

9 Recorded conversation between Thomas Bading and the author, 27 April 2006.

10 Recorded conversation between Annette Kurz and the author, 27 February 2006.

11 Recorded conversation between Ursula Renzenbrink and the author, 23 March 2006.

12 Ursula Renzenbrink, private email, 25 June 2007.

13 Erving Goffman, *The Presentation of Self in Everyday Life* (Edinburgh: Edinburgh University Press, 1956).

14 Recorded conversation between Thomas Bading and the author, 27 April 2006.

15 Recorded conversation between Karin Neuhäuser and the author, 28 April 2006.

16 Recorded conversation between David Ruland and the author, 27 March 2006.

17 Recorded conversation between Horst Hiemer and the author, 23 March 2006.

18 Perceval's note to the actors in rehearsal, 23 May 2006.

19 *Ibid.*

20 *Ibid.*

21 Anon, 'Das Heilsame Gift der Negativität' *Neue Zürcher Zeitung* (31 May 2006).

22 Georg Diez, 'Die Welt als Sofa', *Die Zeit* (1 June 2006) [press archive, Schaubühne].

23 Kerstin Decker, *Tip* (date unknown) [press archive, Schaubühne].

24 Ulrich Seidler, 'Überflüssige Menschen', *Berliner Zeitung* (29 May 2006) [press archive, Schaubühne].

25 Diez, 'Die Welt als Sofa'.

26 Luk Perceval, interview in *Tagesspiegel* newspaper (19 January 2007) [press archive, Schaubühne].

POSTSCRIPT

A springboard for Hans-Thies Lehmann's account of postdramatic theatre is the work of the modernists at the end of the nineteenth and beginning of the twentieth centuries. This was a period of artistic redefinition when, in order to establish new rules of engagement, artists published manifestos. (These included, for example, Filippo Tomasso Marinetti's *Futurist Manifesto* of 1909, the *Dada Manifesto* of 1918, produced by Richard Hülsenbeck and colleagues, Naum Gabo and Antoine Pevsner's *Realist Manifesto*, an argument for constructivism published in 1920, and André Breton's *Surrealist Manifesto* of 1924, among many others.) Manifesto-making is much less fashionable now, nearly a hundred years later – although the Dogme collective in Copenhagen did make something of a splash with its manifesto for filmmaking in 1995.

Making Contemporary Theatre suggests that theatre-making in the first decade of the twenty-first century is plural, contingent, influenced by many sources and open to all sorts of influence and experiment. Nonetheless, our writers have captured a set of resonant principles to do with theatre-making in the new millennium. We wondered what it would look like if we gathered the most compelling of these. Could the work of the geographically dispersed, formally distinct practitioners represented in this book really be boiled down into a manifesto for postdramatic theatre?

Well, it's not quite a manifesto. Postdramatic practitioners do not have a common agenda, a shared animus, in the way that was true of the Futurists, Dadaists and Surrealists. Today's manifesto looks more like a schematic – a diagram rather than a discourse; an advisory and not an argument. It is – appropriately enough for a digital culture – programmatic. In a spirit of contingent conclusion we present the programme for making contemporary theatre here.

Andy Lavender and Jen Harvie

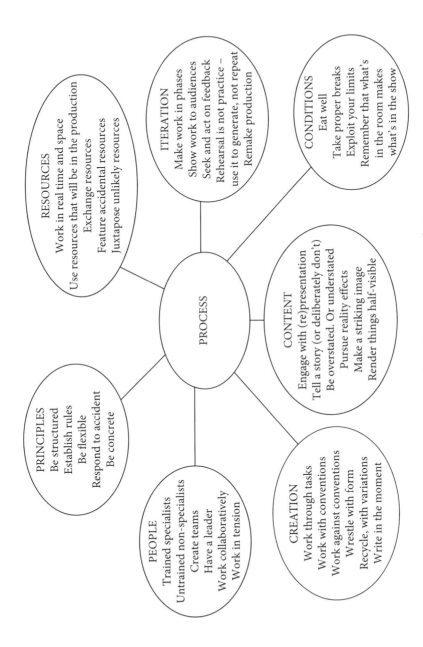

A programme for making contemporary theatre

RESOURCES
Work in real time and space
Use resources that will be in the production
Exchange resources
Feature accidental resources
Juxtapose unlikely resources

ITERATION
Make work in phases
Show work to audiences
Seek and act on feedback
Rehearsal is not practice –
use it to generate, not repeat
Remake production

CONDITIONS
Eat well
Take proper breaks
Exploit your limits
Remember that what's
in the room makes
what's in the show

PRINCIPLES
Be structured
Establish rules
Be flexible
Respond to accident
Be concrete

PROCESS

CONTENT
Engage with (re)presentation
Tell a story (or deliberately don't)
Be overstated. Or understated
Pursue reality effects
Make a striking image
Render things half-visible

PEOPLE
Trained specialists
Untrained non-specialists
Create teams
Have a leader
Work collaboratively
Work in tension

CREATION
Work through tasks
Work with conventions
Work against conventions
Wrestle with form
Recycle, with variations
Write in the moment

SELECT BIBLIOGRAPHY

This select bibliography lists books published in English. Additional sources (including books in other languages, articles and websites) pertaining to the practitioners under consideration are included in the endnotes to each respective chapter.

Ahmed, Sara, *Strange Encounters: Embodied Others in Post-Coloniality*, London and New York: Routledge, 2000.

Allain, Paul, and Jen Harvie, *The Routledge Companion to Theatre and Performance*, London and New York: Routledge, 2006.

Artaud, Antonin, *Artaud Anthology*, San Francisco: City Lights, 1965.

——, *Collected Works,* Vol. 1, London: Calder, 1968.

Auslander, Philip, *Liveness: Performance in a Mediatized Culture*, London and New York, Routledge, 1999.

——, *From Acting to Performance: Essays in Modernism and Postmodernism*, London and New York: Routledge, 1997.

Barrett, Michèle, and Bobby Baker (eds), *Bobby Baker: Redeeming Features of Daily Life,* Abingdon: Routledge, 2007.

Bicât, Tina, and Chris Baldwin, *Devised and Collaborative Theatre: A Practical Guide*, Ramsbury, England: Crowood Press, 2002.

Bottoms, Stephen, and Matthew Goulish (eds), *Small Acts of Repair: Performance, Ecology and Goat Island*, London and New York: Routledge, 2007.

Bradby, David, and Annie Sparks, *Mise en Scène: French Theatre Now*, London: Methuen, 1997.

Bradby, David, and David Williams, *Directors' Theatre*. Basingstoke: Macmillan, 1988.

Bulman, James (ed.), *Shakespeare, Theory, and Performance*, London and New York: Routledge, 1996.

Butcher, Rosemary, and Susan Melrose (eds), *Rosemary Butcher: Choreography, Collisions and Collaborations*, Middlesex: Middlesex University Press, 2005.

Castellucci, Claudia, Romeo Castellucci, Chiara Guidi, Joe Kelleher and Nicholas Ridout, *The Theatre of Societas Raffaello Sanzio*, London and New York: Routledge, 2007.

Chapple, Freda, and Chiel Kattenbelt (eds), *Intermediality in Theatre and Performance*, Amsterdam/New York: Rodopi, 2006.

Clements, Paul, *The Improvised Play: The Work of Mike Leigh*, London: Methuen, 1983.

Cole, Susan Letzler, *Directors in Rehearsal: A Hidden World*, London: Routledge, 1992.

——, *Playwrights in Rehearsal: The Seduction of Company*, London: Routledge, 2001.

Cook, Judith, *Directors' Theatre: Sixteen Leading Directors on the State of Theatre in Britain*, London: Hodder and Stoughton, 1989.

de Certeau, Michel, *The Practice of Everyday Life*, trans. Steven Rendall, Berkeley, CA: University of California Press, 1984.

Deleuze, Gilles, and Félix Guattari, *A Thousand Plateaus* (*Capitalism and Schizophrenia*, vol. 2), trans. Brian Massumi, Minneapolis: University of Minnesota Press, 1987.

Delgado, Maria M., and Paul Heritage (eds), *In Contact with the Gods?: Directors Talk Theatre*, Manchester: Manchester University Press, 1996.

Donohoe, Joseph I., and Jane M. Koustas (eds), *Theater sans Frontières: Essays on the Dramatic Universe of Robert Lepage*, East Lansing: Michigan State University Press, 2000.

Dundjerović, Aleksandar Saša, *The Theatricality of Robert Lepage*, Montreal: McGill-Queen's University Press, 2007.

Eckersall, Peter, *Theorizing the Angura Space: Avant-garde Performance and Politics in Japan 1960-2000*, Leiden: Brill, 2006.

Eckersall, Peter, Tadashi Uchino and Naoto Moriyama (eds), *Alternatives: Debating Theatre Culture in an Age of Con-fusion*, Brussels: Peter Lang, 2004.

Etchells, Tim, *Certain Fragments: Contemporary Performance and Forced Entertainment*, London and New York: Routledge, 1999.

Foucault, Michel, *Power: Essential Works of Foucault 1954-1984*, Vol. 3, ed. Paul Rabinow, New York: The New Press, 2000.

Gekidan Kaitaisha, *Dialogue with Otori Hidenaga and Shimizu Shinjin, Theatre of Deconstruction / Kaitaisha (1991-2001)*, trans. Maeshiba Naoko, Masuda Koji and Adam Broinowski, Tokyo: Gekidan Kaitaisha, 2001.

Giannachi, Gabriella, and Mary Luckhurst, *On Directing: Interviews with Directors*, London: Faber, 1999.

Goffman, Erving, *The Presentation of Self in Everyday Life*, Edinburgh: Edinburgh University Press, 1956.

Govan, Emma, Helen Nicholson and Katie Normington, *Making a Performance: Devising Histories and Contemporary Practices*, Abingdon: Routledge, 2007.

Grotowski, Jerzy, *Towards a Poor Theatre*, London: Methuen, 1968.

Halprin, Lawrence, *The RSVP Cycles: Creative Processes in the Human Environment*, New York: George Braziller, 1968.

Hardt, Michael, and Antonio Negri, *Empire,* Cambridge, MA: Harvard University Press, 2000.

Harvie, Jen, *Staging the UK*, Manchester: Manchester University Press, 2005.

Heathfield, Adrian (ed.), *Live: Art and Performance*, London: Tate Publishing, 2004.

Heddon, Deirdre, and Jane Milling, *Devising Performance: A Critical History*, Houndmills: Palgrave Macmillan, 2006.

Helmer, Judith, and Florian Malzacher (eds), *Not Even a Game Anymore – The Theatre of Forced Entertainment*, Berlin: Alexander Verlag, 2004.

Hill, Leslie, and Helen Paris, *The Guerilla Guide to Performance Art: How to Make a Living as an Artist*, London: Continuum, 2nd edn, 2004.

Holdsworth, Nadine, and Mary Luckhurst (eds), *A Concise Companion to Contemporary British and Irish Drama*, Oxford: Blackwell, 2007.

Johnston, Chris, *House of Games: Making Theatre from Everyday Life*, London: Nick Hern Books, 1998.

Kaye, Nick (ed.), *Site-Specific Art: Performance, Place and Documentation*, London and New York: Routledge, 2000.

Kelleher, Joe, and Nicholas Ridout (eds), *Contemporary Theatres in Europe,* Abingdon: Routledge, 2006.

Krasner, David (ed.), *Method Acting Reconsidered: Theory, Practice, Future*, Hampshire: Macmillan Press, 2000.

Lane, Jill, and Peggy Phelan (eds), *The Ends of Performance*, New York: New York University Press, 1998.

Lavender, Andy, *Hamlet in Pieces: Shakespeare Reworked by Peter Brook, Robert Lepage, Robert Wilson*, London: Nick Hern Books, 2001.

Lehmann, Hans-Thies, *Postdramatic Theatre*, trans. Karen Jürs-Munby, Abingdon: Routledge, 2006.

Lepage, Robert, and Remy Charest, *Connecting Flights*, trans. Wanda Romer Taylor, Toronto: A. A. Knopf Canada, 1998.

Lotringer, Sylvère, and Paul Virilio, *The Accident of Art*, trans. Michael Taormina, New York: Semiotext(e), 2005.

Luckhurst, Mary (ed.), *A Companion to Modern British and Irish Drama, 1880-2005*, Oxford: Blackwell, 2006.

McAuley, Gay, *Space in Performance: Making Meaning in the Theatre*, Ann Arbor: University of Michigan Press, 2000.

McGrath, John, *Loving Big Brother: Surveillance Culture and Performance Space*, London: Routledge, 2004.

Mitter, Shomit, *Systems of Rehearsal: Stanislavsky, Brecht, Grotowski and Brook*, London: Routledge, 1992.

Murray, Simon, and John Keefe, *Physical Theatres: A Critical Introduction*, London and New York: Routledge, 2007.

Nyman, Michael, *Experimental Music: Cage and Beyond*, Cambridge: Cambridge University Press, 1999.

Oddey, Alison, *Devising Theatre: A Practical and Theoretical Handbook*, London: Routledge, 1994.

Phelan, Peggy, *Unmarked: The Politics of Performance*, London and New York: Routledge, 1992.

Quick, Andrew, *The Wooster Group Work Book*, New York and London: Routledge, 2007.

Sandford, Mariellen R. (ed.), *Happenings and Other Acts*, London and New York: Routledge, 1995.

Savran, David, *Breaking the Rules: The Wooster Group*, New York: Theatre Communications Group, 1988.

Schechner, Richard, *Performance Studies: An Introduction*, London and New York: Routledge, 2002.

Schneider, Rebecca, and Gabrielle Cody (eds), *Re:Direction. A Theoretical and Practical Guide*, London and New York: Routledge, 2002.

Scholz-Cionca, Stanca, and Samuel L. Leiter (eds), *Japanese Theatre and the International Stage*, Leiden: Brill, 2000.

Shank, Theodore (ed.), *Contemporary British Theatre*, Houndmills: Macmillan, 2nd edn, 1996.

Stern, Tiffany, *Rehearsal from Shakespeare to Sheridan*, Oxford: Clarendon Press, 2000.

Svich, Caridad (ed.), *Trans-global Readings: Crossing Theatrical Boundaries*, Manchester: Manchester University Press, 2003.

Turner, Victor, *From Ritual to Theatre: The Human Seriousness of Play*, New York: Performing Arts Journal Publications, 1986.

Tushingham, David, *Food for the Soul: a New Generation of British Theatremakers (Live: 1)*, London: Methuen, 1994.

Warr, Tracey (ed.), *The Artist's Body*, London and New York: Phaidon, 2003.

Zarrilli, Phillip B. (ed.), *Acting (Re)Considered: A Theoretical and Practical Guide*, London and New York: Routledge, 2nd revised edn, 2002.

INDEX

Notes: 'n' after a page reference indicates the number of a note on that page. Page numbers in *italic* refer to illustrations.

accident(al) 6, 7, 13, 49, 81, 92, 97-8, 164,
     166, 243
     see also chance; chaos
acting 9-10, 22, 24, 79, 97, 147, 162, 168,
     180-90 *passim*, 199, 200n.2, n.3, n.16,
     208, 215-18 *passim*, 226, 231-8 *passim*
     see also actor(s)
action(s) 7-11 *passim*, 22-7 *passim*, 54, 61-2,
     71, 74, 91, 93, 103-9 *passim*, 123-4,
     127-38 *passim*, 153-4, 161, 163, 168,
     171, 173, 178, 181, 183, 185, 189, 191,
     199, 206, 213, 216, 219, 226, 232, 234,
     237, 239
     see also choreography; dance(s); fight/ing;
     movement(s)
actor(s) 9, 10, 22, 24, 25, 31, 33, 35, 39-41,
     44, 59, 60-79 *passim*, 97, 122-34 *passim*,
     160-73, 178, 180-200 *passim*, 203, 210,
     215-19, 222-40 *passim*
     see also acting
actor-author(s) 161, 163, 166, 168
aesthetic(s) 7-13 *passim*, 19, 31, 53, 83, 86-7,
     106, 108, 115, 118, 123, 133, 181, 202-3,
     219, 222, 224, 229-30, 236, 240

affect(s) 12, 37, 211, 237
     see also emotion; feelings
amateur(ism) 11, 96, 97, 100n.22, 104, 109,
     118
Angelos, Moe 21, 23-25, *24*
animal(s) 13-4, 45, 103, 130, 122-3, 147-9
     chickens/hens 8, 124, *129*, 131, 132, 134, 138
     elephants 76-7
     'sea-dog' 145, 154, 155
     turtle/tortoise 8, 124-5, 130, 134
ankoku butoh or *butoh* 8, 10, 140, 144, 146,
     151
anxiety 7, 13, 63, 123, 126, 133, 146, 156, 209
architecture 29, 61, 171, 228
attention 2, 4, 12-14, 35, 103, 116, 119, 136,
     180, 182, 189, 219, 225, 227, 232, 235,
     237
audience(s) 2-14 *passim*, 20-2, 25, 29-32,
     49, 55, 59, 72, 78-9, 81, 91, 94-7, 103-4,
     107-8, 112-14, 123, 129, 130-8 *passim*,
     142, 151-3, 156-8, 160-78 *passim*, 185,
     186, 188, 193, 195, 197-8, 202-7 *passim*,
     210, 215-219, 224, 232-3, 236-40, 243
     see also spectator(s); witness(es)

audition 50, 64-5, 142, 166, 183
auteur 2, 7, 9, 21, 105, 118, 122, 123
authentic(ity) 13, 76, 86, 130, 180, 182, 223, 225, 232-3, 239
author(s) 2, 14, 42, 106, 111, 160, 163, 167, 170
  authorship 2, 13, 57n.17, 105-16 *passim*, 119
  see also actor-author(s); *auteur*; playwright; writer(s)
avant-garde 11, 82, 106, 203
awkward(ness) 82, 90, 94, 96, 132, 137, 182

Bell, Clive 62, 63, 69, 73-6
Bodow, Steve 84, *85*, 87-8, 91, 97
body/ies 5, 8, 11, 13, 18, 31, 32, 36, 39-49 *passim*, 53-5, 67-71 *passim*, 74, 82, 92, 128, 131, 133, 136, 140-159 *passim*, 167, 176, 202-5, 208, 212-18 *passim*, 220n.20, 223, 231-2
Brecht, Bertolt 60, 197-8, 219
Builders Association, The 5, 17-38
  Alladeen (2003, with motiroti) 18, 19, 20, 29
  Super Vision (2005) 5, 17-38
butoh see ankoku butoh

camera(s) 9, 23-5, 31-2, 36, 125, 133-4, 172, 210-11, 215-9, 234-6
  see also webcam
Carniceria Teatro, La 7, 121-139
  Façon d'aborder l'idée de méfiance, Une (2006) 7, 121-139
cast(s) 11, 21, 70, 183-4, 186, 190-1, 197-9, 227
  casting 6, 8, 64-5, 122, 180
chance 71, 108, 111, 115, 152
  see also accident(al); chaos
chaos 47, 60, 72-3, 101, 163, 164, 170
  see also accident(al); chance
character(s) 5, 6, 10, 12, 22-3, 34, 40-1, 45-7, 49, 53-4, 63, 67, 72, 77, 79, 81, 83, 86, 90-7 *passim*, 123-4, 133, 161, 172-3, 175, 180, 181-99 *passim*, 200n.7, 210, 218, 224-6, 230-4, 237, 239
Chekhov, Anton 10, 223-6, 233
  Platonov 10, 223-5
Cherkaoui, Sidi Larbi 6, 11, 39-58

Foi (2003, with les Ballets C de La B) 40-1, 49, 52
Myth (2007) 6, 39-58
choreographer(s) 1, 2, 6, 88, 121, 123, 128, 163
  see also Cherkaoui; choreography; Hino Hiruko
choreography 8, 62, 89, 126, 132, 133, 136, 143, 145, 148-9, 183, 185, 189, 205, 214, 219
  see also choreographer(s); dance(s); fight/ing; movement(s)
collaboration 4, 6, 18, 19, 21-2, 40, 51, 59-61, 72, 106, 116, 126, 204-5, 207, 217, 243
collaborator(s) 4, 20, 22, 37, 41, 43, 46, 57, 59-60, 73-4, 79, 122, 124, 140, 161, 164-5, 171-2, 181-3, 190, 228
collective(ly) 2, 7, 53, 89, 105, 163-4, 170, 197, 235, 242
  creation 21, 40, 160
Collins, John 85, 87-8, 94, 96
Complicite 6, 11, 59-80, 89
  Elephant Vanishes, The (2003-4) 6, 59-80
composition 2, 33-4, 54, 76, 81-2, 86-7, 92, 94, 100n.18, 105, 108, 124, 130, 176, 205
computer(s) 23, 26, 34, 35, 62, 77, 164, 166, 167, 169, 172
conflict 2, 9, 12, 123, 151, 178
contemporary culture 3, 8, 11, 13, 103, 146
convention(s) 2, 7, 84, 96, 101, 104, 182, 188, 197-8, 209, 218, 243
co-production 6, 11, 17, 60, 222
costume(s) 47, 87-8, 96, 103, 109, 143, 164, 185, 228, 230
critic(s) 4, 79, 157, 165, 175, 181, 185, 198-9, 238-40
cyclorama(s) 19, 22, 25, 29, 30, 32, 228, 237

dance(s) 4, 6-8, 11, 18, 39-58, 74, 81-2, 86, 88-91, 93, 103, 126, 134, 140-159, 163, 203, 206, 218-19, 228
  see also action(s); choreography; fight/ing; movement(s)
'dataveillance' 5, 20, 22, 35
  see also surveillance
dbox 19, 21-2, 31-2, 37n.4 and n.5
Deleuze, Gilles, and Félix Guattari 53, 141, 147, 149
design 3, 8, 10, 17-35 *passim*, 54, 72-3, 76,

87-8, 118, 126, 137, 171, 198, 215-16, 228-30, 240
  see also cyclorama; dbox; designer(s); digital; lighting; projection; scenography/ies/ic; set(s)/setting; set-up; sound; video
designer(s) 1, 2, 6, 7, 9, 20-2, 33, 36, 44, 63, 67, 92, 121, 164, 171, 226-7, 237
  see also design; Laing
devised/devising 2-14 *passim*, 21, 42, 46, 49, 51, 59-60, 63-5, 69-70, 74-6, 83, 85, 88-9, 94, 118, 122, 133, 161, 163-73 *passim*, 178, 203, 206, 208, 218
directing 2-8 *passim*, 11, 15n.2, 180
  see also authorship; director(s)
director(s) 1-10 *passim*, 14, 15n.1 and n.4, 39, 42, 46, 86, 100n.18, 104-6, 116, 118
  see also Cherkaoui; Collins; directing; Etchells; Garcia; Lepage; McBurney; Maxwell; Perceval; Pledger; Shimizu Shinjin; Weems
Dobson, Dan 20, 21, 33-34
dramaturg/y 9, 18, 19, 41, 50, 74, 79, 165-6, 202, 205, 212, 217-18, 224-6

editing 8, 49, 88, 100n.18, 126, 161, 173, 234
Elevator Repair Service (ERS) 6-7, 81-100
  Cab Legs (1997) 7, 81, 95, 97
  Gatz (2006) 7, 83-4, 87, 89
  Highway to Tomorrow (2001) 7, 93, 96
  Room Tone (2002) 7, 87, 89-91, 94-5
  Total Fictional Lie (*TFL* 1998) 7, 91-2, 95
emote/emotion(s) 13, 143, 162, 185-90 *passim*, 194-6, 199, 231
  emotional 9, 17, 22, 163, 188, 230, 234
  see also affect; feelings
energy 65, 83, 87, 91, 96, 127, 133, 143-6 *passim*, 164, 186, 194, 196, 206, 227, 231, 234, 237
ensemble model of theatre-making 105-6, 115, 118-19
ERS *see* Elevator Repair Service
Etchells, Tim 7, 101, 104-119 *passim*
  Certain Fragments: Contemporary Performance and Forced Entertainment (1999), 101, 107, 108, 112, 116, 118
everyday 61, 83, 87-8, 104, 111, 145, 148, 182, 224-6, 232, 234

Ex Machina 8, 160-179
eye contact 10, 24, 186, 197, 232-3

feeling(s) 8, 10, 204
  see also affect; emotion
festival(s) 4, 11, 122, 136, 178n.1, 181
  international 10-11, 19, 161, 165
fight/ing 114, 181, *183*, 185, 189, 196, 199, 205-6
  see also violence
film 8, 49, 54, 90, 109, 160, 168-9, 172-3, 179n.10, 182, 201n.31, 204, 211, 219, 234-7
Flaherty, Peter 20-1, 29, 31-34 *passim*
Forced Entertainment 7, 11, 89-90, 97, 100n.22, 101-20, 188
  First Night (2001) 7, 103-4, 106, 108
  Travels, The (2002) 7, 101-120
Foucault, Michel 141, 148-9, 156, 205
funding 87, 109, 123, 141, 161

game(s) 21, 65, 67, 71, 73, 108, 110, 139n.12, 172, 227, 230
Garcia, Rodrigo 7-8, 11, 121-139
  see also La Carniceria Teatro
Gekidan Kaitaisha 8, 140-159, 207
  Bye Bye: The New Primitive (2001) 8, 140-59
Gignac, Marie 164-9 *passim*, 172-3
global 1, 4, 7, 9-11, 152, 161, 176, 207
globalisation 13, 123, 161, 207

hierarchy/ies 4, 6, 21, 50, 53, 64, 105, 106, 118-19, 128
Hijikata Tatsumi 140, 145, 147-8, 151, 152
Hino Hiruko 140, 143, 146-8, 15-6, 158n.2
history 140, 151-2, 206, 223

image(s) 2, 5, 7-9, 13, 23-5, 29-37 *passim*, 55, 61-2, 67, 74-80 *passim*, 94, 115, 124, 129, 133-7, 141-3, 151, 153, 155, 163, 165-9, 171, 176-8, 202, 210-14, 216-17, 219, 220n.20, 224, 229-30, 243
  see also photograph(s)/y; project/projection/projector
improvisation 2, 11, 20, 33, 43-4, 65-69 *passim*, 73-4, 101, 118, 130-2, 147, 160, 164, 168, 171-3, 178
installation(s) 59, 101, 160, 204, 207, 216

Kempson, Sybil 186-7, 189, 190, 194-5, 199

Laing, Stewart 20, 25-31 *passim*, 34
language(s) 1-2, 4-6, 11, 41, 54, 62, 77-8, 86,
     88, 90, 101, 151-2, 154, 160-1, 165-70
     passim, 186, 207, 223
     see also text(s); translate/translation/
     translator(s); voice(s)
Lecoq, Jacques 6, 59, 64, 67, 70
     L'École 59, 60, 67
Lehmann, Hans-Thies 2, 4, 11-12, 35-6, 86,
     242
     Postdramatic Theatre (1996 [2006]) 11-12,
     16n.7 and n.8, 35
Lepage, Robert 8, 160-179
     Lipsynch (2007) 8, 160-79
light 36, 41, 55, 61-2, 64, 71, 79, 87-8, 91, 124,
     134-5, 143-4, 146, 152-3, 157, 224, 237
lighting 22, 33, 74, 78, 87, 123-4, 126, 133,
     135, 144, 150, 171, 185, 202, 215-16,
     228
listening 115, 203, 233, 239
live 2, 6, 9, 18, 24, 31-2, 35, 37, 41, 94, 103-6,
     108, 115, 124, 160, 178, 188, 206, 210,
     213-18 *passim*, 229, 237
     art/ist(s) 98, 104-6, 111, 115
     see also performance art/ist(s)
liveness 32, 104, 171, 178

McBurney, Simon 6, 59-76
Maxwell, Richard 9, 10, 180-201
     End of Reality, The (2006) 180-201
media/medium 6, 9, 11-13, 17, 37, 59, 86,
     88, 90, 97, 101, 157, 160, 164, 172, 178,
     202-10 *passim*, 215-17
     see also mediation/mediatisation;
     multimedia
mediation/mediatisation 2, 17-19, 22, 24, 32,
     123, 210, 216
     see also media/medium; multimedia
memory 60, 76, 111, 114, 144-5, 152, 158,
     165-9 *passim*, 211, 219, 227, 230, 234,
     237
Mendes, Brian 182-99 *passim*, 200n.2,
metatheatre 14
     metatheatrical/ity 4, 12, 188-9, 205, 207,
     217
microphone(s) 20, 24, 102, 109, 112, 114,
     142, 237

mise en scène 129, 136, 161-2, 168, 176, 180,
     218, 233, 237
mistrust 50, 105, 121, 124, 133
     see also trust
movement(s) 6-8, 10, 12, 22, 34, 46, 67-76
     passim, 82, 85-6, 90-1, 93-4, 124, 140-55
     passim, 166, 172, 185, 189, 193, 203, 208,
     215-17, 232, 237
     see also action(s); choreography; dance(s);
     fight/ing
multimedia 4-9 *passim*, 18, 33-5, 160, 202-3,
     206
     see also media/medium; mediation/
     mediatisation
Murakami, Haruki 6, 61, 63-4, 69-71, 77
music 34, 41, 44, 52, 54, 61-2, 82-3, 85-91
     passim, 101, 104, 124, 157, 160, 166, 181,
     201n.31, 204-6, 215, 231-2, 237
     musical(s) 16, 181
     musician(s) 40-1, 52, 63, 164
     see also song(s); sound; video

Nakajima Miyuki 143, 151-3, 157, 158n.2
narrative(s) 2, 4, 5, 12, 14, 17, 18, 22-5, 34,
     35, 55, 61, 64, 66, 72, 79, 84-6, 103, 115,
     136, 152, 163-4, 166, 170-8 *passim*, 181,
     183, 202, 210
     see also story/ies
New York City Players 9, 180-201
Not Yet It's Difficult (NYID) 9, 11, 141,
     202-221
     Blowback (2004) 9, 202-221

object(s) 2, 53, 61, 71, 85, 87-8, 91-2, 97,
     102-5 *passim*, 109, 110, 124, 130,
     134,136, 145, 147, 153, 160-1, 163, 168,
     171, 198, 228
     see also props

Perceval, Luk 10, 11, 222-41
     Platonov (2006) 222-41
performance art/ist(s) 4, 20, 104, 170, 203
     see also live art/ist(s)
photograph(s)/y 5, 24, 36, 67, 111, 112, 115,
     133, 152, 160
     see also image(s); project/projection/
     projector
play(s) 2, 9, 10, 17, 18, 78, 81, 89, 93, 95, 109,
     116, 122, 134, 161, 167, 180-9 *passim*,

194, 197, 198, 205, 206, 209, 210, 214, 216, 223-40 *passim*
playwright 3, 19, 20, 140
  see also auteur; author(s); writer(s)
Pledger, David, 201-9, 212, 214-19 *passim*
politics/al 9, 11-13, 100n.18, 105, 121, 123, 128, 136, 138, 140, 167, 202-14 *passim*, 219
popular culture 83, 133, 160, 204, 205
postdramatic 2, 4, 10, 11-14, 35-6, 86, 242, 204, 225, 239, 242
postmodern 12, 112, 123, 126,175, 203
  -ism 14, 36
power 2, 4, 8, 9, 13, 49, 79, 81, 105, 115, 121, 128, 140, 148-9, 152, 203, 209, 214, 219, 223, 226
pragmatic(s) 6-8, 73, 92, 118, 133, 136, 229
presence 12, 19, 24, 36, 37n.4, 91, 97, 104, 107, 123, 142, 143, 146, 158, 194, 203, 216, 218, 228, 237
project/projection/projector 7, 9, 18-35 *passim*, *70*, 73, 74, *75*, 102-3, 112, 124, *125*, 127-8, 134, *135*, 136, 160, 172, *175*, 206, 211
  see also image(s); photograph(s)/y; video
prop(s) 2, 87, 91, 96, 97, 101, 191, 198, 210, 233
  see also object(s)
psychological/psychology 96, 123, 124, 131, 132, 180-91 *passim*, 210, 218, 226, 232, 234, 239
  see also realism/ist

realism/ist 9 , 12-14, 31, 124, 180-2, 188-9, 242
  psychological 2, 9-13 *passim*
  see also psychological/psychology
reality 13, 18, 64, 87, 97-8, 104, 157, 188, 196, 209, 217, 219, 228
  effects 9, 96, 243
Reehorst, Nienke 43-4, 46, 50
rhythm(s) 12, 33, 62, 67-8, 71, 76, 77, 87, 88, 91, 124, 129, 181, 217, 218, 231, 237
RSVP Cycles or method 8, 163, 168, 173
rules 7, 108, 114, 186, 230-4, 243

scenography/ies/ic 5, 6, 123, 130, 141-3, 150-2, 171
  see also design; set(s)/setting; set-up

Schaubühne am Lehninerplatz 10, 11, 222-4, 226, 228, 237, 238, 240
screen(s) 23-4, 28-32 *passim*, 34, 61, 64, 72, *73*, 79, 94, 112, 148, 182, 206, *207*, *213*, 216, 219
script(s) 6, 21, 30, 33, 77, 79, 97, 102, 113-18, 124, 173, 183, 185-6, 193-4, 199, 200n.7, 209, 214-5, 227
  see also text(s)
set(s)/setting 20, 21, 25-9, 30, 53, 55, 72, 84, 87, 96, 101, 103, 104, 118, 160-1, 176, 185, 198, 237
  see also design; scenography/ies/ic; set-up
Setagaya Public Theatre 60, 63, 65, 78, 151
set-up 22, 103, 110, 112-13, 118, 215
  see also scenography/ies/ic; set(s)/setting
Shakespeare, William 165, 205-6, 223, 224
Shimizu Shinjin 140-59 *passim*
soap opera 9, 175, 210-18 *passim*
Sokol, Susie 88, 92-100
song(s) 52, 86, 181, 200n.10, 205, 219
sound 17-18, 21, 33-4, 67-8, 73-8 *passim*, 85- 92 *passim*, 124, 126, 143, 149, 153-5, 160, 165-72 *passim*, 182, 199
soundtrack(s) 7, 82, 124, 134
  see also Dobson; music; song(s); voice(s)
space(s) 2, 5, 11, 13, 27, 29-32, 34-5, 39, 71, 87, 89, 97, 143, 145, 148, 151, 160, 171, 203, 213, 214-17, 220n.24, 228-30, 243
  poetic 115
spectacle(s) 13, 82, 83, 123, 138, 157, 160
spectator(s) 12, 18, 32, 84, 86, 94, 123, 126, 128, 132-3, 136, 177, 181, 188, 199, 216, 224, 236
  see also audience(s); witness(es)
Stanislavski, Constantin 106, 118, 162, 225-6
story/ies 5-13 *passim*, 17, 20, 22, 55, 60-79 *passim*, 104, 109, 114-15, 122-4, 152, 161-3, 166-7, 171-6 *passim*, 202, 205, 210-11, 221n.31, 243
  -board(s) 7, 128, 130, *131*, 136, 173
  -line(s) 20, 23, 25, 34, 36-7, 176
  -telling/er 13, 74, 79, 103, 175, 178, 181
  see also narrative(s)
surprise 6, 42, 54, 92, 109, 132, 181, 224, 235
surveillance 9, 19, 23, 31, 35, 207-19 *passim*
  see also 'dataveillance'
system model of theatre-making 105, 106, 108, 111, 114, 115, 118, 119

Tanizaki, Jun-ichiro 60-4, 80

task(s) 9, 21-2, 44-6, 69-70, 74-5, 89, 91, 95, 104, 108, 110-13, 137, 180, 185-96 *passim*, 200n.16, 215, 217, 227, 243

technician(s) 1, 6, 36, 44, 125, 134, 164, 171-2, 176, 227

technology/ies 5, 9, 13,17-22 *passim*, 25, 29, 30, 32, 35, 36, 59, 97, 126, 134, 160, 171-2, 178, 203, 215

television 19, 61, 76, 88, 160, 162, 167, 176, 204, 210-11, 216-9

text(s) 2, 3, 7-13 *passim*, 20, 33, 45, 61-9 *passim*, 74, 76, 79-80, 81, 84-8, 91-2, 108, 116, 118, 122-9 *passim*, 134, 136, 137, 142, 149-52, 154, 162-3, 165, 168, 173, 178, 180, 186, 189, 193, 196, 205, 212, 214-15, 218, 223-7, 231-2, 234, 237, 240
   -based 2, 4, 33, 122, 128
   see also script(s)

time 2-3, 6, 13, 21, 41, 44, 47, 50, 57, 61, 63-4, 67-8, 71, 79, 83-5, 90-2, 95, 104-5, 114, 123-37 *passim*, 141-6 *passim*, 153, 163-4, 168, 173, 175, 178, 186, 193, 196, 198, 203, 227, 233, 236-7, 243

tone 22, 33, 34, 52, 77, 108, 114, 156, 182, 194-5, 218
   see also Elevator Repair Service, *Room Tone*

tour/touring 5, 8, 10, 13, 19, 25, 28, 40-1, 49, 55, 76, 83-4, 99n.6, 101,108, 110, 122, 124, 133, 137, 138n.11, 141, 146, 160-1, 165-6, 178n.1, 207, 222

train/ing 1, 5, 6, 11, 39, 46, 48, 54, 64, 67, 70, 85, 87, 106, 118, 121, 162, 180, 182, 188, 191, 199, 203, 218, 222, 243
   see also Lecoq; voice; yoga

translate/translation/translator(s) 61-2, 74, 77-9, 90, 122, 128, 163, 166-7, 171
   see also language(s)

travel 18, 19, 22, 60-1, 114-15, 161, 163, 205, 210

see also Forced Entertainment, *The Travels*

trust 13, 47, 50, 64, 104, 145, 149, 235
   see also La Carniceria Teatro, *Une Façon...*; mistrust

video 17-25 *passim*, 29-35, 67, 74, 76, 78-9, 89, 91, 94, 101, 113, 124, 133, 139n.12, 154, 164, 171, 176, 206, 215-16, 234
   projection 18-20 *passim*, 22-3, 25, 26, 28-30, 32-5, 124
   see also Flaherty

violence 8, 13, 121-2, 132, 145, 151, 156, 157, 201n.18, *206*, 206, 216, 220n.11, 223, 240
   see also fight/ing

voice(s) 9, 18, 25, 34, 52, 62, 66-8, 116, 127, 161, 165, 166-9, 172-3, 182, 195, 199

warm-up(s) 43-4, 125, 127, 131, *184*, 185

Weems, Marianne 5, 18-21, 25, 28-32 *passim*, 34, 35, 37n.2

Wilson, Robert 16n.7, 105, 130, 139n.15

witness(es) 9, 40, 76, 107
   see also audience(s); spectator(s)

workshop(s) 20, 21, 25-30 *passim*, 40, 42, 51, 52, 60-71 *passim*, 141-2, 152, 155, 162, 203, 218

Wooster Group, The 18, 19, 84-7, 89, 90, 94, 139n.17, 188

work-in-progress 8, 84, 109, 165, 168, 175-7

writer(s) 1, 2, 6, 20, 41, 60-1, 67, 86, 98,121, 160, 163, 164, 167, 173, 224, 225
   see also actor-author(s); author(s); Etchells; Maxwell; Murakami; playwright; writing

writing 11, 20, 42, 46, 54, 61-2, 71, 84, 110-16 *passim*, 121, 128, 168, 171, 205, 212, 218, 223
   see also writer(s)

yoga 6, 11, 43-4, 67, 92